SOUND & FURY: A History of Kansas Tornadoes

SOUND AND FURY: A HISTORY KANSAS TORNADOES, 1854-2008

DANIEL C FITZGERALD

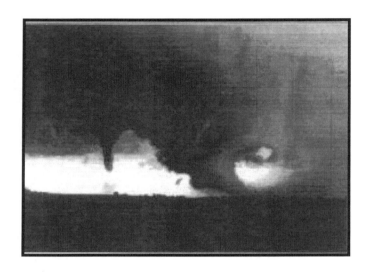

Copyright 2008-2009

The Dan Fitzgerald Company

Produced By Dan Fitzgerald

www.DanielCFitzgerald.com

Table of Contents

INTRODUCTION *15*

   FAVORITE TORNADO LEGENDS 23

CHAPTER ONE: TERRITORIAL KANSAS AND TORNADOES *29*

CHAPTER TWO: EARLY TORNADO DISASTERS, 1860-1880 ..... *43*

   EL DORADO, JUNE 16, 1871 44

   TORNADO OUTBREAK, JULY 1876 47

   COTTONWOOD FALLS/STRONG CITY, 1878 48

   IRVING, KANSAS, MAY 30, 1879 51

CHAPTER THREE: WIDESPREAD TRAGEDIES, 1880-1917 .... *63*

   CRAWFORD, CHEROKEE COUNTIES, APRIL 2, 1880 .. 64

   SOLOMON CITY, JUNE 9, 1881 65

   TORNADO OUTBREAK, JUNE 12, 1881 66

   EMPORIA, SEPTEMBER 29, 1881 68

   NORTH CENTRAL KANSAS, APRIL 5 AND 7, 1882 69

   PHILLIPSBURG, JUNE 26, 1882 72

   SUN CITY, APRIL 22, 1883 74

   KANSAS CITY, KANSAS, MAY 13, 1883 75

   SOLDIER, JULY 10, 1883 77

   SOLDIER, JULY 10, 1883 77

   COFFEY COUNTY, MAY 3, 1884 78

   LINN COUNTY, APRIL 26, 1887 79

   CENTRAL KANSAS, MAY 5-7, 1889 80

   SUMNER COUNTY/WAMEGO, MARCH 31, 1892 81

   CHERRYVALE, APRIL 3, 1892 86

   SHAWNEE COUNTY, MAY 2, 1892 87

   WELLINGTON, MAY 27, 1892 88

OSAGE CITY, APRIL 18, 1893 90

PERRY AND WILLIAMSTOWN, JUNE 22, 1893 91

MT. HOPE, MAY 1, 1895 92

CLAY AND CLOUD COUNTIES, APRIL 28, 1896 93

CLAY AND CLOUD COUNTIES, MAY 2, 1896 97

THE FIVE COUNTY TORNADO OF MAY 17, 1896 98

CUNNINGHAM, MAY 1898 99

CLARK COUNTY, MAY 21-22, 1903 102

GREENWOOD COUNTY, OCTOBER 6, 1903 103

TOPEKA, SEPTEMBER 1, 1904 104

MARQUETTE TORNADO, MAY 8, 1905 105

JEWELL COUNTY, MAY 27, 1908 108

GREAT BEND AND HOISINGTON, MAY 14, 1909 109

NORTON COUNTY, JUNE 24, 1909 110

EMPORIA AND PLYMOUTH, MAY 1, 1910 111

EASTERN KANSAS, APRIL 12, 1911 112

BISON, APRIL 20, 1912 117

MIAMI AND LINN COUNTIES, JUNE 15, 1912 118

SOUTHEASTERN KANSAS, AUGUST 25, 1912 119

TORNADO OUTBREAK, NOVEMBER 10, 1915 121

TORNADOES/SQUALL LINES, APRIL 19, 1916 125

ELLIS COUNTY, MAY 20, 1917 127

SOUTHERN KANSAS, MAY 25, 1917 128

COFFEYVILLE AND OTHERS, JUNE 1, 1917 132

REGISTRATION DAY TORNADO, JUNE 5, 1917 133

CHAPTER FOUR: TECHNOLOGY AND UNDERSTANDING *139*

HAYS, MAY 20, 1918 139

HOISINGTON, OCTOBER 8, 1919 142

GREENSBURG, MAY 23, 1923 144
AUGUSTA, JULY 13, 1924 145
CENTRAL KANSAS, MAY 7, 1927 147
EASTERN KANSAS, JULY 16, 1927 149
STRANGE OCCURRENCES, JUNE 22, 1928 151
ELLINWOOD, MAY 5, 1930 153
PRATT, JUNE 25, 1930 154
WASHINGTON, JULY 4, 1932 159
LOGAN, APRIL 26, 1933 162
LIBERAL, MAY 22, 1933 162
INDEPENDENCE TORNADO, FEBRUARY 24, 1935 163
RAWLINS COUNTY TORNADOES, JULY 10, 1935 165
SALINA, MARCH 10, 1938 166
TRI-STATE TORNADO, MARCH 30, 1938 167
CUNNINGHAM, MAY 1, 1938 169
LEBO, JUNE 10, 1938 171
BURR OAK, JUNE 14, 1939 172
WHITEWATER, VALLEY CENTER, JUNE 7, 1941 172
LINCOLNVILLE, AUGUST 25, 1941 173
OBERLIN, APRIL 29, 1942 174
ALLEN COUNTY, MAY 2, 1942 175
DODGE CITY, MAY 10, 1942 177
MULVANE, JUNE 20, 1942 178
FORT RILEY, MAY 15, 1943 180

CHAPTER FIVE: THE MODERN ERA, 1945-1980 .... *185*

NEOSHO COUNTY, MAY 1, 1948 191
UNUSUAL TORNADOES, JANUARY 1949 192
ROZEL, MAY 19, 1949 193

WILMORE, MAY 20, 1949 193

VIOLENT OCTOBER STORMS, 1949 195

GREAT BEND, MAY 3, 1950 196

McPHERSON AREA, JUNE 8, 1950 196

WESTERN KANSAS TORNADOES, MAY 1951 197

WAKEENEY AND OTHERS, JUNE 27, 1951 198

SEVERE WEATHER, JULY 1951 199

LAWRENCE, BONNER SPRINGS, MAY 22, 1952 200

CENTRAL KANSAS, AUGUST 2, 1952 201

ANTHONY, AUGUST 5, 1952 202

MAY STORMS, 1953 202

JUNE STORMS, 1953 203

WICHITA, JUNE 21, 1953 205

TOPEKA, MARCH 18, 1954 206

MAY STORMS, 1954 207

UDALL, MAY 25, 1955 207

STORMS, MAY 27-31, 1955 214

WESTERN KANSAS, JUNE 4, 1955 214

TORNADOES, APRIL 1, 2, 1956 215

SPRING HILL, OTTAWA, MAY 20, 1957 218

EL DORADO, JUNE 10, 1958 220

MERIDEN AND ELMONT, MAY 19, 1960 224

HUTCHINSON, NEWTON, MAY 24, 1962 228

TOPEKA, MAY 26, 1962 230

HOLTON, AUGUST 6, 1962 231

GARNETT, APRIL 12, 1964 234

GEUDA SPRINGS, MARCH 16, 1965 235

WICHITA, MAY 13, 1965 235

WICHITA, SEPTEMBER 3, 1965 236
EASTERN KANSAS, MAY 12, 1966 239
TOPEKA, JUNE 8, 1966 240
GARDEN CITY, JUNE 25, 1967 248
CENTRAL KANSAS, JUNE 21, 1969 249
REGIONAL TORNADOES, JUNE 23, 1969 251
PRAIRIE VIEW, MARCH 13, 1973 252
NORTH CENTRAL KANSAS, SEPTEMBER 25, 1973 ... 253
HUTCHINSON, MAY 13, 1974 258
EMPORIA, JUNE 8, 1974 259
MORTON, STEVENS COUNTIES, MAY 18, 1977 263
JACKSON COUNTY, MAY 31, 1978 265
THE WHIPPOORWILL, JUNE 16, 1978 265
CLAY COUNTY, OCTOBER 18, 1979 268

CHAPTER SIX: RECENT EVENTS, 1980-2008 .... *271*

LAWRENCE, JUNE 19, 1981 272
SHAWNEE COUNTY, JULY 19, 1981 274
SOUTHEAST KANSAS, MARCH 15, 1982 275
SILVER LAKE, EFFINGHAM, APRIL 26, 1984 277
WICHITA, APRIL 29, 1984 280
CARBONDALE, OCTOBER 31, 1984 281
NORTH CENTRAL KANSAS, MAY 10, 1985 283
BUTLER COUNTY, JULY 5, 1987 285
TORNADOES IN THE SPRING OF 1990 286
HESSTON, MARCH 13, 1990 287
ELLIS COUNTY, APRIL 25, 1990 295
CENTRAL KANSAS, MAY 24, 1990 295
EMPORIA, JUNE 7, 1990 297

INLAND HURRICANE, JUNE 19, 1990 299

CENTRAL, EASTERN KANSAS, MARCH 26, 1991 301

WICHITA AND ANDOVER, APRIL 26, 1991 302

CENTRAL KANSAS, MAY 16, 1991 318

MCPHERSON, GALVA, JUNE 15, 1992 318

RUSSELL, MAY 7, 1993 322

LAWRENCE, JULY 11, 1993 323

KISMET AND MEADE, APRIL 9, 1994 324

SABETHA, JUNE 13, 1998 326

WICHITA AND HAYSVILLE, MAY 3, 1999 327

PARSONS, APRIL 19, 2000 330

HOISINGTON, APRIL 21, 2001 334

KANSAS CITY, SOUTHERN KANSAS, MAY 4, 2003 .. 336

RENO COUNTY, JULY 3, 2005 338

GREENSBURG, MAY 4, 2007 339

PRATT COUNTY, MAY 23, 2008 341

EAST CENTRAL KANSAS, JUNE 11, 2008 342

Appendix 1: Significant Tornado Paths *345*

Photo Credits *369*

Selected Bibliography *373*

Notes *375*

Index to Kansas Tornado Locations *403*

FOREWORD

Five seconds is all it takes. It can change a life. It can end a life. It can change everything as you know it. You can wake up on a sunny, warm morning expecting to go about your day as you did yesterday, the day before, even the week before. Without warning, the skies can turn dark by the end of the day, a tornado can appear, and in seconds everything you own and cherish can be swept away. There are few things in life as devastating as a tornado.

Just ask a resident from Greensburg what can happen in a few seconds. On a humid, windy day in May 2007, Greensburg was wiped off the face of the earth, and hundreds of lives were changed. They will not return to life the way it was ever again. They can only push forward to make things better.

Ask the residents of Udall what happened on May 25, 1955. Many people were in bed and unaware that a giant tornado was heading their way. By the time they heard the tornado, it was too late for many of them.

My first tornado experience was the June 8, 1966 tornado that hit Topeka, Kansas. This tornado sliced a four-block swath down the middle of town, barely missing the Capitol building. I was seven at the time. I may not remember much about it today except for the hundreds of sirens afterwards, but it was a frightening experience that gave me a respect for the awesome power of tornadoes.

There were other scares over the years. I saw my first tornado between Topeka and Lawrence one humid spring day in 1977. I missed another tornado by about two miles in Kansas City in 2003. Each time was as frightening as the last. It was just another part of life in the middle of tornado alley.

Each of the stories in this book depicts a day of reckoning in the life of some Kansas community. Some of the tornadoes were larger and more destructive than others, but does it really matter? The potential for the loss of human life is always there, no matter what the strength of the tornado. But, in addition to death, there are also unbelievable stories of survival. For each person flung through the air a hundred yards and killed, there is a miraculous story of another person flung through the air.... and survived! Call it luck, call it divine intervention, but not every story in my book is one of loss and sadness. Miracles have happened.

Sound and Fury derived its name from an interview I had with a survivor of the June 8th, 1966 Topeka tornado. I thought the name stuck. When I asked him what the seconds were like just before the tornado rolled down Burnett's Mound and hit his house, he remarked, "All I remember, most of all, was the sound...and the fury." I couldn't have said it any better.

I'm not a meteorologist. In fact, my background is in economic history. However, the subject has always fascinated me, and the stories I've heard send chills up my spine. Over the years, these stories and the significant Kansas tornado events have been compiled into this volume.

The goal of this book is to present a pure history of the most significant tornado events in Kansas since territorial times.

Interspersed with these events are major breakthroughs in meteorological history that have allowed forecasters to be more accurate, with a better understanding on how a tornado develops and how to predict them.

This book was an extremely long and challenging project. I started compiling the information and researching Kansas tornadoes as early as 1997. After four years of research and writing, I thought that I was done. Apparently it took another seven years to get it right. In the meantime, more Kansas communities were hit by severe weather and, thus, more topics to discuss. The worst in recent memory was, of course, the Greensburg tornado of 2007.

There are a number of notable tornado resources out there, both on the Internet and in published form. Snowden "Frosty" Flora is perhaps the grandfather of the genre. In the 1950's, he wrote an interesting book called *Tornadoes of the United States*. He combined fifty years of statistics with thumbnail histories of some of the more notable tornadoes in the nation's history. Flora was followed by a few other scientists, meteorologists, and historians, but no one made an effort to compile a state history of tornadoes.

My appreciation goes out to the staff of the Library Division of the Kansas State Historical Society for their assistance in locating information on some of these obscure events. Their resources helped to make this book possible. Among them were Bobbie Pray, Bob Knecht, Darrell Garwood, Karen Schloss, Cynthia Laframboise, and Nancy Sherbert. My fondest regards. In addition, I wish to thank my family: Crissy, Caitlin, Tanner, Connor, and Jacob, as well as my parents, Calvin and Mary Fitzgerald, and Michael Brock, for their patience and recommendations as this book developed. Without them, this would not have happened.

Unfortunately, every spring will bring another active season and more potential for damage, destruction and deaths. There may come a time when this volume may need updating. We always hope that will not happen.

INTRODUCTION

It is certainly not the goal of this book to concentrate on a generalized history of tornadoes. There are literally hundreds of articles and books that deal exhaustively with this subject. The *Weather Channel* even runs special features on tornadoes, especially in the spring months. However, in order to educate the novice tornado reader, I will briefly describe how a tornado forms.

The tornado, which in Latin means "tornare" or "to turn", is the most violent storm that nature produces. It is a vortex of destructive, whirling winds with air currents of great lifting strength. The speed of a tornado's winds was estimated in the nineteenth century at around 800 miles an hour; in the mid-twentieth century at 450-500 miles per hour, and in recent years, the speed has been downgraded to a more realistic 150-300 miles per hour, even in the most turbulent storms. Sometimes it is considerably less. The dynamic force of these wind currents results in a partial vacuum at the center of the vortex, which causes an explosive effect as it passes over structures.

Tornadoes can occur at any place and at any time in the United States. According to U.S. Weather Bureau statistics, in tabulating tornadoes from 1916 to 1954, they found that, on average, 179 tornadoes are reported each year. The four states with the greatest average number of tornadoes were Kansas, Texas, Oklahoma, and Iowa respectively.

A second study was conducted covering the years 1954 to 1988. In this study, Texas led all states with an average of 123 tornadoes a year, followed by Oklahoma with 53; Florida with 44; and Kansas with an average of 42 tornadoes a year. Kansas dropped from number one to number four in the second study.[i] Some years were worse than others at contributing to the overall averages. For example, the year 1973 was a bad one for everyone–a record 1,109 tornado were reported, causing 87 deaths.

Since 1880 when records were first kept, Kansas ranked first in the number of F-5 tornadoes, although this high ranking might be due to Kansas being one of the best-documented states in the region. In the state's history of F4 and F5 tornadoes, Kansas had 125 since 1880, the second highest in the nation. The state averages five tornadoes per 10,000 square miles, around 35 killer tornadoes with 899 deaths.

Tornadoes are most frequent from March to September. Sixty-eight percent of these tornadoes occur from March to June; 21% during late summer and early autumn; and about 8% in the winter months. In a study done in 1953, the Weather Bureau found that 148 of 500 tornadoes occurred in June. Most tornadoes take place from 4:00 p.m. to 7:00 p.m., when local conditions are at their warmest.[ii]

In the entire world, no single place is more favorable for the development of tornadoes than the Plains region east of the Rocky Mountains, and Kansas is located in the center of this region. A term known as "tornado alley" has been adopted to describe the area from Northern Texas to Oklahoma, Kansas, and Iowa, which seems to be the most susceptible territory for tornado development. What happens is the warm moist air from the Gulf of Mexico collides with dry air associated with late spring cold fronts originating in Canada and the Northern Pacific. On the Central Plains there are no mountain barriers to modify this tropical air, which leaves it free to drift far to the north. The ensuing mix of these air masses results in severe thunderstorms, and with them, tornadoes. Several hours of humid, unstable air creates a volatile mix that can precede the formation of super cell thunderstorms and, with them, tornadoes.[iii]

The cold air behind a front wedges itself underneath the warm air, forcing the warm air to higher altitudes. Sometimes in advance of the cold front, a portion of the cold air is forced upward several thousand feet. If upper air winds are strong, such as the jet stream, the cold air and the warm moist air converge sharply to form a swirling vortex of low pressure, which grows and deepens with a twisting motion. Resultant cooling starts the formation of a corkscrew-like cloud that builds downward to the surface. In this wall cloud, a tornado can appear. Coincidentally, tornadoes will generally form about fifty miles ahead of a cold front.[iv]

The weather preceding a tornado often gives tell-tale signs that danger is near. Unusually hot, humid conditions with high dew points coupled with a strong southerly wind flow can be a prediction of severe weather. As clouds gather and thicken, the bases appear to bulge downward in pendulous forms not unlike huge grapes. These are called mammatocumulous clouds. Sometimes these clouds are a greenish-black color. Tornadoes will often develop on the southwest side of a storm cell, or sometimes at the tail end of the storm. If there has been heavy rain, hail, strong gusty winds, and then it suddenly becomes deathly still and quiet, this is an age-old sign that a tornado is in the vicinity. If the cloud base is too high or the vortex is too weak to reach the ground, it is just a funnel cloud. Thunderstorms with low cloud bases are more likely to have stronger tornadoes.

Some tornadoes are described as resembling the trunk of a huge elephant, while others look like snakes and drift backward almost horizontally. On rare occasions when the funnel is not in evidence at all, it is described as a black massive cloud that descends to the ground. The second tornado that hit Irving, Kansas on May 30, 1879 was just such a rarity. This tornado was described as a "cloud of inky blackness with an almost perpendicular front, apparently two miles wide." Some tornado paths have been scarcely a hundred feet wide, while others have been two to three miles. The average width of a tornado is around 396 yards.[v]

The tornado is considered the most violent of all storms. About 70% of all tornadoes have winds of 75 to 100 miles an hour. About 25% are considered strong with winds of 110 to 200 miles per hour, and about 2.5% are considered violent with winds that surpass 250 to 320 miles an hour. Rarely have tornadoes surpassed the 320 mile mark. All of these figures are open to conjecture, as no equipment has survived a direct hit by an F5 tornado. Tornadoes travel along the ground at an average speed of 30 miles per hour. Some have been known to stand still, barely moving at all, while others have been clocked at 150 miles an hour on the ground. In most cases tornadoes move from the southwest to the northeast, but they can turn at any time and go in another direction. Tornadoes have been known to make U-turns and even complete circles.

Tornadoes can and do occur at all hours. They are especially dangerous during the middle of the night when it is difficult to see them. However, most develop between three and seven p.m. In the northern hemisphere, tornadoes revolve in a counterclockwise direction, and in the southern hemisphere, clockwise. There does seem to be occasional exceptions to this rule. J.P. Finley, the noted nineteenth century meteorologist and pioneer of the U.S. Signal Service, did a study of 350 American tornadoes and found 29 that he claimed rotated clockwise in our hemisphere.[vi]

Little is known, even today, about the interior vortex of a tornado. The 1996 Warner Brothers film, *"Twister,"* had a primary storyline about two conflicting groups trying to get a device close enough to the vortex of a tornado to lift it into the funnel and record wind velocity and barometric readings. This goal among scientists in the field is to accomplish just that. In reading this book, you will find only two accounts of individuals who actually saw inside the vortex of a tornado. Both of these people were extremely lucky to survive. It has been a tough task to take readings of wind velocity, humidity, and temperature in the whirling winds at the surface of a tornado.[vii]

Witnesses often describe a tornado as sounding like a freight train speeding through a tunnel. The source of this noise could be within the tornado itself or in the lower part of the thunderstorm, since the sound is present even when the funnel doesn't touch the ground. People close to a tornado have noticed their ears pop, which is due to the difference in air pressure, and, in fact, this change in pressure causes the most damage -- it can literally make a house explode. When a sudden reduction in pressure occurs, air in many enclosures will rush outward, which causes windows to shatter, buildings to collapse, and automobiles to lift.[viii] The odor that accompanies a tornado is similar to the smell of sulfur or a person's bad breath. What individuals are inhaling at this point is difficult to imagine. It may be a combination of dust and other natural ingredients caught in the swirling vortex.

The color of a tornado depends on the natural background behind the cloud and the stuff the funnel has sucked up from the ground. Depending on the type of soil, the vortex can turn into shades of yellow, brown, or red. And then there are those tornadoes that are invisible. Just imagine the fear this can invoke.[ix]

What are the chances of any one person seeing a tornado in Kansas? In examining the routes and locations of tornadoes over the past century, native-born Kansans who live an average life of 70 years, will have an 80%

probability of seeing a tornado. The possibility of having your home destroyed by a tornado during the same 70 year[x] period is less than 1%, but there is a 43% chance that their property will incur sufficient damage to result in an insurance claim within that same 70 years. Tornadoes are not the only weather-related phenomenon that causes property damage. Hail, high winds, heavy rains, and floods from severe storms cause more damage than a tornado. Actually, there is only 1 chance in 1,613 that any square mile in Kansas will be struck by a tornado in any given year.[xi]

H.L. Jones, a scientist and tornado expert, concluded that the lightning discharged in tornadoes is brighter, bluer, and has a higher voltage than in any other storm. Some eyewitnesses have described the lightning in funnel clouds as bright sheer lightning, almost like lacework. It's theorized that certain lightning patterns could be a means of detecting the presence of a tornado in a thunderstorm when the funnel is not visible.[xii]

From 1916 to 1954, a total of 8,776 lives were lost in tornadoes, making an average of 225 deaths per year. As for injuries, thirteen persons are injured for every one killed by a tornado. In Kansas the chances of being killed are 1 in 5,736 and of being injured, 1 in 441.[xiii]

The earliest recorded tornado in history struck London, England, on October 17, 1091 and demolished 600 homes and churches. The first documented U.S. tornado battered Massachusetts in 1643 and killed one Native American. Other early American twisters were recorded in New Haven, Connecticut in 1682, and Charleston, South Carolina in 1761. The Charleston tornado sank five ships anchored at port. The deadliest tornado outbreak was known as the "Tri-State Tornadoes." The outbreak occurred on March 18, 1925. Seven tornadoes passed through Missouri, Illinois, and Indiana, killing 695 people and injuring 2,027 along a 437-mile path.[xiv]

Waterspouts were recognized as early threats to sailing vessels and they are related to tornadoes. This is an early 1869 view of waterspouts threatening sailing vessels, location unknown.

Another significant tornado outbreak occurred on April 11, 1965 when 40 tornadoes cut across Wisconsin, Iowa, Illinois, Indiana, Michigan, and Ohio, causing 256 deaths and 3,000 injuries. The longest storm system in recorded history struck on April 3-4, 1974 when 148 tornadoes cut a path of destruction 2,400 miles long. On May 20, 1949 witnesses saw 36 separate twisters in Oklahoma, Colorado, Nebraska, and in Kansas, where newspaper headlines read, "Tornado Army Hits Kansas."[xv]

Tornadoes have been recorded almost everywhere in the world. The deadliest twister struck on April 26, 1989 at Dhaka, Bangladesh, where the storm killed 1,109 people and injured 15,500.[xvi]

Wherever tornadoes strike, most regions are unfamiliar with the very nature of them. If you grow up in the Midwestern United States, tornadoes become a fact of life. Growing up anywhere else, and it is an unfamiliar terror.

Early View of a tornado from an 1869 publication by J. Rambosson

Between 1916 and 1953, Kansas ranked thirteenth in property damage from tornadoes with $24,534,010. The 1966 Topeka tornado was the first $100,000,000 tornado in the United States.

In early accounts of Kansas tornadoes certain terms were used interchangeably. Many people used the word "cyclone" when describing a tornado; in fact by 1900 the term "Kansas Cyclone" became a well-known phrase. The word "cyclone" describes several different types of storms, but actually a cyclone is any storm that has winds spiraling around a low-pressure system. A tornado is merely one example of a cyclone; others are hurricanes and the large-scale storms that occur in the mid-latitudes.[xvii]

The first Kansas settlers knew about hurricanes because many of them came from either New England or the Middle Atlantic States, where they experienced hurricanes firsthand. Unfortunately, this knowledge was useless when they encountered tornadoes and severe thunderstorms on the Plains. Even though they knew little about the true nature and severity of these storms, after several frightening years on the prairie these residents became wary and sought shelter when dark clouds appeared. The "cyclone cellar" was the first place the pioneers headed for cover, and they knew if they reached the cellar in time and closed the door securely they were safe.[xviii]

Settlers who were caught out in the open had two options: either run out of the storm's path or lie down in a depression on the ground. Near Topeka a farmer and his wife saved their lives by crouching in a shallow hole used to store potatoes. In the same storm, a neighbor dropped down next to a tree and threw his arms around it. Although he took a terrific beating as the wind buffeted him about, he came through the ordeal alive.

From the 1920s to the present, the basement afforded the best underground protection. Early recommendations were to take cover in the southwest corner, but after further studies, scientists discovered that the northeast corner was the safest. Now they suggest hiding under a sturdy table or piece of furniture in a central room away from windows and doors. In a house without a basement, they advise going to an interior closet or windowless room, lying down, and throwing a mattress on top for added safety.[xix]

FAVORITE TORNADO LEGENDS

Tornadoes have left behind a legacy of peculiar incidents, and some of these were recorded repeatedly in 19th century eyewitness accounts. Most of them have been explained, but some remain a mystery. The following section describes a few of these tornado legends.

*Women and Children First.

Many of the deaths, especially in the 19th and early 20th centuries, were primarily women and children. This myth is valid. When a storm struck, most men were working outside in the open where they could see a tornado coming and take cover. Women and children were not so lucky. Since their domain tended to be inside the home, they were oblivious to the rapidly changing weather conditions outside. When a tornado approached, they took refuge in rooms that afforded little protection, and if the house collapsed, they often suffered death or severe injuries.[xx]

*Plucked Chickens.

One story repeated many times is that tornadoes can strip a chicken of all its feathers. Witnesses have described how the feathers appear to explode off the chicken. This is untrue. Scientists discovered that when a chicken becomes frightened it loosens its feathers. The wind merely blows them off the chicken. This peculiarity is known as "flight molt." After the Registration Day tornado on June 5, 1917, a man kicked over a box that landed upside down in his field.[xxi] Out popped a de-feathered hen squawking and running as fast as she could. Another citizen reported seeing a rooster blown into a jug with only his head protruding. This oddity is questionable.

*Straws Penetrating Trees.

Some images show wood straws that appear to have penetrated trees and lodged there. The theory is that the wind is so strong it can actually drive a straw into a solid tree. What really happens is the wind turns in a cyclonic fashion, twisting the tree and ripping open the bark. Then the wind blows the straw and other flying debris horizontally into the tree. The straws actually penetrate the trunk as it cracks open. After the tornado passes, the tree returns to its original position, leaving the straws stuck in the bark.

After a tornado hit Scottsbluff, Nebraska on May 30, 1951, a newspaper reported the wind imbedded a bean into an egg one inch deep without cracking the shell. This story is open to speculation.[xxii]

*Dust Devils and Micro Bursts.

These two weather anomalies have been closely associated with tornadoes, although neither one really has anything to do with the other. Dust devils are vortexes created at the surface and generally form on hot days under a clear sky with light prevailing winds. The surface of the earth becomes extremely hot, causing the excess heat to surge upward in a plume. If there is a slight breeze, the in-rushing air has enough momentum to cause rotation. The highest winds are usually about 30-60 miles per hour, although around 25 miles per hour is most common. The life span of a dust devil ranges from a few minutes to longer than half an hour.[xxiii] Though dust devils may look imposing, damage is usually minimal; however, a few of the stronger ones have been known to overturn trailers and down power lines.

Microbursts (or downbursts) are completely different. There is a fine line between a microburst and a small tornado, as both can cause significant damage. In the past these "bursts" were called "straight winds", "prairie hurricanes", or "derechos." Dr. Theodore Fujita defined the concept of a microburst in 1976, after he analyzed hundreds of aerial photographs from the "super outbreak" of April 3-4, 1974. A typical micro burst will last from 50-60 minutes and can produce widespread roof and tree damage. Some houses that are twisted off their foundations give the initial impression of tornadic activity. The exact process that triggers the rapid descent of air resulting in a micro burst is not completely understood. What is known is when a cumulonimbus thunderstorm begins to weaken; air currents laden with moisture plunge downward to the ground, which causes the air to spread out in a 400-foot layer containing winds of 40-50 miles per hour. Some winds have been clocked as high as 150 miles per hour. The front of this air mass spreads out in an arc.[xxiv] The source of the flow is exhausted in a few minutes, but the outflow keeps expanding with a curl-back motion that can carry small debris for a half mile.

There have been debates among weather forecasters over the concept of a micro burst vs. a small tornado. The difference between the two is almost negligible. A presumed microburst caused public outcry in 1998 when it severely damaged a Lake Jacomo, a lakeside community near Kansas City. The weather service issued no watches or warnings, and the residents cried foul when the weather service downplayed the event from a small tornado to a microburst.[xxv]

*Animal Behavior Prior To a Storm.

Before the age of modern-day forecasting, one of the primary methods used by pioneers to predict severe weather was to observe the erratic behavior of their animals. Some interesting folklore and superstitions include:

- Horses run fast in the corral before a storm.
- Cows lie down and refuse to go out to pasture.
- When dogs eat grass, expect severe weather or a tornado.
- Ants are busy, gnats bite, crickets sing louder, and flies gather at the screen door before a storm.[xxvi]

*Large Cities Protected by "Heat Dome."

One theory contends that large cities create higher temperatures in the spring and summer, similar to a "heat dome" that saves them from tornadoes. These theorists claim that tornadoes will develop outside of this urban heat dome, and then drop to the ground. Most large cities that support this theory are those that have not had a tornado in recent years. Their good fortune is based on luck, not increased temperatures.[xxvii]

*Tornadoes Strike Twice in the Same Place.

Unfortunately this is true. Two of the most terrifying tornadoes in recorded history hit Irving just 45 minutes apart on May 30, 1879. The first moved in from the southwest, and the second and most violent entered the town from the northwest. One-third of Irving was in ruins. Tornadoes struck the town of Codell in Western Kansas three times in three consecutive years—1916, 1917, and 1918. Even more peculiar is the fact that each of these storms occurred on May 20 at about the same time of day. A fear that spread immediately after the June 8, 1966, Topeka tornado and the Ruskin Heights tornado in 1957, was that another tornado was following the path of the first one. This same rumor nearly caused a riot after the 1991 tornado that hit McConnell Air Force Base and Andover near Wichita.[xxviii]

*A Tornado Can Suck a River Dry.

This is true. The suction effect of a tornado vortex is powerful. U.S. Signal Service administrator J.P. Finley related a story about a farmer's wife who left two buckets of milk hanging in a well to cool. A tornado, hovering aloft, pulled up both buckets and then disappeared. Finley also spoke of wells being sucked dry as the vortex passed overhead. Waterspouts, or small tornadoes, often suck water out of lakes, along with live fish.

* Atmospheric Pressure Causes Most Damage.

Tornado damage is caused by the combined action of strong rotating winds and the impact of wind-borne debris. Houses seem to explode, but actually the force of the wind pushes the windward wall inward, and then the roof lifts up and the other walls fall outward.

Opening windows does not make a difference, although it can limit the spread of broken glass. The house will be damaged just the same, but not necessarily due to a radical drop in air pressure.

*A Tornado Can Be Outrun.

Although most tornadoes travel at about 30 miles per hour, some can move at greater speeds, such as 70 miles per hour. Their paths are erratic, and they can change directions suddenly. In more populated areas citizens can lose sight of a tornado while fleeing and end up directly in its path. Many people have died trying to outrun a tornado. The Wichita Falls tornado in 1979 recorded several deaths caused by this foolish action.[xxix]

*Hills and Valleys Afford Protection from Tornadoes.

This is a false rumor. Tornadoes have no geographic limitations. Emporia residents believed that building a city between two streams afforded them protection, but they have been hit by tornadoes several times. Topeka citizens just knew that a high hill on the southwest side of town, called Burnett's Mound, would protect the city. This theory was wrong—a huge tornado struck on June 8, 1966.[xxx]

CHAPTER ONE: TERRITORIAL KANSAS AND TORNADOES

Before Kansas Territory was opened for settlement in 1854, various Indian tribes inhabited the region. The interaction between these tribes and the weather is a subject we know very little about. We don't know if any of their villages were destroyed by tornadoes; we don't know the mysticism that some tribes believed about severe storms and tornadoes; we don't know how many lives might have been lost by massive tornado outbreaks that escaped recorded history. We can only imagine what it was like being out on the open prairie and, without any warning, seeing a tornado bearing down on a village.

We know that Native Americans were great weather forecasters and some of their predictions have survived to the present day. Here are a few gems that have endured:

"When the moon wears a halo around her head, she will cry before morning and the tears (rain) will reach you tomorrow."

"When locks turn damp in the scalp house, it will storm on the morrow."

"When the night has a fever, it cries in the morning."

"When the buffalo band together, the storm God is herding them."

"When the sun sets unhappy, the morning will be angry with storm."

--Zuni Indians[1]

Records of tornadoes in America date back to 1804; reports of this information is scattered throughout the bulletins of the U.S. Signal Service.

In the early 19th century, a great divergence of opinion existed concerning the climate on the Great Plains, which lay beyond the fringe of eastern civilization. Was this really the Great American Desert, as explorers such as Zebulon Pike professed? Did this "desert" make agricultural development impossible? These questions remained unresolved throughout the settlement of Kansas Territory. At that time the main source of climatological data came from the U.S. Army detachments stationed at the western forts. It was the responsibility of the Medical Department surgeon at each post to keep a "Diary of the Weather," with a view to compiling a "medical topography" of the region.[2] Though of doubtful quality, their observations did give an indication of the general climactic conditions west of the Mississippi River. Beginning in the late 1840s, the military weather records were supplemented by the reports of volunteer observers from the Smithsonian Institution in Washington, who supplied an array of thermometers, barometers, and rain gauges to these qualified individuals.

The first weather records recorded by the Medical Department began at Fort Snelling in Minnesota and Fort Leavenworth, Kansas in 1836, and a year later at Fort Row, at St. Louis Missouri.[3] The observer's records did not show any weather anomalies for several years and indicated only a passing interest in severe storms and tornadoes.

By 1850, after thirty years of record collecting, the weather observers gathered enough data for an analysis. This monumental task fell to a youthful statistician by the name of Lorin Blodget. His final report was a 400-page book entitled, "Climatology of the U.S. and the Temperate Latitudes of the North

American Continent." This invaluable weather record earned Blodget the title of "Father of American Climatology."[4]

While it appeared that weather observers were making strides to understand the science of meteorology and forecasting, it was apparent that even the simplest of weather theories were unpopular. It would take disaster after disaster to spur further study and acceptance.

The first major meteorological breakthrough came from across the Atlantic Ocean. On November 14, 1854, the French warship *Henri V* sank off the coast of Balaklava during a fierce storm that claimed 400 lives. The French minister of war asked noted astronomer Urbain Leverrier to look into the circumstances surrounding the disaster. By showing that the "surprise" storm was actually no surprise, that it formed on November 12 and then swept across Europe from northwest to southeast, Leverrier proved that weather phenomena travels across the earth' surface.[5]

The French government theorized that cities could exchange information and use it to locate storms and predict their movement. In 1855 the government established a special observation network of 24 stations linking 13 of these by telegraph. Other European nations followed suit, and by 1865 Europe's weather observation network boasted 59 stations.[6] A similar weather service wasn't established in the United States until 1870, and the advent of the telegraph led to its development. Without the telegraph, no instantaneous link of information could exist between cities.

The first significant encounter between early Kansas settlers and nature at its worst occurred in October 1844. Some early Kansas residents were missionaries appointed to bring Christianity to Native Americans living on reservations. One of the largest of these missions was the Shawnee

Methodist Mission located in present Shawnee Mission (a suburb of Kansas City). In the 1840s the mission became a popular gathering place for both settlers emigrating on the Plains and members of the Shawnee Indian tribe.

On October 24 a tornado struck the mission. Elizabeth Hayward recorded in her book, *John McCoy, His Life and His Diaries,* the following passage: "In the evening a dreadful hurricane passed over Shawnee Methodist Mission, demolishing many of the buildings and injuring some few individuals, but no lives were lost."[7]

East of the mission, the tornado damaged more settlements. The Fort Leavenworth Indian Agency, located near the Missouri state line, was "torn to pieces . . . all the roof was carried off several hundred yards, and torn all into pieces and scattered, hardly two pieces at the same place.[8]

At the village of Westport, Missouri, the tornado demolished a schoolhouse and one dwelling, killing a little girl. McCoy certainly had reason to make mention of this storm as his two-story frame house was "thrown from its foundations," and the "gable ends… were carried upwards of 50 yards… Some of the large beams were taken 50 feet. Pieces of furniture were found a great distance in the woods." Near the town of Independence, Missouri, the tornado reportedly killed ten people.[9]

Two days later, on October 26, 1844 Shawnee Indian missionary Jotham Meeker, curious about the rumors of death and destruction in the area, rode east to Westport. He recorded in his diary: "Ride to Westport and other places, where I witnessed terrible destruction from a tornado which passed about a mile from us… Nearly all the fences, trees, houses, in its course are prostrated. Many people are wounded. Hear of eight lives being lost."[10]

Two years later on August 19, 1846, several companies of Missouri volunteers driving a thousand head of cattle westward camped on Coal Creek in Douglas County. That night a severe wind and hailstorm struck the party, spooking the animals and stampeding them across the plains. It took the men several days to round up all of the cattle.[11]

Encounters with severe weather were a new and frightening experience for emigrants on the Oregon, California, and Santa Fe Trails. Francis Parkman in his famous work, *The Oregon Trail,* does not describe any contacts with tornadoes but does mention thunderstorms and bad weather.

Parkman, who was in an Oglala Sioux village when a severe storm struck, wrote the following about his experience:

"After eating a bowl of meat and inhaling a whiff or two from our entertainer's pipe, a thunderstorm that had been threatening for some time now began in good earnest. We crossed over to Reynal's lodge [A Frenchman in the Sioux village]...Here we sat down, and the Indians gathered around us.

"'What is it,' said I, 'that makes the thunder?'

"'It's my belief,' said Reynal, 'that it's a big stone rolling over the sky.'

"Old Mene-Seela, or Red Water . . . said he had always known what thunder was. It was a great black bird, and once he had seen it, in a dream, swooping down from the Black Hills, with its loud roaring wings, and when it flapped them over a lake they struck lightning from the water.

"'The thunder is bad,' another old man said, 'he killed my brother last summer.'"

Parkman learned more about the man killed by the lightning:

"He belonged to an association which, among other mystic functions, claimed the exclusive power and privilege of fighting the thunder. Whenever a storm which they wished to avert was threatening, the 'thunder-fighters' would take their bows and arrows, their guns, their magic drum, and a sort of whistle, made out of the wing-bone of the war-eagle, and thus equipped, run out and fire at the rising cloud, whooping, yelling, whistling, and beating their drum, to frighten it down again. One afternoon, a heavy black cloud was coming up and they repaired to the top of a hill, where they brought all their magic artillery into play against it. But the undaunted thunder, refusing to be terrified, darted out a bright flash, which struck one party dead as he was in the very act of shaking his long iron-pointed lance against it. The rest scattered and ran yelling in an ecstasy of superstitious terror back to their lodges."[12]

Early Kansas settler Ely Moore, who was a resident of Lawrence for decades, left behind a legacy of speeches, letters, and journals on every aspect of life in nineteenth century Kansas. In one account, he told of his first encounter with a Kansas tornado in 1855, and his reminiscence is the only known record made by a white settler about the Indian's perspective on these storms.

Moore was out hunting buffalo with a party of Miami Indians when a storm approached. Suddenly the Chief of the Miami tribe pointed skyward at the millions of grasshoppers winging their way east obscuring the sun. The Chief exclaimed to Moore, "They know. The devil winds they come kill all. Maybe." Moore realized that they were all out in the open facing a gathering storm so they banded together with the Indians to protect themselves from the severe weather.

Moore wrote that the men worked feverishly cutting a trench wide enough to hold the wagons. They brought all the ponies into an enclosure and herded the cattle close so the guards stationed around them could prevent a stampede. Moore said:

"About five o'clock in the afternoon a greenish purple cloud hung close to the horizon and revolved as it approached. This balloon shaped lowering monster had many laterals that were licking up beasts, water, earth and air to satiate the ponderous paw of this fiend of might... Our awed cattle with lolling tongues and stamping feet were pitiful to see... Our chief mounted up his favorite horse and occupied the center of the encampment, the squaws packed the empty wagons, and the hunters with their arms thrown around their horses necks stood and awaited the result. Just then a sound as of muffled drums reached us, and as a rift in the clouds shot a glare of light upon the camp, I stole a hasty look around me. There stood the Indians, stolid, and in a humble supplication to the Great Spirit. The storm descended with violence upon the dusky forms that seemed to literally await their doom. After the wind came the hail of great size and sharp enough to force cattle's eyes from their sockets and lacerate the backs and flanks of their ponies.

"Some of our wagon covers were tattered or shred in strips. The 'cyclone' as it was known then, appeared egg-shaped to the north, a half-mile wide in length. As it neared the encampment it deposited with our corral of wagons a downpour of sand, earth, grass, weeds and limbs of trees. We were literally covered—wrapped in an electric cloud.

"Some of our wagon covers were tattered or shred in strips. As the electric sparks snapped from the tips of our horse's ears, the mooing shivery creatures were circled by the electric fluid and bolts were drawn from our wagon beds. Fortunately as the tornado approached, it seemed to bound in the air some hundred feet. Just as one of the drag-nets, or feeders of the parent dragon reached our encampment it was apparently struck by lightning.

"The breaking of the dragnet was all that saved us---the force was broken and contented itself by destroying only a few wagons."

Ely happily reported, "As the disappointing fiend passed, over us came feelings of light and joy and jolly, then supper. What a transition! The faces that were but a few moments before blanched with despair, now were warm with a smile and a jest."

On their way home and just a few miles from their camp, they saw where the tornado had stripped acres of sod from the prairie. They found two dead buffalo, both completely devoid of hair and each had broken bones. "These animals must have been picked up by the tornado and carried high and then dashed to the earth," Moore noted. His account of this tornado is the first one recorded in Kansas.[13]

The early years in Kansas Territory were not only violent with free-state and pro-slavery skirmishes but also plagued by destructive tornadoes. David Ludlum in his *Early American Tornadoes* noted on May 15, 1859, a tornado dipped down in the small town of Manhattan. On June 8 a strong tornado hit Lawrence, destroying buildings, tearing the roofs off houses, and injuring many residents.[14] The storm moved on to Osawatomie where it killed three people.[15]

One account of this storm's passing was written by O.C. Brown and appeared forty years later in the *Jefferson County Journal* published in Adams, New York. Although his account was off by two years (he states it occurred in 1857), it was actually the 1859 storm that he was describing. This is his version of what happened:

"In gratitude to a watchful providence, which so signally protected our lives, I will give a minute account of the wind demon, which well might be denominated the 'spirit and power of the air.' It was a Sabbath afternoon, when returning from a meeting at the Geers Hotel, casting my eyes west I saw a black cloud the size of a man's hand. A moment later its proximity and size filled me with terror. I sent my son Spencer to the river [Marais des Cygnes] to secure the ferryboat. My wife with the bronchitis, unable to increase her speed, with my arm around her waist I almost carried her bodily, reaching the door of our cabin as the bolt struck us, burst it in, and prostrating us upon the floor with great violence. That saved our lives, for a moment later the roof of the adjoining building was of the adjoining building was ser down by the terrible wind just in front of the door we had so quickly entered, as not to have time to raise the latch.

"My son having made the boat secure, started back through the woods some forty rods for the house, reaching the timber just as it was struck. He ran the gauntlet of the falling trees, leaping the downed and dodging the falling ones, and limbs. He came to us in our moment of peril.

"Into the northwest corner of the room my family, about half a score, was grouped. The west part of the roof over our heads was carried away, but the puncheon floor above us protected us from any falling debris. The rain fell in torrents after the wind subsided. Rushing in came many of the hotel people. Happy that no lives were lost and no one seriously injured, we set about disposing ourselves for the night. The two-thirds roof remaining on the east end of the house shielded the thirty or more people from the pouring rain.

"Having had some experience in 'the field bed line,' having seen the beds and floor filled we had to send some away to other cabins with unoccupied floors, we spread our blankets and bedding so as to cover the protected part of the floor for night rest as best we could."[16]

Brown and his party surveyed the damage the next morning with renewed respect for the storm's awesome power. He noted, "The force of the cyclone may be understood better when I state that the entire building was lifted bodily over a pile of glazed sash, for the entire building landed on the ground some 20 or 30 feet away and landed in my garden beyond. No glass was broken… the power of the storm was much greater here when it first landed, so to speak, than a mile farther east, when the hotel only was crushed and some few buildings moved from their foundations."[17]

On June 20, 1859, settlers witnessed another tornado in the sparsely populated region around Minneapolis. This storm proved to be the end of severe weather for over a year.

A lack of precipitation was troublesome to the settlers through most of 1859 and into 1860. A drought that year destroyed their crops and forced the settlers to eat weeds and pumpkin rinds to survive.[18] During 1860 nearly 30,000 people left Kansas, and those that remained had to borrow money at a high rate of interest against their claims. Subsequent foreclosures caused many of those who survived the drought to lose their land.[19]

The only break in this drought was a storm that formed in extreme Eastern Kansas, where a tornado virtually destroyed every building and house in the Missouri River town of Sumner in Atchison County. This storm marked the end of Sumner; the town had been in competition with Atchison for the county seat.[20]

In 1922, Thomas F. Doran made a speech to the Topeka Saturday Night Club about the trials of the drought:

"1860 was a dry year. It did not rain for 14 months, and practically nothing was produced except wild grass, which never fails."[21]

Stephen Spear told of life on Dragoon Creek in Wabaunsee County during the drought of 1860, "During the fall and winter of 1859 scarcely any rain or snow fell, and during the spring of 1860 barely enough fell to sprout and bring up the crops… The hot winds blew and the grasshoppers came in swarms from the southwest and devoured what little vegetation there was… The drought was so severe that the streams stopped running, and most of the pools in the creek beds went dry. The prairie grass was short and eaten close to the ground by the cows and young stock."[22]

Peter Bryant, a Jackson County pioneer, noted in a letter dated May 20, 1860 the gloomy prospects due to the drought, "It is very dry. There comes a shower once in awhile but not enough to do any good. The old chaps around here shake their heads and say they are afraid that they are not going to make any crop." In a May 13 letter, Bryant wrote that the winter wheat around Holton was only about three inches high and that "The Missouri River is very low. Steamboats do not run up any higher than Atchison, and they all wear 'grasshoppers' to lift them off the sand bars. I waded the Kaw yesterday and drove across four yoke of cattle. Deepest spot was 3 ½ feet."[23]

Independence Day 1860 brought the first significant summer rains, and also the first destructive storm in nearly a year. Funnel clouds accompanied by heavy rains raked northeast Kansas.

"Great quantities of timber were destroyed on the Missouri River by a tornado," according to David Ludlum. On July 31, tornadoes caused damage in Burlington, Leroy, and Ottumwa in Coffey County and Marysville in Marshall County.[24]

In Marysville, the thermometer that July day reached 102 degrees, and a brisk wind blew from the south. It seemed to be just another day of drought not unlike so many others. Then all of a sudden a dark cloud appeared in the northwest and moved up the valley of the Blue River. A man by the name of Weisbard, a storeowner in Marysville, watched the cloud change into "a dark gray cylindrical mass of vapor." The storm swept through the town, ripping the roofs off of houses, uprooting trees, and carrying away fences.[25]

Weisbard recounted in a newspaper interview, "When the tornado struck . . . Marysville it filled the air with dust and a dark mass of clouds, until it seemed like midnight. The first crash burst in the front door of my store, and then carried the roof off. I went out the back door to save my trunk, when the wind hurled me south towards my stable, where I grasped an elm post, around which I was several times whipped, but managed to hold on until the storm was over. A man was blown from my side and carried several hundred feet over the ruins of a house and deposited in Spring Creek Valley. On the prairie in the center of the storm track, the grass was completely stripped, as in winter after the prairie fires..."[26]

On July 28, 1860 the *Neosho Valley Register* of Burlington ran the headlines, "A Frightful Hurricane, Houses Blown Down, Miles of Fences Scattered About." The editor noted, "It commenced about five o'clock and lasted nearly an hour, during which the rain fell in torrents, Jove's artillery made the heavens and earth tremble and the vivid lightning darted from cloud to cloud, which added brilliancy to the lurid scene... Large trees two feet in diameter were twisted in two by the wind and fences by the mile, barns, outhouses, and many dwellings, with people inside, yielded to the tornado and were scattered everywhere." In Burlington the tornado leveled Mr. A. Fleming's house, but the family escaped injury. The high winds pushed the

Davis & Post building off its foundation and jolted the newspaper office, cracking the plaster inside.[27]

In Leroy the storm damaged six buildings, including the Neosho House, Smith's log store, and the roof of Amsden's saw mill. The twister destroyed Mr. Hough's house and seriously injured him.[28]

At Ottumwa, north of Burlington, the tornado damaged the Methodist parsonage, which caused a devastating fire that burned all the furniture and household items. A man identified as Mr. Mills was in the upper floor of the building when the storm hit. It threw him several feet in the air and out through an opening in the roof. Rescuers found him unconscious a hundred yards away. The twister destroyed much of the town, including the blacksmith shop, a cabinet store, and a hotel.[29]

The newspaper editor concluded that everyone should pay attention to the tornado damage to wooden structures and should construct stone buildings, which would save their property the next time a tornado appeared. For Ottumwa it was too late. The town ceased to exist shortly thereafter.[30]

The brief respite from tornadoes was over, but the drought continued to have an impact in Kansas Territory. A letter from a soldier in the First U.S. Cavalry, dated October 22, 1860, summed up the year: "The heavy drought that prevailed in Kansas the past summer has caused a great many to abandon their homes on the frontier for homes farther east, where they could gain a livelihood during the coming winter. In a great many cases everything too cumbersome to carry away, was left behind… The streams we crossed were nearly all dry." [31]

The mass exodus of people from Kansas Territory continued until the end of the year. All the settlers blamed the drought for their failure to succeed on the prairie, but some of the blame rested directly on their own shoulders. Few of them bothered to study the climate or the land and to time the planting of their crops accordingly.

James C. Malin, in a 1941 study of winter wheat production in Kansas, had this to say: "The drought year of 1860 yielded no crop, the harvesting of winter wheat was done with butcher knives, each man carrying a sack to put the heads in… these farmers did not remain long enough in one place to learn anything of the peculiarities of either soil or climate, and as certainly would contribute little accumulated knowledge to those who succeeded them."[32]

The settlers viewed their experiences with severe weather and tornadoes about the same as they did the drought. Kansas Territory was so isolated that few of them could gain any real firsthand knowledge of the destructiveness of a tornado. Those who witnessed the tornado's power were indeed awe-inspired, but they lacked the desire to pass the information on to the new settlers.[33]

The ordeals of the pioneers during the next twenty years would change their lives forever. Although the tornado would lose some of its novelty, it would become a manifestation of terror and ferocity. Newspapers of the day described its characteristics as having an almost super-human, monstrous quality, and the impact of one horrendous tornado would lead to another migration out of Kansas.[34] By 1860, 500 stations were making regular observations and sending their findings back to the Smithsonian Institution. Weather forecasting had made significant inroads in less than fifteen years. But along came the Civil War.....

CHAPTER TWO: EARLY TORNADO DISASTERS, 1860-1880

Sometimes it takes a war to bring about new technology for positive change. In the Civil War, military strategy depended upon the cooperation of the weather. Forecasting was not a top priority until military movements and battles became stymied by bad storms. The war that waged in the Atlantic Ocean and the Gulf of Mexico depended upon warnings of approaching hurricanes and tropical storms. A large hurricane could, in fact, destroy an entire fleet of ships.

Samuel F.B. Morse, with his "Morse Code" and the telegraph, brought about our first experiments in weather forecasting. The telegraph proved an invaluable tool for informing troops concerning the whereabouts of the enemy and in alerting armies that an approaching storm front could ruin their military movements.[1]

The U.S. Government had never created an agency to further the development of weather forecasting until 1870 when Morse and weather theorist James Espy founded the United States Army Signal Bureau.[2] Quite often officers of the Signal Corps went galloping across the plains in an effort to track meteorological aberrations and tornado aftermaths. This agency sent Sgt. John P. Finley west to investigate the Irving, Kansas tornadoes in 1879, and another tornado outbreak in 1881. Finley was directly responsible for calling Kansas "The Cyclone State"[3]

The U.S. Army Signal Bureau became the U.S. Weather Bureau. General Albert J. Meyer became the first acting director. Finley served as a field scientist. He became fascinated with tornadoes and he resolved to learn how they formed and if they could be predicted. In 1880 he made an unprecedented effort to document tornado activity. He recorded nearly 100 tornadoes that year. By 1884 Finley had a hundred correspondents in the field that sent him newspaper clippings about severe storms and tornadoes. Unfortunately, many of these resources disappeared; about 60% have since been reorganized and they are available on microfilm.

Finley's efforts were remarkable, given the limited knowledge and technology of the day. He is directly responsible for increasing our understanding of weather phenomena at a time when tornadoes were seldom documented. Without Finley's perseverance, there would be few records about weather happenings in the 19th century.

Finley recognized the need for tornado warnings, and during the 1870s he endeavored to bring about more accurate forecasting. At that time daily weather forecasts were known as "probabilities" and were sporadic in nature. Actually, Finley initiated a tornado warning system in the 1880s but the fact that he soon discontinued them indicates that his success ratio was slim. A lack of surface observations and the absence of upper air readings made it impossible for him to obtain any data on the structure of these storms.[4]

EL DORADO, JUNE 16, 1871

The decade of the 1870's came in like a lion. While Finley was in the first years of the U.S. Army Signal Bureau, Kansans were experiencing one of their first significant tornado disasters.

An account of how the day unfolded was recorded by B.F. Adams, who lived through the tornado that day:

"Its appearance... seemed indescribable; apparently a great wall of inky blackness, from which came the vivid lightning flashes, grand in one sense, yet behind it were the missiles of destruction and death. Soon there was a rumbling sound 'as the rushing of a mighty wind,' and so it was. A moment later, about 7:30, that bank of blackness had burst upon us in all its fury, and continued with but little cessation for an hour and a half. The appalling destruction at such times cannot be described; it is only realized when felt, and at these times do we fully feel how frail we are and our utter helplessness. Our house, although rocked like a cradle, was left standing."

Several neighbors were not as lucky. Several lost their homes, and they somehow made their way to the Adams place for help and shelter. Many were beaten by hailstones while making the trip.

Twenty-one houses in El Dorado and vicinity were destroyed. The Silas Welch place lost a kitchen and porch. Where these sections of his place went were unknown.

Several people were killed, including a three-year-old child that was ripped from his mother's arms and blown several hundred feet away. El Dorado would eventually rebuild but the town became an early reminder of things to come.

In 1874 Kansans were plagued by another phenomenon---the grasshopper invasion. On July 28, millions of grasshoppers darkened the sky across Kansas; they ate everything including crops, gardens, and posts, even the clothes off the backs of the settlers. When they crossed rivers and streams, their droppings fell in the water, killing all the fish. The following winter was so mild that the grasshoppers and their eggs lay dormant in the ground. As a result, when the weather warmed up in the spring, another grasshopper plague occurred equally as devastating as the one the year before.

Occasionally other insects and animals would annoy Kansans, including locusts and the "toad outbreak" in 1879, but none were as destructive as the grasshopper invasion.

As more settlers moved to Kansas during the 1870s, the reports of tornadoes became more frequent.[5] The pioneers, who had little experience with these storms, were uncertain about what they were facing. In 1976 Emma Kinner wrote an article about her grandparents, Anna and Frank Doubrava, who encountered a tornado in Ellsworth County in 1878. She had this to say about her grandmother Anna:

"This spring day had been warm and quiet, with fitful gusts of wind. In the far west a few thunderclouds were rising but they would not reach this area until nighttime. Grandma had washed the blue work shirts for grandpa and the boys, and had hung them on a rope line stretched between two trees... Suddenly she was conscious of a strange sound— a low roar, apparently from the west. She stepped out and saw something she had never seen before. Spinning like an immense top, and moving upright down the slope towards her, was a big brown barrel. As she watched it, spellbound, it passed a few feet in front of her, and engulfed the line of shirts, storing them, line and all, somewhere within itself... She was so angry at it that she ran after it, screaming and waving her arms. She did not catch it, and it lifted into the sky and disappeared. Where would you find five new work shirts?"[6]

TORNADO OUTBREAK, JULY 1876

A series of severe storms, some with tornadoes, caused widespread damage to several communities during the first weeks of July 1876. On July 5th a tornado struck Chase, a railroad stop in Marion County, where it turned over several railroad cars, tore off a corner of the depot, damaged two stores, a church, and some residences. Flying glass injured several people. The next day another tornado hit the town of Stafford, destroying nearly every building in town and killing Mr. A. Crooks. The high winds at Woodbine also blew a flourmill off its foundation.[7]

The storm moved northeast to Abilene, demolishing a Baptist church, three houses, and a blacksmith shop. At Enterprise it damaged several stables and unroofed a store.[8]

On July 6 a tornado hit Stafford, destroying nearly every house in town and killing one man. Then it moved to Woodbine where it knocked a flourmill off its foundation.

North of Abilene on July 9, lightning struck the home of Tom Perry, killing his son. In the same neighborhood, a small tornado demolished several houses and killed other settlers. At Chapman it wrecked the Methodist church, and in Manhattan it destroyed another Methodist church as well as causing widespread destructive damage. At Fort Riley the wind unroofed nearly all the buildings and injured two soldiers. A tornado struck El Dorado where it wrecked three houses and killed one person. It demolished three houses and killed Mrs. John David. The wind picked up Mrs. K. Plant's son, swept him to the tops of the highest trees, then set him down on his feet uninjured. This storm system soon moved out of the state, striking several towns in Iowa and Michigan and killed more people before it dissipated. [9]

COTTONWOOD FALLS/STRONG CITY, 1878

For a while in the mid-1870s, tornado activity lessened but then it came back violently in 1878 and 1879. During a major storm outbreak in 1878, a tornado dropped out of the clouds near Cottonwood Falls in Chase County. Cottonwood Falls is located about a mile and a half from nearby Strong City. The *Chase County Leader* of April 18 reported the storm's events as follows:

"A tornado struck this city and Cottonwood Station [Strong City] about half past four o'clock last Saturday afternoon, which for terrible fury and disastrous results surpassed anything heretofore known to the oldest inhabitant. For half an hour or more before the terrible crash, our citizens watched the conflicting elements for the destructive onset. The sky appeared to be one boiling, surging mass of clouds, terrible, grand, which finally assumed the shape of a funnel."

When the funnel hit the outskirts of Cottonwood Falls, it struck the Catholic church first, forcing it about eight feet off its foundation. Then it turned the residence of George Estes upside down. The twister lifted up the home of J.W. McWilliams and "sot it down across lots." The wind carried Mrs. McWilliams, who was busy cleaning house when the storm hit, across the street and dropped her unhurt in a neighbor's yard. Before the tornado moved east, it damaged a barn and three other homes. The *Leader* noted that the tornado was "accompanied by a perfect deluge of rain and hail, the latter doing immense damage to windows. The pecuniary loss to this city will foot up to somewhere around $2,500. No one was injured but the excitement and terror for an hour after the storm was intense and about one-quarter of the inhabitants sought safety in the courthouse."[10]

Actually, the excitement had only just begun. Strong City, then known as Cottonwood Station, owned the railroad depot about a mile and a half north of Cottonwood Falls. It was situated on Main Street directly in the path of the tornado.

First, the funnel smashed John Miller's two-story house southeast of the railroad depot and scattered it along the road for half a mile, seriously injuring Miller, his wife and three children. The wind lifted Mrs. Miller over thirty feet in the air and hurled her against a picket fence. She died within the hour. The tornado swept away the Walter family residence, injuring three people. Rescuers found Mrs. Walters underneath part of the roof, still clutching her newborn baby beneath her. Then the tornado hit a row of new homes, destroying four of them, and badly injuring two more people.

North of the railroad tracks, the funnel leveled four more houses, injuring Mrs. Ike Matthews and carrying Mrs. John Filson 150 yards under a roof support.

On Main Street the tornado unroofed the Cottonwood Hotel; flattened the back of the Harris Store; tore the roof off the smokehouse, where several hundred pounds of freshly-cured meat disappeared; and knocked the Hildrebrand residence and the Plumberg house off their foundations. The storm removed the roof from the Wharton store and hurled it against the Hildrebrand Brothers' warehouse.[11]

When the funnel reached the John Morton house, it tore the kitchen from the main building and carried it over a hundred feet, then scattered furniture, clothing, utensils, and other items all over the site. "For several minutes," the *Leader* noted, "the air was black with dirt, grass, stones, and timbers and the wonder is that so few were injured."[12]

The twister continued on. It blew fourteen loaded freight cars off the tracks; one car contained a threshing machine, several wagons, and other large farm implements belonging to the Hildrebrand Brothers' store. Arch Miller was loading one car with wheat and he had just unhitched his team when the tornado struck. It overturned the car and smashed his wagon. Miller and the team escaped injury. Mr. Bomgardner had three freight cars loaded with household goods, farm machinery, and a complete house frame. After the tornado hit the cars, it rolled the items over and over, crushing all of them. The railroad section boss had $820 cash in his house before the storm swept it away; he finally located $500 in an adjoining field.[13]

After the storm passed, the *Leader* described the scene:

"Cottonwood Station, immediately after the tornado, presented a pitiable sight. But five houses were left intact. Men, women, and children, with faces and bodies blackened and bleeding and with clothes torn to shreds could be seen in every direction, almost crazed with pain and fear. The [most] severe injuries were to women and children; the men were mostly out of doors and at work in the depot or at the stores... The damage at Cottonwood Station will run over $50,000."

The tornado moved east, touching down again near the community of Diamond Springs in Morris County. It caught Tom Morton out in the open in a spring wagon and after blowing him several feet in the air, it spun him around like a top and dashed him to the ground; he escaped with only bruises. The storm then moved to some settlements near Peyton Creek, where it destroyed the Thompson house and injured the occupants. On Jacobs Creek the funnel demolished the Osborne house, killing three members of the family; and at the Davis home, it singled out and killed one child. The twister turned up Phenis Creek, killing three more people, a six-year old boy and two women. The wind carried a child of the Bogue family two miles away. Rescuers found her later, only slightly injured. In all, the tornado destroyed over twenty farmhouses in a ten-mile area, leaving only one farmhouse undamaged.[14]

The tornado moved on, striking the town of Safford, where it destroyed three store buildings, including one stone structure. Hailstones damaged the north side of the Safford railroad depot, leaving large dents in the siding. The tornado then headed for Emporia where it demolished several buildings on the outskirts of town, including the Lyon County Poor Farm, the high school, several business buildings, a flourmill, and furniture factory. At times this tornado appeared to be four to six miles wide. Right before it rose back into the clouds two miles east of Emporia, it blew a twenty-five-car freight train off its tracks.[15]   Map Available, Appendix 1.

THE TORNADO OF THE CENTURY:

IRVING, KANSAS, MAY 30, 1879

The tornadoes responsible for giving Kansas the label, "The Cyclone State," were the Irving tornadoes of 1879. These horrendous storms were a wake-up call to provide more adequate storm warnings to settlers. These tornadoes were the most violent in the history of Kansas, and if they had occurred fifty years later and struck any of the larger cities in the state, a major disaster would have resulted.

This storm front was responsible for a series of tornadoes reported in Kansas, Missouri, Nebraska, and Iowa on May 29 and 30. Although there is no reliable list of casualties and property damage from these storms, it was unusually high considering the sparsely settled region where they occurred. Few people caught in this storm system's path had ever seen or heard of anything quite like these tornadoes.[16]

Sergeant J.P. Finley, one of the founders of the U.S. Signal Service, thought these storms were so significant that he came to Kansas just to retrace their paths. He published his findings in "Professional Papers of the Signal Service No. 4." Most of Finley's detailed report formulates the basis for our knowledge of this destructive tornado outbreak.[17]

The morning of May 30 dawned bright and clear, giving no warning of what was in store for the settlers. One citizen, however, reported in the afternoon that the wind blew harder than normal from the southeast, and the air became unusually sultry. About 4:00 p.m. the sky turned ominously dark in the southwest near the town of Randolph, where a small tornado formed and caused severe damage to three farms. It followed Walnut Creek for about seven miles to Fancy Creek, and then veered off down "Hanson's Ravine," where it destroyed a barn. This seemed to be the last of this small tornado. So far there were no fatalities.

A larger tornado then formed at Fancy Creek and destroyed the Weisdanger house. At that point, the high winds were carrying 150 to 200 pound stones more than 300 feet. The tornado continued northeast where it hit the house of Adam Schwein. Inside were his family and three school children. All became buried beneath the ruins. The father and mother were not seriously hurt, but the twister killed an infant in its mother's arms, and falling timbers crushed their daughter's head. The tornado destroyed this home and family in an instant without giving them any warning or opportunity to escape. The wind blew all of their belongings a mile away, some items dangled from the tree tops.[18]

Most of the residents of nearby Randolph saw what was happening, and when several funnel clouds appeared they had time to take cover in their storm cellars or dugouts. Right before the storm, the air around Randolph became deadly calm, but after the tornadoes passed, heavy rain and hail hit, along with cold northerly winds.

The tornado continued moving along North Otter Creek, where it unroofed a stone schoolhouse. The students had left just minutes before. The funnel was now estimated at 300 feet wide. After reaching the open prairie, the tornado skipped back and forth until it crossed into Marshall County where it descended again and became a quarter of a mile wide.[19] There the funnel destroyed four farm houses. Gaven Read was inside his home unaware of what was happening outside. When he stepped out the door, he fell twenty-five feet to the ground, seriously injuring himself. The tornado lifted his house that high in the air.

The twister moved to Game Fork Creek where it destroyed a cluster of homes, including George Martin's house. Falling timbers killed Mrs. Martin. Henry Wilson's log house now lay in the path of the twister. It lifted the house, dashed it to the ground, and then carried it away piece by piece. Thirteen people were in the house, mostly small children, but none of them were seriously hurt.

Now the tornado began to bear down on Irving, a thriving community of 300 inhabitants. J.P. Finley described the tornado at this point as "demonic, whirling with most frightful rapidity, the intense black column would at times seem to level the whole bluff as it disappeared from view within the huge rolling mass of darkness"[20] On the outskirts of town at the home of the Brumbells, all the tornado left was a few foundation stones and part of an old stove. Nearby, the Buckmaster house completely disappeared. The family suffered horribly— the father was lying on the ground by the foundation with fragments of his clothing still clinging to him. The tornado killed the mother and five children instantly.

As the funnel entered Irving, the first house it hit was that of the John Gale family. The wind blew them outside and stripped them of their clothing. Dorothy Gale was wedged head first in the mud, her body sticking straight up in the air. The visual picture was gruesome, and newspapers described it that way all over the country.[21]

In a later reference to this tornado, it was noted that L. Frank Baum, author of the "Wizard of Oz" books, had as his main character a young girl named Dorothy Gale. At the time of the Irving tornado, Baum was a salesman who traveled all over the Midwest. No one knows whether he ever visited Irving, but he could have read about it in any newspaper. Is it a coincidence that the Kansas girl in the Wizard of Oz had the same name as the young woman killed in Irving? Readers can only surmise.

The Gallop house was next. The tornado lifted it in the air, along with the family of five, and carried it to a height of twenty feet, then twisted and dropped it.[22] Miraculously no one was killed. The tornado then moved on through the southern part of town, destroying Captain Armstrong's new farm buildings— nothing remained standing. Later a farmer found his own letters seven miles northeast of town. Armstrong stated that there was complete destruction in about ten seconds.[23]

After this storm disappeared to the east, a warm southerly wind blew over the town, accompanied by a soft rain. Then the sun came out, the warm rays soothing the terror-stricken inhabitants, who were witnessing firsthand the terrible destruction all around them. But hardly had they emerged from their cellars when there appeared to the west a cloud of enormous proportions; it covered the sky with a perpendicular front of inky blackness nearly two miles wide. The cloud looked so threatening that some people actually believed judgment day had arrived and were offering up fervent prayers that they might be saved.

With a roar "like that of a thousand cannons," the cloud covered the whole town - it was a cross between a hurricane and a cyclone. In an instant it swept everything from the earth, and the settlers experienced death in its most dreadful form. The power of the tornado destroyed in a few minutes what took the townspeople twenty years to build.[24]

The twister hit Mr. J. Preston's place about 6:20 p.m. and he noted:

"Our first sensations upon the contact of the storm were as though the building had been picked up, violently shaken, and then set down again. The next instant the doors and windows were broken in, the furniture whirled around the room and broken in pieces, and I, standing in the east room, picked up, whirled around and carried through the folding doors into the main room to the west and laid upon the floor uninjured… Upon rising from the floor I found my clothing torn into shreds, but not a bruise upon my body. While in the act of taking hold of a door knob to descend into the basement, where I had sent my family, I found both hands benumbed as though asleep and I was unable to open the door.

"...During the passage of the storm electricity ran over the walls of my house, throwing off sparks like an emery wheel, but of a paler color, but I attribute this effect to the particles of sand and plaster blown from the walls by the extreme violence of the wind."[25]

At the Keeney home, the tornado blew three small boys out into a field and tore their clothes from their injured bodies. It carried their father, mother, and grandfather 200 yards, killing all three. Mrs. Keeney was upside down with her head buried in the soft ground stripped of her clothing. The funnel lifted up the Sabin house, twirled it around several times, and shattered it; the family landed on the ground seriously hurt. The wind blew Frank Seaton, who had been at the Sabin's, through the top of the unroofed house and carried him forty feet, lifted him up again and rolled him another hundred yards, then he disappeared. At the Sheldon's, the tornado blew Mr. and Mrs. Sheldon east of their house, critically injuring them. Rescuers found a sister Emma Sheldon dead, her body completely nude and barely recognizable.[26]

The storm moved on, destroying the depot and overturning all the railroad cars. It demolished a stone schoolhouse and lifted the heavy cornerstones from their base, dumping them into the center of the building. By this time the roar of the tornado was so loud that when it struck the church, the women inside were unaware of the terrible destruction until they emerged from the wreckage.[27]

Now the tornado appeared so enormous an eyewitness described it as being two tornadoes side by side. J.P. Finley defended this account when he examined the debris as being caused by two tornadoes moving together.[28]

The W.J. Williams house was the next one destroyed. The kitchen, where several families had taken refuge, remained intact. The tornado killed Mrs. Williams, but her baby was still in her arms, alive and unharmed.

After the storm reached the eastern limits of Irving and disappeared, all that could be seen for two miles was debris from the demolished businesses and homes. The ultimate power of the tornado was indescribable. It actually moved an 800-pound boulder to the top of a bluff and rolled it down the other side. Never before has such a feat been recorded. The storm blew many wagons and carriages away, and no one ever found them, not in pieces or as a whole. Someone found Mr. Kenney's pants with $1.60 and an account book in the pockets three miles away.[29]

The storm had an immense pull. James Patterson noted certain oddities concerning objects and the tornado, "…on their extreme edges an upward pressure (formed), which acted so powerfully as to apparently reduce a man's weight about two-thirds. Small articles of every kind were observed rising from the ground from localities where no strong wind was felt, and finally drawn into the tornado cloud. It was necessary to hold your hat on, even when you felt no pressure against the side of your body. Shavings, straws, and other light objects would ascend in a straight line for a considerable distance and then all at once dart with lightning rapidity downward to the base of the funnel cloud, then upward through its vortex and out the top."[30]

Drawing of the Irving Presbyterian Church after tornado damage. The drawing shows the wind direction.

In this storm were many near misses. The first tornado hit Irving about the same time the railroad ticket agent was expecting the Union Pacific. It was on time, but the engineer saw the tornado and stopped the train outside of town. He waited until he knew approximately where the funnel might cross the tracks, and then he quickly brought the train into town. Two minutes later the tornado passed over the exact spot where the engineer had waited out the storm.

The first tornado reached the railroad track at 5:35 p.m.; the second tornado, which actually hit the railroad depot, stopped the clock at 6:45 p.m. This exact timing told J.P. Finley that the tornadoes struck Irving a little over an hour apart. Storm number one was a half-mile wide, but the second tornado was 1 ½ miles wide. The second tornado had a deafening roar far louder than the first, and the first was described as that of a hundred trains. The first tornado took 1-½ minutes to move through town; the second took about three minutes.[31]

Persons who lived through these tornadoes said the air was filled with fumes not unlike sulphurous smoke; the sky had a reddish tinge bordering on purple; and the ground rocked as if by an earthquake. Some people said they saw waterspouts swinging back and forth like elephant's trunks, taking away everything in their paths.

After the first tornado left Irving, it formed again, killing several more people near the towns of Beattie and Axtell. Beattie was a new community of about 150 people. Although the tornado was smaller by this time, its destructive force had not diminished, and it destroyed many homes and businesses. When the storm passed, an intense cold wind and a hard rain set in, causing more problems for those assisting the hurt and homeless. They were huddled together in the ruins, shivering from the chill.[32]

At St. Bridget the tornado destroyed an old schoolhouse and damaged the Catholic mission. Severe storms also hit the towns of Stockdale, Delphos, Waterville, and Wakefield. At Stockdale, falling debris crushed a woman to death, but the baby she held was not injured. At Delphos someone found two hailstones weighing 6 ½ pounds each.

Death did not elude the community of Delphos. A tornado carried Mrs. Voshman through the air for 200 yards and lodged her against a barbed wire fence, killing her instantly. Thick black mud covered her naked body and splattered her hair and face beyond recognition. Mud was a problem; in fact it filled people's eyes, ears, and hair and plastered their clothes.[33]

A twister killed Jacob Garber after rolling him over and over across the muddy terrain. A wagon with one horse attached went up in the air together, and neither one was ever seen again. The force of the wind removed the 200-pound cast iron wheels from a harvester and carried them through the air a half mile. At the Rev. Joy Bishop's home, six members of the family made it to their storm cellar, but when the tornado hit, it threw a lot of debris in with them, including two hogs. If the debris and mud had been a few feet higher, it would have buried the family. At Wakefield the tornado destroyed eleven buildings, killed one person, and injured three others.[34]

Finley noted in his report:

"The ground was soaked with water and the surface covered with thick heavy black mud. As the terrible scene of desolation was approached the cries of the wounded people and the moans of the tortured animals were plainly heard, which, mingled with the distant roar of the storm, filled one with an indescribable fear and dread of the awful monster that was still in sight, and was a fearful reminder of its terrible force. Upon arriving at the ruins... a dreadful sight was presented. Human beings could not be distinguished from animals as all alike were covered with mud and mingled with an interminable mass of debris in the most sickening manner. Women and children striped of their clothing were found lying by the side of horses and hogs. Now an arm or a leg would be raised up from the filthy mass surrounding them, attending with a piercing shriek for help and upon examination ugly gaping wounds were filled with mud, straw, and bits of wood. This was the worst destruction in the whole course of the storm and was confined to a path about 60 yards wide."[35]

The Irving tornadoes left behind a legacy of terror, which caught the attention of scientists and the general public from coast to coast. The

Scientific American of July 5, 1879 devoted an entire story to the Irving twister, to tornadoes in general, and made the following colorful remarks concerning the storm:

"Much of the country traversed has been but recently settled and in the absence of complete telegraphic communication, it is impossible to form a connected idea of the course of either of the whirlwinds or gain any definite...idea of the destruction wrought by them. Forty or fifty persons were reported killed... and many houses were wrecked at points so situated as to make it certain that no single whirlwind could have done all the mischief... It was a funnel shaped cloud with terrific rotary motion and irresistible suction leaving in its path a looped and sinuous line of ruin and death. Whatever came within its range was lifted bodily, torn to pieces, and scattered broadcast over the country. Nothing was blown down; everything was twisted and whirled into ruin. Horses, cattle and hogs were caught up and carried considerable distances then thrown aside crashing often into shapeless masses. In some places it took the straight and narrow, in others the terrible trunk would sway from side to side leaving a belt of partial destruction a half a mile wide with here and there a section entirely unharmed, perhaps an island like space in a loop of complete devastation.

"It is impossible to estimate the violence of the air movement at such times. Houses are swept up like straws, heavy wagons and machinery are crushed and carried for long distances and the toughest trees are twisted like reeds."[36]

Settlers did not soon forget the horror of these tornadoes. Night after night following the storms, some of them never went to bed but just kept peering into the darkness watching for another tornado or a recurrence of those dreadful scenes they had witnessed. Every dark cloud brought the fear back to them, causing many unnecessary trips to the storm cellar.

Since this storm occurred 130 years ago, little comment is made about these tornadoes anymore. In fact now they are no more than a footnote in meteorological history.

The big land boom overshadowed the impact of severe storms on emigration to Kansas in the 1880s.

As for Irving, the town rebuilt and prospered for many years until the construction of Tuttle Creek Reservoir in the 1950s forced the townspeople to leave when the Corps of Engineers purchased the town site. However, Irving has never been under water and is a ghost town today. People can still walk a few of the empty streets and see where the buildings once stood. At the center of the site there's a stone monument and a mailbox. Inside the box is a notebook for travelers to write a message or their impressions of the area. In scanning the notebook, some of the comments are from meteorologists who consider Irving "sacred ground" in the annals of tornado history. Mention the name of the town to a gathering of weather forecasters and chances are at least one will have heard of the community and its dark days of 1879— this alone, 130 years later, is a testimonial to the town's legacy.[37] Map Available: Appendix 1.

CHAPTER THREE: WIDESPREAD TRAGEDIES, 1880-1917

The Irving tornadoes had a widespread impact on Kansans— it scared them to death. Many settlers left the state, never to return. Others chose to stay but they decided that it was time to protect their families from these horrendous storms. The problem was they were trying to protect their households against a natural killer about which they knew nothing. Kansas writer Henry Inman told a newspaper reporter he believed tornadoes were "magnetic and have their origin in the sun." His theory was not uncommon.

Kansans began constructing "cyclone cellars" or small caves dug into the ground near their houses. They formed these cellars by scooping out a small area of earth about six feet deep, and then placing a frame support around it nearly six feet high. They piled dirt over the top of this support. Each cave had a door that opened outward and stairs just inside leading down into the cellar. This undertaking was a positive move that saved lives and it was the single most important endeavor that brought down the tornado death toll. Much to the chagrin of the families, however, the cave also became a haven for insects, spiders, and snakes.[1]

Ada Zeruah Stites brought the fact that storm cellars actually protected homesteaders vividly to light in an early account in the spring of 1881. After a tornado hit Axtell damaging several buildings, Ada wrote, "Everyone was preparing their home for a storm. After [running an errand], when I got back all the folks were in the cellar but papa. He rushed me in, fastened the door and hurried me downstairs in front of him. His feet had just left the bottom step when it lifted up right back of him and the whole house raised up far enough so we could see the lumberyard back of the house go up in the air like a straw pile. Then the house settled down on its foundation, 3 or 4 inches out of line."[2]

In 1977 Emma Kinner gave this description of the family storm cellar in an interview: "The early settlers tried to protect themselves from the violent prairie storms by going underground, because actually it was the only place that they could go. So they built cyclone cellars, or storm caves. Sometimes these were only pits covered with planks and sod, with a wooden door flat on the ground. Later they were more elaborate and permanent, usually lined with stone. They were always close to the house as possible, and they served a double purpose because they were used for the storage of vegetables and fruits, and as a cool place to keep milk and butter... When the door was pulled shut, it was DARK."[3]

Kinner also told about some fancy caves she had seen in her life:

"I know several families who had cyclone caves connected by tunnels to the basements of their homes. The de-luxe of all of them was one built like a bomb shelter; a vault of concrete, entered from the basement, but shut off from it by a heavy door with iron bars, and with its own exit, an iron manhole cover over the top. As far as I know, the owners never had to come out that way."[4]

Since accurate tornado forecasting was years away, families often spent most of the evening in the storm cellar. There were many false alarms, but the settlers took heed of the saying, "better safe than sorry."

CRAWFORD, CHEROKEE COUNTIES, APRIL 2, 1880

At 6:30 p.m. on April 2, 1880 a tornado moved toward Girard, passing just south of town. The twister leveled a half dozen farm homes southwest of

Girard, killing four people. The storm then went on east to the Missouri border.

At the same time, another tornado moved northeast from Chetopa, passing five miles west of Columbus, where it destroyed three homes. A "balloon-shaped tornado" headed for Ottawa, where it unroofed the railroad depot and overturned several railroad cars, along with a few passengers. The twister demolished seven homes in Ottawa and damaged thirty others. One child was killed instantly and a woman died several days later.[5]

SOLOMON CITY, JUNE 9, 1881

About 4:00 p.m. on June 9, 1881, storm clouds appeared northwest of Solomon City and began to move in a circular motion. By 4:30 a small tornado dropped from the sky about three miles from town, but once on the ground it began to increase in size. The funnel was moving northeast, and the settlers watched it with great interest until it disappeared. Within ten minutes, the wind changed directions and increased to gale proportions, and then large hail began to fall, crashing through windows, stripping limbs from trees, and pounding crops into the ground.[6]

A reporter from the *Topeka Capital* stated on June 10th that, "Stones were seen that were from one to three inches through. As we were leaving [to go to Salina] a report came in that 3 people were killed in the cyclone. Then later we got word that 2 more people were killed. I took a horse and started in the morning to go over the path of the cyclone and send back a full report. Everyone is wild with excitement. I found that where it did extend, it was goodbye to everything in the way of crops—also there were 6 houses demolished and 30 people injured."

The next day the same reporter noted several oddities about the tornado: "The monster took up two horses belonging to a farmer in the area, carried them over the Solomon River and landed them easily on the opposite bank. It also carried a Randolph header weighing 2,500 lbs into the air and it has not been heard of since. In the east part of Solomon City a large hay press weighing 6,500 lbs was raised into the air several feet and deposited upside down. A team of horses was thought to have been blown across the river and left unhurt."[7]

The reporter went five miles south of town where he discovered another house that had been hit, and inside he found a man in bed with a fractured leg. Beside him sat his six children, a wife, and a farmhand. The tornado tore the upper part of the house away, leaving the family scared but fortunately unhurt. Just down the road, other residents were not so lucky—he found both of them dead in the wreckage of their home.

The tornado moved on to Bennington, where it destroyed five houses and killed two men. The same tornado also heavily damaged buildings in the towns of Glasco and Ashville.

TORNADO OUTBREAK, JUNE 12, 1881

A significant tornado outbreak struck the counties of Osage, Cowley, and Ottawa on June 12, 1881. The aftermath of these storms was so noteworthy that it caught the attention of the U.S. Signal Service, whose representatives came west on horseback just to do a survey of the damage. Not since the tornadoes that hit Irving in 1879 did Kansas attract so much attention.

In Ottawa County the town of Minneapolis suffered considerable destruction. The high wind shattered all the windows in every building on main street facing north. The hotel, which was a large multi-storied structure, had all its windows broken by the hail. The residents saw numerous small tornadoes in the area that day.

As the squall line moved east, more tornadoes followed. At 4:00 p.m. a black cloud from the northwest headed toward the Marais des Cygnes River west of Melvern. At the same time a similar dark cloud came from the southwest and moved over the same area. As both storms approached Melvern, the lightning display was vivid and intense.

The *Osage City Free Press* of June 13 described the scene as follows: "The whole heavens in the vicinity appeared to be in a towering rage, and the furious contortions of the clouds, the sharp piercing thunder and lightning formed a terribly grand and impressive picture that no one would soon forget. The wild wrangling of the mad elements lasted for nearly an hour, after which the lightning suddenly ceased and the thunder hushed. A dark, ugly funnel-shaped cloud formed about the center of the storm, and as it rose and fell, it began to sweep down the river. Everybody knew what it meant. Everybody knew that ruin and death would mark its course."

The funnel actually dropped to the ground near Olivet, where it tore up trees and carried off buildings, leaving nothing standing. One home owned by the Powells was not in the tornado's path until the funnel turned suddenly and tore the house from its foundation, smashing it to the ground. The family was in the cellar, which soon became filled with debris. Fortunately, they all escaped with only minor cuts and bruises.

The next day Mrs. Tweed found her watch in a field a quarter mile away but never found any of her other possessions. After the wind tore her clothing from her body, she had nothing left to wear. The tornado destroyed the Plaunty farmhouse, where three children had been left home alone. All three were badly injured, and one died the next day. Two other people, John Harper and A. Rosencrantz, were killed. Seven others were badly hurt near Melvern.

The tornado moved on to Quenemo, where it destroyed the Presbyterian church. It literally blew it apart and scattered pieces of the building for miles. After the storms had passed, assistance came from all over the area. Although many were left destitute, their recovery appeared to be quick.[8] Map Available, Appendix 1.

EMPORIA, SEPTEMBER 29, 1881

Emporia has seemed a magnet for tornadoes and severe weather. The town has been struck more times than any other Kansas community. Fortunately, it is located in the beautiful Flint Hills where there is ample visibility in all directions.

On September 29, 1881 a late season twister struck the town, causing severe damage and several deaths. The first house hit was that of a Mr. French; his home was nicknamed "Old Firey Place." Eleven people were visiting him when the tornado struck. It threw Mrs. Ewing against a barbed wire fence, gashing her face. Falling timbers from "Old Firey Place" crushed Mrs. Newby, and flying debris killed Edith Bradford, 9, and a baby belonging to the Richards family.

Next, the tornado destroyed the O'Neil house, killing their four-year old daughter by crushing her skull. The storm demolished the Ruggles schoolhouse, and then moved east where it smashed the Walkup schoolhouse and a slaughterhouse.[9]

After the tornado hit Reading, it finally subsided near Lawrence, where hailstones weighing over a pound broke windows and killed livestock. The high winds unroofed a few houses and blew down trees.

NORTH CENTRAL KANSAS, APRIL 5 AND 7, 1882

A widespread outbreak of severe weather affected every section of the state during the first week of April 1882. In the Manhattan area, heavy winds and rain did extensive damage. A 100-mile an hour gust took the roof off the schoolhouse, knocked down chimneys, outhouses, and stables. A small tornado hit Chapman in Dickinson County on April 5, destroying the Methodist church, blowing the roof off the railroad depot, and damaging several houses and barns. At Woodbine, the twister destroyed the flourmill, Baptist church, three houses, and a blacksmith shop. Farther east at Valley Falls in Jefferson County, hail larger than hen's eggs broke windows.[10]

A tornado nearly obliterated Stafford in South Central Kansas. Of the seventy-five or eighty residences in town, only two houses remained standing. The county was holding an election that day, and the tornado scattered the ballots everywhere before they could be counted. This tornado, although a small one, skipped all over town, killing one person and injuring many.

Al McMillan, editor of the *Macksville Enterprise*, recounted that:

"Stafford was filled with people and it was so cold that many men wore heavy overcoats. During the afternoon, threatening clouds formed in the west and southwest. The elements were in turmoil all afternoon. The voting place was on Main Street 100 feet from the old Vickers sod hotel. We happened to be inside the little building when the cry 'cyclone' was heard.[11] Our first view was a mighty black wall a half mile southwest, and a close look showed that it was moving in a direction to strike the town. We started to run in a northwest direction but the storm, as black as midnight, was upon us before we reached the center of the street… Something struck us on the back of the head, but our overcoat collar softened the blow, else we might have been knocked senseless. The worst injury we received was to our right knee. We had difficulty walking when we got up, and though we walked all over the wreckage that day, we were on crutches next morning and for nearly a week."[12]

Two unusual insights can be gleaned from this narrative—it appears that someone had established a system in town where anyone could sound a warning, and the concept of escaping at right angles seemed to be the right thing to do.

The damage to Stafford was extensive, and McMillan wrote, "What a sight! Wrecks of buildings covered the street from one end to the other. Looking around we found a pair of coveralls partly covered with debris, and by a closer look discovered a pair of shoes at the bottom. Tearing away the covering we found an eight-year-old boy, apparently dead. We carried him into the hotel, and he was placed on a couch. In a little bit he began to breathe and in a few hours he was able to walk home." McMillan concluded his article by stating that, "If you have never been in a cyclone you have yet to hear the most devilish, terrifying, alarming noise that ever was made on the earth."[13]

This same tornado entered Pratt County and destroyed everything in its path. It killed four women at the Peak residence, and at the Frisby home, it buried the wife and children beneath the debris of the house, wounding all of them. Tom Moore suffered injuries while riding his horse to the Peak home. The twister lifted him from his saddle, carried him 150 yards, and dropped him on his back. The force of the wind blew his horse into a well.[14]

The storm outbreak was not over— a tornado struck Clay Center, killing the Reed family and Mrs. Mann. It destroyed Red's Hotel, the Chatten General Store, the Eckles Brothers Store, the post office, Miller's store, the Sutton, Swisher and Duprees Store, the Congregational church, the Speer drug store, and several other small buildings.

Two days later a tornado swept over northern Dickinson County, overturning three houses and killing Mrs. David and three of her children. The wind carried the seven-year-old son of Mr. Plants over some high trees and set him down on his feet, running from the storm.

Another funnel passed over Junction City, tearing roofs off of buildings at Fort Riley and injuring two soldiers. The loss was estimated at $25,000 to $30,000.

At Canton a tornado missed the town but hit Wesley Bryant's house, killing his wife and two children.

In Marysville a tornado struck about 4:00 p.m. All day the sky looked threatening, and then suddenly a funnel-shaped cloud appeared to the south. Many residents, who visited Irving just three years before, knew what was about to happen. As the funnel drew closer, the frightened citizens panicked. Businesses shut down and the residents fled to their cellars for protection. Then the thunder, lightning, and hail began; kegs, barrels, and outhouses swept through the streets, and the wooden sidewalks were rising to the second stories of the buildings. Although the tornado took no lives, it demolished houses, blew railroad cars from the tracks, and damaged bridges.[15]

Next, the tornado passed over the city of Waterville, causing extensive damage to houses and barns, injuring many people and killing livestock. The storm subsided around midnight, but started up again about 2:00 a.m. Apparently there were two different storms, one out of the southwest and another out of the northeast, and they met just west of Waterville, where they destroyed the G.D. Bolling residence, seriously hurting the family. Upon hearing the roar of the storm as it approached, the Silas Halbert family sought refuge in the cellar. Just as they lifted their child from his bed, a hundred pound stone fell on the bed, smashing it.

Tornadoes damaged buildings near Kimeo in Washington County, Mayday and Parallel in Riley County, and south of Greenleaf, where the storms destroyed four homes. Last but certainly not least, Irving was hit again by a tornado that unroofed Peter Lane's house and the stone building formerly used as a Methodist church.[16]

PHILLIPSBURG, JUNE 26, 1882

A tornado struck Phillipsburg late in the afternoon of June 26, 1882. A reporter for the *Topeka Capital* described the climactic conditions before the tornado struck as unusual: "About 5 o'clock p.m. after a hot and sultry day, the wind commenced blowing from the north and blew quite a gale for perhaps an hour, meeting an opposite current of air not more than two miles south of the city, for a few minutes there seemed to be a mighty war among the elements, black clouds going hither and yon."

The twister formed just south of town and destroyed the Ross Hale house by lifting it twelve feet off the ground and dropping it on one end. Mr. Hale, his wife and child, were surprised by the tornado, and they fell into the debris. Hale, when interviewed later, said he only remembered sliding down the floor into the cellar. The tornado then slammed into Phillipsburg.

The reporter noted that, "The heavens were lighted with a red glare and terror reigned supreme; buildings went to pieces as if by some power besides the wind." The tornado destroyed a Baptist church, a billiard hall, several granaries, a livery stable, and injured at least ten people. It unroofed part of the county courthouse, blew down numerous chimneys, and broke nearly every window in town. As soon as the tornado left, it disappeared into the clouds. Its entire existence was spent creating havoc in Phillipsburg.[17]

Three days later severe weather struck Central Kansas in Rice and Barton Counties. A tornado developed that would have gone unnoticed except that a party of men on a trip west had a clear view of the storm. Since the Kiowa Indians inhabited much of the region, white men were a rarity. D.B. Long, a fish commissioner, and Z. Jackson witnessed the scene:

"Just as the sun was setting we were going down the slope towards Cow Creek just below the mouth of Plum Creek… As we rode along we saw a herd of buffalo up Plum as far as we could see… Our attention had been so taken up watching the buffalo that for some time we had failed to notice a very black cloud coming up from the southeast promising heavy rain. We hastened on so as to make camp before it began to rain… A narrow belt from the large cloud stretched out like a man's arm, extending from east by south to northwest by north… The arm to the left gradually seemed to drop at two points… The second drop of the arm began to lengthen out so it looked like a large saw tooth. All this took place faster than I could write. In a few moments a dark cloud rose from the ground behind the tooth, making a complete inverted funnel and the whole tooth and ground cloud now united and swept through the densest portion of the herd of buffalo– they ran wildly in every direction.

"We never investigated the cyclone's path. In fact, we did not then… know that we had perhaps the only view of a cyclone from a box seat, complimentary at that… A goodly number of Kiowas appearing in the southwest next morning postponed any investigation of the cyclone's path."[18] Map Available: Appendix 1.

SUN CITY, APRIL 22, 1883

Under headlines "Work of the Storm Fiend," the *Medicine Lodge Cresset* reported all the gory details concerning a particularly devastating storm that struck southwest of Wichita.

According to the *Cresset*, a tornado hit Sun City around midnight with "terrific force. The winds came in with a whirring noise, but the majority of the people were wrapped in slumber and heard nothing until they were awakened by the crashing of timbers, unroofed houses, sharp sounds of thunder, and debris flying through the air with the lightning that followed in the wake of a seething, howling cloud."[19].

In Sun City the tornado damaged or destroyed several stores including the Saunders general store, the Douglass store, and the livery stable.

Although the tornado also demolished the house of Lizzie Fishburn down to a height of seven feet, no one was hurt. Captain Ayers reported that lightning struck his house fir, and then the tornado wrecked it. Since the wind blew all of his books, papers, and clothing away, the Captain "consoled himself with the thought that some poor stranger could enjoy a clean shirt and respectable literature."

Oddly enough, the storm came out of the east and moved northward. Most of the buildings in town were damaged but not completely destroyed, indicating that perhaps the tornado was aloft when it hit the community.

In the Turkey Creek valley, the tornado dealt a death blow at the residence of B.B. Allen, when in an instant the storm destroyed the house, killing three people— B.B. Allen, David Shumate, and Shumate's wife. Their bodies were 200 yards away, stripped of their clothing. The path of the storm was "littered with fragments of flesh, bones, hair, and brains. The top of Mrs. Shumate's head was crushed down to the lower jaw. David was found beneath the waters of Turkey Creek, badly mangled and torn. The rest of the family made it to the storm cellar and survived."[20]

The twister tore a heavy lumber wagon to bits and scattered it everywhere; a cow had a rail driven through her body; and someone found a feather bed, untouched, in the top of a tree.

KANSAS CITY, KANSAS, MAY 13, 1883

One of the few tornadoes to hit the Kansas City metropolitan area came on May 13th, 1883. The storm demolished at least fifty buildings, damaged two hundred, and killed four persons— Mrs. David Reed, two employees of Cole's Circus, and a boy named Willie Silben. Although the path of the storm left the downtown area untouched, it did extensive damage in outlying areas, which included Kamps Brewery, the German Evangelical church, and a Methodist church. The path of the tornado was about three miles long, and it scattered trees, bricks, rafters, boards, and household effects everywhere. Heavy rain and large hail accompanied the tornado, which only added to the turmoil.

The tornado critically injured ten people. Mary Jackson died from her injuries, and Capt. Joseph Burns died from a broken neck. A woman sitting at the piano on the second floor of her home was still there after the wind lifted the upper part of her house; she and the piano were not disturbed.

South of Leavenworth, the storm caused a landslide that obstructed the passage of the Missouri-Pacific trains. The tornado also did considerable damage at Easton before it moved into Missouri, where it caused destruction at Oronoga and Liberty. At Missouri City on the Missouri River, the winds tore the steamboat "Bright Light" from its moorings and blew it across the river to a sandbar near Atchison. [21]

This tornado came at a critical time for the steam boating industry. The industry was already losing commerce from the railroads. High winds and tornadoes were one of the principal reasons it was not a stable form of transportation. During the boom years of steamboat navigation on the Missouri River, a high percentage of boats were lost due to weather. Map Available: Appendix 1.

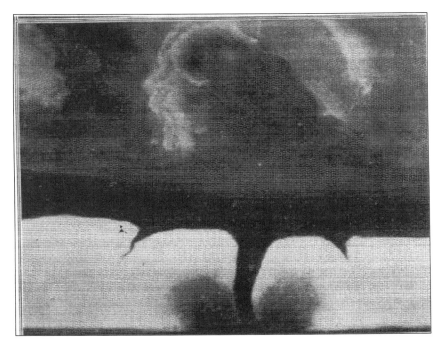

This is reputed to be the first picture ever taken of a tornado. This image was taken somewhere in the Dakotas in 1884. However, a picture of a tornado taken in Garnett may pre-date this view.

SOLDIER, JULY 10, 1883

Less than two months after the Kansas City tornado, another violent tornado struck Northeast Kansas and hit Soldier, a small town north of Topeka. Under the headlines "Half of the Town Blown to Atoms," the *Holton Recorder* described the harrowing experience several days later:

"Some citizens had gathered in front of the Wilson Brothers store about 10:00 p.m. to watch the progress of the storm, when without any warning, a tornado lifted the store from its foundation, carried it thirty feet and smashed it to the ground. The roof from the store blew across the railroad tracks a half-mile away. Luckily, everyone in the building escaped with only minor cuts and bruises. The tornado demolished the hotel next door, but not before the patrons fled to a nearby cave. A drug store, general merchandise store, a livery stable, and the residence of Dr. Channel were all destroyed. His mother and sister were killed. The John Owen residence was smashed, and his wife and child were killed. The Charles Hungeford house was damaged, and he was caught under some timbers. An axe had to be used to free him."[22]

In all, the storm killed four people before it left the town and continued south.

COFFEY COUNTY, MAY 3, 1884

This tornado was not particularly noteworthy except that a photographer from Garnett was successful in taking what is believed to be the first pictures of a tornado. General Harrison Kelley, a witness, stated that it was a "dry tornado" and that it had the shape of an ale barrel at fifteen miles away. The actual diameter of the little twister was only about 150 feet and wherever it touched the ground it swept the surface bare. The funnel did tear a wagon away from some horses and sucked the vehicle up sixty feet before dropping it.[23]

The following picture does not show any indication of a barrel of ale. It does appear to be a tornado that may have been about 150 feet wide. The buildings in the background appear to be Garnett. If this was the first picture, it would be an historic occasion. However, the tornado taken in the Dakotas in 1884 is significant as well because it shows two other tornadoes that are forming beside it. The Dakota tornado did not cause any damage and primarily traveled over open prairie.

This picture of a Coffey County tornado also dates from 1884. Could this be the oldest known picture of a tornado in existence?

LINN COUNTY, APRIL 26, 1887

A tornado moved through Linn County on the night of April 26, 1887, killing one man at Prescott and injuring twenty others.[24] The *Topeka Daily Capital* noted that, "A long funnel shaped cloud was formed rapidly, black in color, and an intense rotary current was created, and as the cloud swept southward our attention was riveted on the sight left to full view. At this instant the sun shone from behind the whirling mass, while the north end was draped with a dense black cloud. Rapidly this monster approached, growing wider and gathering everything up in its awful mouth and many stood riveted to the spot. Hundreds of people are without homes. Prescott was literally blown to pieces."[25]

CENTRAL KANSAS, MAY 5-7, 1889

A severe windstorm raged through Central Kansas for almost three days before moving on east. On May 6 a tornado hit northern Pratt County, eastern Stafford County, and southern Rice County, striking first five miles southeast of Stafford, where for miles it left nothing but a barren countryside strewn with parts of houses, barns, trees, and fences.

The tornado killed William Crawford and injured thirty other people. It demolished several houses, scattering them in all directions. The John Bartlett house blew away like a "feather before a gale." The wind tossed his wife a hundred yards behind the house, where a hay rake hit her. She lost an eye, had her nose broken, and sustained internal injuries. The funnel picked up Bartlett's son and carried him thirty feet before he landed on a combine. This machine and the boy were airborne for a quarter of a mile. He stated that for most of his wild ride the combine was actually off the ground. The wind blew the three other Bartlett children into the haystacks by the barn. Flying timbers struck farmhand William McVey, severely injuring him.[26] Some object hit Joseph Perris on the head, which caused excessive bleeding from the ears, and one of his daughters, also struck on the head, was still unconscious the next day. The twister carried another daughter for two hundred feet before dropping her unhurt.

While Stafford was not directly hit, it sustained damage from heavy hail that broke nearly every window in town. The storm left more than a hundred persons homeless and without food or clothing. The townspeople formed a committee to aid those who had lost everything. This brought some immediate relief to the destitute that needed it so urgently. Map Available: Appendix 1.

SUMNER COUNTY/WAMEGO, MARCH 31, 1892

A monstrous tornado hit Sumner and Butler Counties on March 31, 1892. Its path was a mile wide. In addition, it formed around 10:00 p.m., a scary time for a tornado to develop.

The twister first appeared around South Haven, where it injured several people and destroyed much of the town. According to witnesses, the whirling black cloud stayed close to the ground and the sound of crashing houses and cries of the wounded only added more horror to the roar of the storm.[27]

The tornado also damaged homes near Kiowa and Wellington, where it killed five people on the William Little farm. At the Sam Butterworth house, the twister blew a hired man, a son-in-law, and a couple of children 200 yards, but they survived with only a few bumps and bruises.

From Wellington the tornado moved to Augusta, where several houses were "blown to pieces." The *Wichita Beacon* of April 1 stated that little was known about damage and lives lost between South Haven and Augusta due to the bad roads and no telegraph lines. The storm killed Albert Barnes and an infant on an adjoining farm, where the wind sucked the baby out of the house and dropped it into a small pond nearby.[28]

Much of the damage centered on Towanda, a small town of 300 on the Missouri Pacific Railroad. There three people lost their lives and twenty were severely injured. The tornado destroyed every business in town, including a large hotel. The *Beacon* stated that George Douglass of Wichita passed through Towanda the next morning and reported that two-thirds of the buildings were "smashed to pieces." All the stores were 'blown down and many of the residences reduced to kindling wood. It had the appearance of being knocked in a heap by some mighty power."

All the streets and roads were blocked. "Piles of bedding, broken furniture, boards, brick, and iron being mixed together and scattered over the area that but yesterday was a well laid out and clearly defined little town."[29]

The *Beacon* described the condition of the bodies of the three that were killed. "In one of the little houses that withstood the effects of the storm were the remains of three people who lost their lives. The remains were disfigured; the cruel blows that caused death in every case were visible on the bodies of the victims."[30] One of the bodies was that of a small baby. "The body of the little baby," the *Beacon* noted, "was a silent witness to the fury of the cyclone. Its little head was completely severed from its body, which was in the wreck of his home, while 20 feet distant was the head. The head was cut from the neck as though with a sharp knife, the severing was done by a post or some heavy piece of timber… Sadly the different parts of the little body were picked up and deposited in the cottage that at the time acted as a dead house."[31]

This makeshift morgue attracted a sizable number of curious residents. The *Beacon* reported, "The little house was the center of attraction and the half-crazed and half-clad people wended their way aimlessly about the place invariably winding up at the dead house where they gazed at the three victims of the storm and spoke softly to each other about the terrible work of the storm and the little baby whose dismembered remains told such a sad story."[32]

Survivors transported the injured to another home, which served as a temporary hospital, and about twenty-five people gathered there, mostly women and children. The *Beacon* noted, "The groans of the little ones were heard above the words of calm resignation of the brave women, who tried to forget their own suffering in their efforts to soothe and quiet their little companions. Among the injured who were crowded into the house, the only one left in the center of town, were many whose legs and arms were broken and others whose injuries were of an internal nature."[33]

C.A. Aikman, a Towanda resident, remembered the terrible tornado and recounted his story forty-six years later for the *Wichita Eagle*. He recalled the ominous roar of the approaching storm, and that he warned his father they needed to take cover. They rushed to the storm cellar about fifty feet from the house, but the tornado was already upon them by the time they reached the door of the cave. The wind blew him and his mother to the ground; he crawled on all fours, holding his mother's hand, the rest of the distance to the floor of the cellar. During this time, the tornado blew the barn with fourteen head of cattle to pieces just 150 feet away. When they emerged from the cave, they found the house intact but missing windows, doors, and chimneys.

Aikman recounted the story of an African-American man named Martin Reynolds, who was the father of seven children. The tornado flattened the family's log cabin and scattered the children in every direction. Mr. Reynolds fell to the ground, praying that all the children would return unharmed, and sure enough, one by one the children came back home, a bit shaken but unhurt.[34]

Those who miraculously survived the storm walked about Towanda in a "dazed kind of way, not fully realizing the extent of their loss and not being able to collect their thoughts."[35] The next morning many of them were still walking around with "blankets and quilts pinned about them to keep out the chilly wind. They had not thought of digging in the ruins of their former homes to get their wearing apparel and some did not seem to care whether they lived or not."[36]

William Sorter, proprietor of the town hotel, was a hero. Despite the fact that his hotel was in ruins, he managed to save his wife, child, and one guest single-handedly by pulling everyone out one by one. His wife was trapped next to a wood stove that had a fire burning inside. Although she received injuries from flying debris, she was only slightly burned due to her husband's quick actions.

J.H. Porter and family escaped from their home with only bruises because Porter's little son who was unable to sleep kept everyone else awake. As Porter stood in the middle of his son's bedroom, the house disintegrated around him, leaving them unhurt.

The wind blew the railroad depot from its foundation along with the telegraph office. This left the town cut off from the outside world; they were unable to summon help. The next day (April 1) word of the tornado reached other communities in the area, but since it was "April Fool's Day," many residents thought it was only a cruel joke. When they realized the truth, the rescuers boarded a train for Towanda, but it had to be diverted to a sidetrack due to debris. The other track had the Towanda depot piled across it, and the rescue train ran into the already damaged building. No one was hurt.[37]

Although the *Augusta Gazette* reported that a tornado "blew away" Towanda, killing and injuring more than a score of people, the newspaper didn't list actual names or numbers.

Wichita barely escaped the brunt of the storm. The wind broke some windows, uprooted trees, and damaged roofs, and derailed a freight train near Derby. Other than that, the tornado missed Wichita.

The same storm system didn't stop there. Seven were killed near Wamego, in Pottwatomie County. Three were children under the age of ten.

The house of Albert Taylor was completely wrecked and scattered around the farm. Mrs. Albert Eggers was found dead clasping the dead body of her younger child in her arms. The body of her older child was found some distance from his parents. Pieces of their house were found a mile away. One of the kitchen chairs was found a half mile away undamaged and sitting upright.

The *Aspen, Colorado Weekly Times* of April 9, 1892 said this about the storm:

"The faces of all the [victims] had the appearance of being powder burned, dust and dirt having been forced below the skin by the force of the wind. Albert Eggers was found about midnight wandering about his farm. He was in a dazed condition and sustained a fracture of the right arm and other bad bruises. His injuries may result fatally. His mind now appears to be completely lost, and result of learning the dreadful fate of his wife and children.

"The house of John Taylor was moved some distance from its foundation and then was crashed to the ground with terrible force, wrecking it completely. Taylor's body was found among the debris crushed and mangled beyond recognition. His 9-year old child met death in the ruins, its body being found near that of its father. Mrs. Taylor was rescued from the ruins in an unconscious condition. She cannot recover."

Nearly every building in Wamego was damaged or destroyed. Emergency supplies had to come from neighboring communities. Many residents lost all their clothes and needed new clothes quickly. One man, James Taylor, had to wear his wife's dress because all his clothes were blown away. Map Available: Appendix 1.

In the 1890s the U.S. Signal Service ceased to exist and it became known as the National Weather Service. With regard to forecasting, however, they had the same problems as the signal service; they were unsuccessful in pinpointing locations where tornadoes were likely to strike. Forecasters began to use the term "violent local storms," when forecasting tornadoes. In this manner, even if a tornado did not appear, the bureau was still warning communities of severe weather. In the Midwest and in Kansas, where these storms were frequent, warnings in advance could make the difference between life and death. For years forecasters recognized what was commonly called "cyclone weather," or weather likely to spawn outbreaks of tornadoes.[38]

CHERRYVALE, APRIL 3, 1892

Three days after the Towanda tornado, disaster hit again. This time it was in Cherryvale, in Southeast Kansas. The situation might have been worse except that the tornado barely missed town, skirting the city limits a mile to the east. Six houses were destroyed and two people were killed. One of the individuals killed was struck by lightning.

The tornado caught everyone by surprise because it happened at 10:45 at night. Everyone was asleep and they were unaware of the changing weather conditions. Telegraph lines were down across the county, which delayed assistance.

A cow, which was standing in a stable lot near Cherryvale, was carried up to the roof of a house and left there. Several attempts were made to get the cow down, but the effort was apparently futile and the cow had to be killed.

SHAWNEE COUNTY, MAY 2, 1892

Topeka and the surrounding countryside were hit by a tornado on May 2, causing considerable damage. In some places the bark was actually peeled off the trees. The house of James Mitchell, a farmer, was in the path of the storm. He was killed instantly but the rest of the Mitchell family somehow survived. An unidentified woman, who had just moved into the Thomas Brooks house, was also killed.

The house of Joseph Hurd was ripped apart and Mrs. Hurd was killed. James Plaxton's house was carried from its foundations and wrecked, and Plaxton was instantly killed in the debris. Swan Anderson, a farm hand, was working in a field when the storm came up. He was hurled against a stone fence and killed. Gabe Halderman, a farmer, was fatally injured when his barn was destroyed.

The most serious situation was when the Pleasant Valley schoolhouse was hit by the tornado. The building was demolished. A number of children had taken refuge there from the storm, but they all miraculously escaped death, though a few were seriously injured.

WELLINGTON, MAY 27, 1892

After an extremely sultry day on May 27, 1892, it began to rain. Around 9:00 p.m. the tornado struck before the townspeople had time to take cover. The funnel entered the city near the railroad tracks, where it picked up two large boxcars and tossed them into a ravine. The tornado then struck two houses, severely injuring Jesse Brower, and carrying his small boy a block away and dropping him in the mud, unhurt.

The funnel was now 200 yards wide, and it demolished two churches and damaged three more houses. It lifted the Lutheran church from its foundation and dumped it on the dwelling next door. It picked up large stones and deposited them into the second stories of roofless buildings. It lifted a horse to the top of a tall building and left it there. It raised a baby from its cradle, carried it for two blocks, and then laid it softly on the ground, unscathed.

When the tornado hit Main Street, it intensified and completely obliterated a row of buildings on Washington Avenue. It struck the Phillips House Hotel, where it killed six people. Just beyond the hotel it wrecked ten more buildings, including the printing office, cigar factory, seed store, mortgage company, real estate office, coal yard, feed barn, a marble company, carriage works, and the schoolhouse.

The schoolhouse situation might have been far more serious than it actually was. Timing is everything, and timing saved the lives of children. The cigar factory became a smoker's dream: literally hundreds of shredded and damaged cigars scattered to the winds.

View of a nearly flattened building in Wellington

Minutes after the tornado passed, a fire broke out in the wreckage of the Cole-Robinson block. Firemen were soon on the scene hoping to rescue several women caught in the building. First they pulled out a nearly lifeless Mrs. Murphy and her son. After searching for an hour, they found the bodies of two sisters crushed by toppled bricks. Rescuers took a railroad worker to a hotel, where he died an hour later. They carried another man home unconscious; he never woke up. During the night firemen found two more bodies at the Phillips House; and the next morning, after searching through the debris, they brought out three more bodies—the hotel barber, a professor, and a man from Belle Plaine. All together, this tornado killed thirty people.[39]

This tornado became one of the most photographed storms to date. Amateur and professional photographers came from all over to capture the images of wrecked buildings and wrecked lives. It went far to describe the wild weather that Kansans tolerated.

Map Available: Appendix 1.

More tornado damage in downtown Wellington, 1892.

OSAGE CITY, APRIL 18, 1893

Two or three tornadoes may have visited Osage City the afternoon of April 18 at the same time. The storm that spawned them formed around 4pm that day. It first struck on the north side of the city and then divided. One funnel may have gone to the southwest and the other to the southeast based on multiple wind speeds and directions.

The course of the storm was very irregular. In the northeastern portion of the city, where the greatest damage was done, one house would be left standing, riddled by flying debris, while those surrounding it were completely blown away.

The *Aspen, Colorado Weekly Times* of April 22, 1893 said this about the storm:

"Furniture, clothing, bedding and everything pertaining to housekeeping could be seen intermingled with boards, lath, plaster, brick and building material, all one mass of debris. Trees, barns, fences and outbuildings were scattered in every direction and the appearance of the territory in the track of the storm is almost indescribable. A mass meeting was held today to provide means for the relief of the homeless and destitute. In the northeastern part of the city, the destruction of property was very great, several houses being blown down. Several loaded cars were blown from railroad switches."

Near the Missouri Pacific Railroad depot over forty buildings were destroyed. Half of the buildings in town were damaged. Despite the property damage, the list of dead and injured was relatively short. One person was killed and two dozen were badly injured, including the Swanson children, both of which escaped barely with their lives.

PERRY AND WILLIAMSTOWN, JUNE 22, 1893

A short-lived but violent tornado left death and destruction along the Kansas River between Topeka and Lawrence.

Early in the evening of June 22, 1893 a tornado formed near Perry on the Union Pacific Railroad and followed the river to Williamstown, where it devastated a strip of land four miles long and a mile wide. Along its path the twister destroyed the residence of Sara Kincaid, killing Mr. Kincaid, his wife and four children. Farther down the river at the Hutchinson home, debris from the tornado cut Mrs. Hutchinson's body in half, one leg was in a tree a quarter of a mile away. Mr. Hutchinson had both arms and a leg broken. The twister killed two more people at the home of Sill Davis.

This tornado killed nine people, and apparently it caught these communities by surprise.[40] Map Available: Appendix 1.

MT. HOPE, MAY 1, 1895

On the first day of May 1895, a tornado formed close to Mt. Hope and stayed on the ground for twenty-five miles, going past Halstead to the Moundridge area. It left in its wake seven people dead and more than twenty injured.

It was 4:30 in the afternoon when this twister started its rampage. A witness, Dag Hall, was watching some tag ends of black clouds when suddenly they started to circle, and then a tornado swung to the ground in front of him. A reporter noted that, "all agree that there was no regularity of form or gyration, although the rate was regular enough, and the velocity was variously estimated. There was a boiling chaos vapor with occasional throwing off of coils and unrolling of sheets of vapor which were immediately reabsorbed by the incredible suction of the mass."[41]

The funnel demolished Joseph Wear's house, killing Mrs. Wear and her daughter Grace, and a few feet away lay the bodies of a son Herman and the Wear's baby. Although Mr. Wear wrapped his arms around a tree and hung on; he was critically injured by flying glass. Another son and daughter successfully reached the cellar and escaped with only minor injuries.

A quarter mile west of the Wears, the storm widened to nearly a mile, and the Armstrong farm was in its path; it caught the family by surprise and killed two of them.

Cyrus Hinkson saw the funnel approaching. He rode his horse to the house, tied it in the barn, and hurried his wife and four children into the cellar. Just after the house flew over their heads, his horse was lifted by the wind and dropped into the cellar with the family. The gentle animal, unhurt, stood quietly while Hinkson dug his wife and family from under the stones piled on the stairway.

Daisey Neff and Mrs. Coates were outside when they attempted to outrun the tornado, but the wind caught up with them. Mrs. Coates suffered fatal injuries, and Daisey died several hours later.[42]

Just about the time the tornado reached Moundridge, it lifted into the air and disappeared, but not before depositing a shower of debris on that town and on Canton.

For years, survivors of this storm still remembered the horror of that day and reacted emotionally every time the wind howled a bit too loud, or a storm seemed too severe.[43]

CLAY AND CLOUD COUNTIES, APRIL 28, 1896

Clay and Cloud Counties were hit hard in 1896. Both counties had their share of destructive storms, and if "tornado alley" really exists, they are directly in the middle. Whether these counties are at the center of storm tracks during the spring months, or whether it is a coincidence that they have been hit so many times, either way, the residents have learned to live with severe weather.

The storm that hit on April 28, 1896 was particularly destructive. The headlines of the Clay Center Dispatch for April 30 gave the usual graphic details of the day, "AWFUL! Seven Killed Outright, Many More Probably Wounded Unto Death… Nothing Could Withstand the Storm King's Fury. Livestock Cut and Mangled Frightfully."

Two tornadoes moved through these counties on a Saturday night about 9:30 p.m. The larger of the two funnels entered Clay County from the French settlement of St. Joe. It varied in width from 150 yards to a mile wide and headed northeasterly, where it converged with another tornado. The electrical display was "fearful and the thunder came crash on crash"; the roar of the storm was heard twelve miles away in Clay Center.[44]

Along with the wind came the rains— creeks and ravines overflowed their banks, and within four miles of Morganville, hail fell that was nearly eight inches in diameter. The storm smashed and scattered houses, barns, fences, and granaries about the fields; the loss of livestock was appalling.

The news of the tornadoes didn't reach Clay Center until 2:00 a.m. Sunday when a telegram came from Morganville relating that five people were dead and twenty injured. Physicians, reporters, and rescuers headed for the scene of the disaster, following the path of the storm until they came to Morganville.[45] From St. Joe the tornado hit farm after farm, doing extensive damage and destroying outbuildings. Fortunately, no one was killed, although there were some close calls. At the Julian Tromble house, the twister blew a little girl about twenty yards south and stripped off her clothing, otherwise she was not hurt.

In Cloud County, the first death was Henry Dufresne's wife, who was out in the open and killed instantly. Mr. Dufresne had a broken arm.

The destruction in Clay County began at the little settlement of Bloom, where the storm surprised the Eli Belthazor family. They had just started for their storm cellar when the tornado struck. They didn't make it. He and his wife died in the cornfield, each had a hand reaching out above them as though forcing the debris away from their faces. The wind from the storm wounded six of their children, three severely. At the McCullough house, the tornado destroyed everything and injured Mrs. McCullough.46

The storm jumped over the Republican River three miles north of Morganville, scooping up water from the river and dumping it on the lowlands nearby. The tornado destroyed the home of Frank Wilkerson. He and his wife were so badly injured they barely survived. When rescuers found Mrs. Wilkerson, she was standing waist deep in water holding her baby out of harm's way. Walter Haynes saw the approaching storm, grabbed his wife and jumped through a window into the cyclone cellar. They just made it in time, for in the next instant their house "exploded."

The *Clay Center Dispatch* noted, "For a distance of four or five miles all around, the ground is covered with wreckage, pieces of all kinds of furniture, shingles, boards, clothing, carpets, wagon wheels, ears of corn, and everything else that goes into making a home."[47]

Moving on northeast, the tornado destroyed the home of Ole Halverson, killing Mrs. Halverson and injuring her husband. At the Frank Peterson residence, the twister killed Mrs. Peterson and one daughter. Mr. Peterson and another daughter were so badly hurt that it was doubtful they would recover. Eric Johnson, who lived alone next door to the Petersons, was trying to hold a door shut against the wind when he fell through the floor into the cellar. The tornado lifted the house over him and smashed it into kindling. Miraculously, he was not injured. The twister destroyed the home of J.J. Derringer, or "Indian John." Nothing was left of the entire homestead. Derringer was caring for a sick boy when the tornado struck, and although he succeeded in escaping injury, the wind dumped him in a farm pond some distance away.

Elizabeth Bong saw her walls crumble in such a way that she found herself imprisoned within her house. When rescuers came by and heard no cries for help, they gave up and moved on. Upon returning later, they removed a rock from the doorway and found her alive and unhurt.

Ten people were staying at the Peter Anderson farmhouse, where the storm wrecked everything, seriously injuring all the residents. Rescuers found Jesse, 5, dead sixty yards from the house. On down the road, the storm blew a different Peter Anderson about eighty yards from his barn and killed him.[48]

As with every tornado, there were oddities. On a pile of debris at the Frank Peterson farm, a mirror lay unbroken. At another farm the wind jammed a wagon wheel down over the top of a tree at such an angle that the tree had to be cut down to remove it. Chickens without feathers were a common sight. The wind pulled a water pump up out of a well and twisted the pipe into knots. The storm turned a section of wire fence around from south to east in a straight line and every post had disappeared. At one home a washing machine was the only thing left standing. One farmer found his 300 pound sow dead with a stake driven through her body, but nearby her little pigs were not hurt. At the Anderson household, the wind blew two pocket watches away, and Anderson found one of them in a field the next day. It was still running.[49]

Henry Gardner gave this horrifying account of the storm:

"About 20 minutes past 9 we were sitting in the house. Suddenly we heard a roaring coming from the southwest and before I had time to make any preparations the house was lifted off the foundation. I saw my wife pick up the baby and a great crash came.

"I remember nothing more until I felt the rain falling on my face. I rose and looked around. The house had disappeared. I called to my wife, she answered and going toward her I found her with the baby in her arms. She was uninjured and the baby was safe. One of my boys was under a part of the wall and his legs were broken below the knee, I took a stick and pried him loose. My boy 5 years old had disappeared, but after some search I found him 60 rods from the house in the mud, not seriously injured. His eyes were full of mud and so was his mouth. I gathered my family together and went to the neighbors for assistance."[50]

The *Clay Center Dispatch* printed a final report on the devastating storm:

"…The path followed by the storm is 400 feet in width and over 20 miles long. The power of the storm was terrific; nothing could withstand its force. Not houses, not barns, not people— the latest reports give the number killed as 11, while nearly 30 were injured. The air seemed hot with an odor resembling burning sulphur. Looked at from a distance it appeared to cut like a sword, crush like a falling mountain, grind like a millstone, and move with such energy as irresistible as the mighty surging of the ocean."[51]

This was not the last tornado to hit the Clay Center area. The worst was yet to come. Map Available: Appendix 1.

CLAY AND CLOUD COUNTIES, MAY 2, 1896

Clay and Cloud Counties were hit again a couple of days later. The day began overcast, humid, and rainy. By the end of the day, clouds became thicker, darker, and the winds picked up. About 9:15pm, a rumbling noise was heard about three miles southeast of Miltonvale, and in the next instant, persistent lightning revealed a large tornado. Before long, there were two tornadoes, following each other.

The tornadoes moved northeast toward St. Joseph, Missouri. It leaped the Republican River between Clifton and Morganville, and they finally lifted on the Washington County line. They were around ¾ of a mile wide and had a path around twenty miles long.

The home of Eli Baltagor was destroyed. Both Eli and his wife were killed, and all of their six children were badly hurt. In Clay County, four lives were lost and seventeen were badly injured. Many homes were destroyed and scattered.

THE FIVE COUNTY TORNADO OF MAY 17, 1896

A particularly dangerous and lengthy storm swept through Clay, Riley, Marshall, Nemaha, and Brown Counties on May 17, 1896 killing more than thirty people and injuring many others.

The tornado destroyed most of the town of Frankfort's residential district; the storm then made a path through Baileyville, Seneca, Oneida, and Sabetha. At Seneca it destroyed the courthouse and several homes.

The tornado struck Sabetha just before 7:00 p.m. and made a swath three blocks wide through the town. After leaving there, the funnel dropped down east of Sycamore Springs, cutting a path across the county eight miles long and two miles wide before passing into Nebraska.

Several people told interesting personal accounts of the storm. Reverend E.W. Parker stated that although the wind was blowing from the east, there was a black cloud approaching from the northwest. Suddenly it became ominously still. "I said to my wife, 'I don't like this!' I had scarcely got the words out of my mouth when we were struck and the house fell in. I remember Mrs. Parker had the baby in her arms and that I put my arms around her, and that my little girl came to us and took hold of us. That is all I remember."

Harry Thompson remarked, "I was fixing a hole in the window when the wind lifted the house off the foundation. The partition fell on my wife. I helped her up and started with her to the cave. The wind caught us up and carried us over a hundred feet against the barn."[52]

The storm was gone but not forgotten by the residents.

CUNNINGHAM, MAY 1898

Late in May 1898 a devastating tornado struck the town of Cunningham. Although intermittent showers had fallen during the day, by late in the afternoon most farmers were in the cornfields southwest of town. Suddenly a small but severe thunderstorm appeared in the west, and a tornado dropped from the clouds immediately. The scene was surreal— the sun was shining at the same time a tornado was bearing down on Cunningham.

The tornado's path, only about a hundred yards wide, went through the center of town. The railroad section house was wrecked. Harvey Howell's general store was in ruins as was McPeek's Drug store and Hick's General Store, and the Branstetter Hotel was totaled. Fortunately, not a single life was lost.

The Cunningham tornado left behind some vivid memories. Mason Wetherall, a pioneer of the community, recalled having a horse tied up in a neighbor's barn, and when the tornado blew the barn away, it left the horse standing alone, unharmed. He also noted that the wind carried an end gate from the Ratcliff Brothers Grain office down to the Lish Ratcliff residence, where it sailed through the kitchen window, across the room, into the dining room, and down in front of the door leading into the living room. The Ratcliff's dog, huddled under the kitchen stove at the time, escaped frightened but unscathed though the house was badly damaged. The wind blew a trunk out of the Jack Manual home and deposited it in the attic of the Casper Foster house. Someone found a razor from the barbershop three miles north of town.

At the railroad section house, Bertha Morton and her father sought refuge in the cellar. When the storm passed, debris filled the cellar except for the corner where they were crouched. Unfortunately, molasses covered Bertha's hair from a jug that tipped over on a shelf above her head.

The tornado trailed Mr. Branstetter. When he realized the funnel was heading right for him, he ran at a right angle out of the funnel's path towards a cellar located next to the railroad depot. After running fifty yards, he noticed that the tornado had turned again and was heading right towards him. Then he decided to backtrack to a spot where he had been originally, but the funnel followed him. Branstetter gave up, threw himself to the ground and clung to the grass while the funnel peppered him with broken glass, lumber, and other debris. He survived.

Harve Howell and his friends watched the tornado until it destroyed the section house. Then they jumped into a storm cellar, holding down the cellar door from below. When the tornado hit the cellar, it ripped the door off and drove a two-by-four into the cellar floor just two feet from where Mrs. Howell was sitting.[53]

Charley Cooley was watching the storm next to Branstetter's Hotel when the tornado hit. His only choice was to run. A block down the street, he crawled into a ditch and lay flat. Suddenly, something came down on him that felt like a load of bricks. He imagined all sorts of things including trees, building debris, or maybe a cow. But then it spoke—it was his friend Cal McNamee! When the rain and the hail commenced pounding them, the two sought comfort beneath Cooley's overcoat.

The tornado picked up Tom Long and carried him over several buildings. He stated that he sailed around for a long time before the twister deposited him gently on the ground, unharmed.[54]

Someone found a cow with barbed wire wrapped around her neck, but otherwise unhurt. One farmer found a calf stuck in the fork of a tree, and the tree had to be cut down before he could remove the animal. A huge safe, contents untouched, made a trip through the air and landed at the rear of Howell's store, but no one ever found its massive door that had been wrenched from its hinges.

Photo of a Smith County tornado in 1902.

CLARK COUNTY, MAY 21-22, 1903

Western Kansas has had fewer tornadoes than the eastern half of the state. This fact is based on 150 years of recorded information, but that doesn't mean that an occasional tornado doesn't "knock on the door" of some Western Kansas community. Such was the case in Clark, Clay, Ford, Hodgeman, Saline, Dickinson, Marshall, Riley, Pottawatomie, Norton, Morton, and Wallace Counties in May of 1903. John R. Walden, editor of the *Clark County Clipper* at Ashland gave the following account of the two day siege:

"I was a witness to both the tornadoes of May 21, 22, 1903. I was working in the Clipper office at that time... The first one was Thursday afternoon just after the passenger train had arrived from the east about 4:30 p.m. At that time the Clipper office was over the Stock Growers State Bank. I could see quite a bit of territory from the window to the west and southwest.

"It looked as though two clouds met near where John Rankin's house is located... It was just a short time when the winds assumed cyclonic proportions and was heading toward town at a terrific rate. The first house it struck was completely demolished, then a few blocks farther north it struck the C.B. Nunnemacher house, tearing it up.

"The wind came near tearing the roof off the bank building and in the Smith building it tore off the doors and caused quite a commotion. We had to suspend printing the paper until the next day.[55]

"Just as I went off to work about 12:30 p.m. the next day, I went to the back window for some papers and looked out and saw a black cloud in the neighborhood of Englewood. It looked like a long elephant's trunk. It was coming northeast. I called to get a camera. About that time the cloud was directly west of the town and the first place it struck was north of the railroad tracks and killed several horses in the pasture. Then it struck in another pasture and killed 38 head of cattle. One large bull was blown through two wire fences and into another pasture. He was completely wrapped in barbed wire. Trees were broken down. From there it struck the schoolhouse, completely demolishing it. The tornado continued northeast but no further damage was reported."[56]

Lone tornado captured near Goddard, Kansas, on May 26, 1903.

GREENWOOD COUNTY, OCTOBER 6, 1903

Greenwood County has a widespread rural population, but in spite of the spread of inhabitants, two people died during a tornado that struck early in the 20th century. The two deaths occurred on the Bailey farm located ten miles north of Eureka. W.E.W. Bailey, three children, and J.A. Hellman were in the house when the storm hit and killed Edith Bailey, 11, and Hellman. Both had their necks broken by falling timbers. W.E.W. took the youngest child in his arms and that is how she escaped serious injury. He had a gash on his head and a badly sprained back. Rescuers found Ollie Bailey buried under the ruins of the farmhouse unconscious and paralyzed.

The tornado that began four miles northwest of Eureka and traveled in a northeasterly direction across the county destroyed or badly damaged nearly a hundred buildings in its path.

At the John Henley farmhouse, the twister tore the porches off and damaged the roof. It also leveled the Highland church, and a Santa Fe Railroad section house disappeared. Thirty-two families had homes, barns, or outbuildings destroyed, and the storm demolished the Prairie Bell schoolhouse.

Actually, the only town struck by the tornado was Aliceville, where much damage occurred.[57]

TOPEKA, SEPTEMBER 1, 1904

The first tornado in recorded history to hit Topeka occurred on a late summer day in 1904. It struck near a high hill known as Burnett's Mound on the southwest side of town. Its path was only about thirty feet wide, but it caused considerable damage on the Washburn University campus before disappearing into an open field north of the Euclid School. The twister then moved northeast on Lane Street, where it carried a wagon and several cows airborne for a short distance. It also lifted a glass door over 100 feet before depositing it unbroken in the grass. At Huntoon and Washburn Streets it went back in the clouds and dissipated.[58] Sixty-two years later, the path and destruction would be quite a bit different.

MARQUETTE TORNADO, MAY 8, 1905

Monday, May 8, 1905 was a day of extreme weather over central Kansas. During the noon hour a severe thunderstorm passed south of Marquette. In the afternoon another storm drenched the central part of the state, but Marquette remained dry.

About 10 p.m. a light rain started falling. People went to bed feeling that all was well. At 11 o'clock, without warning, a tornado dropped down about ten miles south of the city and moved northward at what can best be described as 100 miles an hour. It struck the city west of Pete Hopp's property, crossed the river and hit Charley Brown's house, and veered north straight for Louis Johnson's barn. Then the twister disappeared.[59]

The tornado left behind 28 dead: Olof and Minnie Hanson; Mrs. A.C. Postier and baby; Gottfred Nelson and wife; Elmer Nelson; V.A. Anderson and wife; Gust Anderson; Clyde Norris; Tillie Ellerson; Mrs. E. Hultgren; Vivian Roberts; A. Sjogren; N.P. Nelson and wife; Carl Nelson; Lillie Nelson; Eric Nelson; Blanche Switzer; Nina Switzer; Charley Vernquist; Elmer Carlson; Myrtle Coulson; and Ruth Coulson.

The twister struck H.R. Haywood's home, destroyed Frank Nelson's house, and plowed into Olof Hanson's buildings. The funnel toppled over Olson's farm buildings where Andrew Peterson lived. A short distance away it struck Gust Carlson's house where A.C. Postier stayed. It came close to Chet Skinner's, and wiped out J.M. Johnson's house where Gotfred Nelson lived. It then went straight north and passed J.M. Johnson's, Gust Peterson's and destroyed Muller's orchard. As the tornado advanced, it sucked up great quantities of mud and water from the river and sprayed it all over town.

Those who heard the tornado said it sounded like a passenger train at full speed. A roar, a rush, a cloud of dust, and it was all over. In the still night air, the cries of the wounded could be heard, and within ten minutes the entire population was out with lanterns seeking the dead and rescuing the injured. By dawn they had accounted for everyone. Doctors, undertakers, and nurses came from all over the county. They buried the dead within two days in the best manner possible. It was a sad sight to see two or three funeral processions going at one time and from one to six dead in each. Sadness was everywhere.

One remarkable incident occurred concerning the Postier family. They were on their way to the cellar when the wind blew Mrs. Postier and the baby about thirty rods north of the house. Mr. Postier landed near Andrew Peterson's property forty rods south, and Peterson lit just across the hedge from Postier. Although they were able to help each other, they were unable to find their families. It was too late for them.[60]

Aftermath of tornado damage in Marquette. In the background is the Fuqua family home nearly ripped apart and shattered to pieces.

The storm scattered Olof Hanson's home, barn, outbuildings, and trees for miles, and it killed him and his wife instantly. The two sons, four daughters, and Anna Swanson at the home were injured–two of them critically; a daughter Minnie died two days later. Andrew Peterson lost everything, and both he and his son were in critical condition. A.C. Postier's wife and little baby were killed, and he was seriously injured. Chet Skinner's daughter Myrtle Coulson and her daughter Ruth were listed among the dead. Skinner's three grandsons were all that was left of the Coulson family. Gottfred Nelson, his wife and his brother Elmer were all killed.

The tornado destroyed the new house of V.A. Anderson and killed both the parents and their son Gust. S.N. Norris, his sick wife, and two sons were home when the twister hit. One son Clyde was sitting with his mother. He succeeded in saving her but lost his own life. The wind carried J.M. Ellerson's house across the street and dropped it upside down. The family was badly hurt. His daughter Tillie and her baby were staying with Mrs. Hultgren; they were all killed. The beautiful home of Charles Roberts blew away, killing little Vivian instantly. Mrs. M.L. Berg was fatally injured, and her property was a total loss.

The twister demolished the Nelson home, killing N.P. Nelson, his wife and three children. The wind destroyed the property of A. Sjogren and killed him. L. Switzer and his three girls were at home, but after the storm, rescuers found two of them mangled in the railroad tracks a thousand feet away. Little Nina's body was west of the house. Switzer's loss was the saddest of all.[61]

The injured were not listed because there were so many. Such a catastrophe brings many people together. A thousand friends unknown before had the city's profound thanks for help in its hour of need. Map Available: Appendix 1.

JEWELL COUNTY, MAY 27, 1908

A late night thunderstorm roared through Athens and Browns Creek Townships in Jewell County on May 27, 1908. Without warning a small tornado formed and demolished farms and homes, killing one man and injuring nineteen other people.

The tornado destroyed George Hahn's house, barn, and outbuildings. It also fractured his skull. He spoke only once to his wife before he became unconscious, saying that he didn't think he was badly injured. By the time help arrived, he was dead. Mrs. Hahn had internal injuries and some cracked vertebrae. Relatives found the little baby that usually slept between them rolled up in the bedspread uninjured.

At the McFarland farm the twister demolished the house and barn, but the family escaped with only minor cuts and bruises. The Ellis Crites family watched the storm approaching, and upon hearing a roar, they ran for the cave. The high winds scattered their house and barn over the nearby fields and caused some of the wreckage to pile up against the door to their cave. They had to dig their way out the backside. At the Bowman farm every structure blew apart, and some members of the family were badly hurt. Mrs. Bowman had a broken shoulder and a large splinter run through her hip. One family member was blown out a window into the yard while resting on their bed. The ride, however, left them uninjured. The twister blew the rest of the family into adjoining fields, where it dropped them. The storm caught Will Moshier out in the open. When the wind slammed his body to the ground, it mangled his arm so badly it had to be amputated.

The tornado destroyed the C.B. Durant homestead, leaving many dead calves, pigs, and naked chickens lying in the cellar and amid furniture, stoves, books, and other wreckage. Mr. Durant was not hurt, but Mrs. Durant had a severe gash on her leg. She heard the tornado coming and roused the family. When the storm hit they were on the cellar stairway, and she was holding the lantern. She fell and doused the lantern, leaving the family scared and in complete darkness.[62]

Shortly afterwards the tornado rose back into the clouds and disappeared, leaving behind immense uninsured losses. Local committees collected donations and contributed large sums of money to help everyone rebuild and get back to normal financially.[63]

GREAT BEND AND HOISINGTON, MAY 14, 1909

On May 14, 1909 a tornado moved into the Great Bend and Hoisington areas. About 3:00 p.m. Friday afternoon, a black mass of clouds began to gather twenty-five miles southwest of Hoisington. This storm extended halfway to Great Bend, and on the southern edge of these clouds a long snake-like tornado touched the ground. It moved northeast toward Hoisington, just missing the community by four miles. In this area it destroyed several homes, barns, and a schoolhouse. When Robert Doonan saw the storm coming, he said it was so dark he could hardly see to get everyone safely in the cellar. The tornado destroyed his farmhouse before leaving and heading east. At the George Walker ranch, his wife was at home with two small children when the tornado approached. She barely had enough time to escape to the cave before the wind crushed the house, barn, granary, and all the buildings, scattering them for over a mile.[64]

William Beck was approaching Walker's ranch when he saw the storm coming and he drove in behind the house for protection. After the storm passed someone found him buried but still alive in a pile of broken boards.

His horses were not hurt, but the storm smashed his buggy beyond recognition. The tornado left 200 chickens scattered about the farmyard, some of them decapitated, others had legs and wings pulled off, and all were stripped of their feathers.[65]

The twister struck a Santa Fe railroad work crew a mile east of Heizer, where they had just finished working on a bridge. It blew the train from the tracks and scattered some of the cars into the adjoining fields. William Ackley was pinned under the wreckage and killed instantly. Ten others were seriously hurt. Rescuers immediately transported them to Great Bend for medical care, and then they transferred them to the company hospital in Topeka. Two of the workers, Arthur Dillinger and Walter Murray, died two days later. In all, six people died and thirty-eight were injured in one of the worst tornado outbreaks in the region.

Twenty-five people were injured in Mount Washington and Fairmont Park, two suburbs of Kansas City. Three people were also killed at Hollis, Kansas, near Concordia. Hollis was wiped off the map. One of the largest buildings destroyed in Hollis was the grain elevator. The town had a population of 150 at the time. Map Available: Appendix 1.

NORTON COUNTY, JUNE 24, 1909

Northwestern Norton County was devastated by eight tornadoes which destroyed farm buildings, injured men working in the fields, killed livestock, and mowed down trees.

Six tornadoes formed around 4pm, following a sultry day. One of the funnels came within ten miles of Norton before it dissipated. Hail measuring six to seven inches in circumference was also recorded.

The death toll was small primarily because the storms formed early. Had the tornadoes formed after dark, the outcome might have been more severe. Later in the evening, two other tornadoes formed a dozen miles south of Norton, traveling eastward.

View of the tornado that struck Norton, Kansas

EMPORIA AND PLYMOUTH, MAY 1, 1910

A tornado struck the western section of Emporia, tearing roofs out of several houses and carrying one off its foundation. A large cow barn was crushed like an egg and smaller barns were completely blown away. More than a hundred buildings were wrecked. Fortunately, there was no loss of life.

Mrs. George Davis was blown into a hedge surrounding her home and was badly injured. Neosho Rapids, nine miles southwest of Emporia, was also hit hard by the wind. A store building and several frame residences were destroyed.

The town of Plymouth a town of 400 people six miles southwest of Emporia was nearly destroyed that night. A large number of dwellings and buildings were destroyed but no lives were lost. Map Available: Appendix 1.

EASTERN KANSAS, APRIL 12, 1911

One of the worst tornado outbreaks of the century occurred on April 12, 1911. Late in the afternoon, the storm struck Eskridge in Wabaunsee County, where it swept across Main Street, damaging the Commercial Hotel. It skipped over part of the town and then dropped down near the railroad yards, destroying everything in its path. One witness, Mrs. Wray, reported, "one-half of the town was severely damaged or destroyed. House after house went down before a storm that left a mass of wreckage behind." The tornado injured dozens of people, including thirty-five school children, who were just being dismissed when the storm struck.[66]

The twister then moved northeast and killed two people between Hiawatha and Holton. At the farm of Leonard Dorte near Germantown, the family escaped death from the storm, but it killed all of the livestock. Lightning struck J.E. Rosenbalm at his farm and killed him instantly. Four small girls remained in the Diamond District schoolhouse near Hiawatha, and when the storm hit and demolished the building, it killed one of the girls.

At Hiawatha the tornado hit another schoolhouse, killing one child and breaking the teacher's legs. A student, Nolan Mellott, led the small group to safety but after he opened the outside door the twister leveled the school, crushing the teacher and four children beneath the walls. Nolan pulled himself over the wreckage and called for help. Some people in a cellar nearby came immediately to the rescue. Apparently the school building had imploded. The wind did not disturb the student's desks but crushed the teacher's desk, and carried the school bell several hundred yards to the center of the street.

The storm moved on through Whiting, but destroyed the Manville Grain elevator between Hiawatha and Robinson. The wind blew the telephone lines down and wrapped some poles in tin from nearby sheds. The storm killed one person at Robinson.[67]

About 6:55 p.m. the tornado slammed into Lawrence, killing two people. The storm was not over until around 8:20 p.m., when an ominous lull fell over the city. The funnel first touched down southwest of town, then dipped back and forth and dropped again, sweeping across Mississippi, Indiana, and Louisiana Streets. Lifting briefly on Kentucky Street, it didn't touch down again until it hit the Eldridge House Hotel. At the old Eldridge, Mrs. H.T. Hutson was on her bed reading a newspaper when she heard the storm coming. Remembering that her daughter and children were in the front room, she jumped off the bed and hurried to help them to safety. A few minutes after she left her room, the ceiling collapsed, burying her bed under a pile of bricks.[68]

The twister finally passed across the river, leaving swaying buildings and a demolished factory district in its wake. Debris was piled high on Massachusetts Street and adjoining avenues, which hampered rescuers.[69]

Tornado damage on Massachusetts Street in Lawrence

The *Lawrence Journal World* described the damage as follows:

"Wilder's shirt factory and laundry is a total loss. The roof and entire fourth story was listed off by the furious wind. The stone walls are cracked, rendering the building extremely dangerous to enter. When the roof was torn off, the wind picked up a roomful of shirt boxes and swirled them all over the block. The Paper Mill was in the vortex of the storm and sustained severe damage. The egg case and corrugating departments were unroofed. The brick walls were torn away. The roof of the bleaching building was blown away and both the east and the west walls were crushed in by flying timbers.

"The foundry and cabinet works were unroofed and the top of the east wall demolished. The Boener Cigar Factory was unroofed… The Bowersock Mills have a few corners crumpled at the top and the wooden awnings torn loose. The big electric sign on top of the flourmill was converted into a tangled mass of wire and broken incandescents… .The front of the brick building occupied by the Brown Cash grocery was destroyed–the walls on the second story were lying on the sidewalk, exposing to view the bedroom with its furniture and pictures. The roof of the old jail was blown off, and the west wing partially wrecked."[70]

Massachusetts Street Looking South in Lawrence

The tornado killed three women— Ethel Wheeler, Mrs. Joe Sullivan, and Laura Childs.

Wheeler was a domestic on the Doubleday farm when the storm appeared. "I'm not going to remain in here around that stove," she said as she dashed out the door to her death. When they recovered her body an hour later, her neck was broken, her face crushed, and one leg dangled limp. She and her husband Dave had settled in Lawrence just three weeks before. The wind destroyed the Doubleday Farm and a nearby chicken house. Of the hundreds of chickens, nothing but a few feathers remained.

Mrs. Joe Sullivan paused a moment to close a transom. This brief pause cost Sullivan her life. The storm had become violent, and her son George urged her to take refuge in the cellar. Mrs. Sullivan remembered the open transom, and fearing that the rain would stain her carpet, she paused to lower the sash. Before she could join her son, the tornado swept the house from its foundation and buried both mother and son beneath the wreckage. Some neighbors rescued her quickly but she lived only a few minutes.[71]

The tornado was about a block wide north of the river and did extensive damage in the residential area, especially on Walnut Street. The wind tore one house occupied by Charles Powell from its foundation and threw it sideways against the Hackney home, which also collapsed. The Powell family had to be rescued through a window. At the home of William Browning the storm drove a large timber through the house, leaving a hole as big as a cannon ball.[72] The twister lifted A.N. Dankin's new water pump from the ground, mangled it and dropped it in the yard. J.T. Curbey, a barber, found an open razor carried from a neighbor's house firmly imbedded in the siding of his shop. At Bismarck Grove the storm lifted the cupola from the schoolhouse and tore away one corner of a barn.

Rumors were rampant that the tornado picked up a woman and child from the Kansas River Bridge and dropped them into the water below. Although no trace of either one could be found, several so-called eyewitnesses repeated the incident. Later it was determined that no one was crossing the bridge during the storm.

Just as the tornado was about to strike Lawrence, a Santa Fe passenger train was nearing the town. The engineer in his darkened cab noticed the threatening storm about three miles back. By the aid of lightning flashes, he could see the black clouds and the flying debris rotating in a mass above the skyline. Suddenly some gusts of wind struck the train, shaking the cars. Fearing that the full force of the storm would knock the train off the track, he opened the throttle, allowing the train to spring forward. Heroically risking derailment to avoid a tornado, he raced the storm to Lawrence. However, the tornado gained rapidly on the long line of cars, and a mile out of town, the wind rocked the train so violently that the engineer believed the storm was upon them. With a final burst of speed the train ran under the protective embankment at the Kansas River Bridge, just as the tornado passed over.

This storm system claimed twenty-five lives and injured hundreds more. Many of these deaths occurred in Missouri as the storm continued on to the border. This outbreak was one of the worst of the decade.[73] Map Available: Appendix 1.

BISON, APRIL 20, 1912

On April 20, 1912 spring came early to central Kansas. On this day a tornado hit the small town of Bison in Rush County, killing two people. One of the heroes in town that day was Dr. Robinson. He was the first to notice the strange cloud hanging over the town. He ran from his office to warn the residents, but it was too late for them and for him. Caught out in the open, he threw himself against a telephone pole, but the force of the wind snapped the pole half way down and carried him a hundred yards before dropping him in the mud. In spite of his cuts and bruises, he went on caring for the many injured and dying. Only when two more physicians arrived from La Crosse to assist did he treat his own wounds.

The tornado did odd things that night. The floor of Henry Swindt's demolished barn was carried a hundred feet with his motorcar completely wrecked on the top floor. The wind blew William Witt five blocks and let him down easy on the same spot where the German Baptist Church had stood just minutes before. William Reinhardt claimed the wind blew him out of his wagon north of town, and when he came to his senses, he was standing in the yard of his house, a half mile away.

Before the storm hit, Bison had a population of 400, but the wind flattened half the town. The path of the tornado was nearly 300 yards wide.[74]

MIAMI AND LINN COUNTIES, JUNE 15, 1912

A large tornado outbreak occurred in the rural areas of Miami and Linn Counties, as well as portions of Oklahoma and Missouri, on June 15, 1912. It killed eleven people and injured sixty, although most of these were residents of Oklahoma.[75]

In Linn County the storm left scarcely anything at the C.W. Bishop residence. It tore away barns, outbuildings, and even foundations. The Bishop family took refuge in their cellar and thus escaped serious injury. At the McFadden farm, six miles southwest of Parker, the tornado caught the family by surprise. Before they could reach shelter, it picked up two members of the family and carried them some distance before throwing them against a tree.

At the W.H. Hearn home, southeast of Parker, the Hearn's and seven children just sat down to dinner when the storm struck. Since they had no cellar and no time to go to the neighbors, all they could do was await the fury of the storm. It tore their house to pieces and tossed all of them into the debris. They were injured but not seriously.[76]

At the Wettke farm, Mr. Robbins noted, "The storm tore the house wrong side out–the front door which formerly opened in, now opens out."[77] The tornado destroyed the Harry Parker farm, the George Pollman farm, and the residence of Reuben Cox. At the Pollman farm, the storm killed all his pure bred horses. At the John Weir home, the twister demolished the house, crushing Mrs. Wier. In spite of her life-threatening injuries, she was tough and she eventually recovered. The Weir family was unlucky; three months earlier they had suffered a devastating fire that burned most of their belongings. The house and the furnishings scattered by the tornado were all new purchases.[78]

At the Grant Main house, the only thing left standing was the cook stove. The Louis Russour residence suffered extensive damage, but Mr. Russour had a premonition that a storm was coming and took out "cyclone insurance" that same day. Map Available: Appendix 1.

SOUTHEASTERN KANSAS, AUGUST 25, 1912

A tornado outbreak on August 25, 1912 killed three people and caused widespread property loss. The storm hit Elk City first, where it demolished schools, homes, and barns. Those killed included a woman near Farm Ridge, a man at Wauneta, and another man at Sedan. The tornado nearly obliterated the little town of Monett and leveled many houses south of Dearing. This same storm system hit Neodesha, Coffeyville, and Independence, causing widespread damage. The hotel at Dearing caught fire during the height of the storm and forced fourteen guests to run outside wearing only their nightclothes.

A destructive tornado hit Omaha, Nebraska on Easter Sunday, March 21, 1913. Milton Tabor, then editor of the *Topeka Daily Capital*, witnessed a phenomenon that few have lived to talk about. Tabor looked up into a funnel cloud and wrote this account of what he saw:

"The tornado formed where a group of students, including myself, were enjoying a picnic just east of Lincoln, Nebraska, and whirled furiously over our heads. We looked up into what appeared to be an enormous hollow cylinder, bright inside with lightning flashes, but blackest night all around. The noise was like ten million bees, plus a roar that begs description."[79]

Foster Dwight Coburn, secretary of the Kansas State Board of Agriculture from 1894 to 1914, attempted to modify the image the state had as a tornado region. He purposely dropped from his vocabulary embarrassing terms such as "drought," "cyclone," "grasshopper," and "blizzard." Unfortunately, every time a tornado occurred, there was little he could do to disguise it, and Kansas continued to be the state everyone thought of when the word "tornado" came up in the conversation. Wealthy Kansas City philanthropist William Rockhill Nelson did nothing to help Colburn's cause. He described Kansas as a "scriptural kingdom-a land of floods, droughts, cyclones, and enormous crops of prophets and plagues."

Julian Street in his book, *Abroad At Home: American Ramblings, Observations, and Adventures,* painted a grim picture of Western Kansas as he traveled across the area in 1914. Street saw only a drab, treeless wasteland of brown and gray---"nothing, nothing, nothing"--images of incessant wind, violent cyclones, dust storms, and tragic desolation. As the train he was riding approached the small town of Monotony, which he felt was appropriately named, he listened sympathetically to the remarks of a fellow passenger: "God! How can they stand living out here? I'd rather be dead!"[80]

Unfortunately, this was not a valid description of Kansas. Things were changing and concepts like socialism were popular in some areas, especially in Southeast Kansas around the coal mining fields. The eastern part of the state was becoming urbanized, especially around Kansas City, Leavenworth, and Topeka. There were few voices conveying this image of the state.

Interesting view of a tornado photographed in Smith County, 1913

TORNADO OUTBREAK, NOVEMBER 10, 1915

Late in 1915 South Central Kansas was the recipient of a nasty storm, dispelling the theory that tornadoes only occur during the spring and summer months.

A large tornado roared through northern Sumner County and destroyed the small town of Zyba, and then, continuing on north, it cut a path of destruction through southern Sedgwick County. The *Wichita Eagle's* headline read, "Zyba Wiped Off the Map." Outside of town, the tornado destroyed some farmsteads and killed four people. Mrs. Dave Gordon was one of the witnesses, and in 1979 she had this to say:

"Zyba was on the old Meridian Road just south of the Ninnescah (River) where the Rock Island Railroad crossed the river. There wasn't much there—a country store, depot, stockyards, and a few houses. My dad Henry Hartle bought a store and we moved from Oklahoma in 1911. We had a two-story house. I slept upstairs. My dad, mother, little sister, and one hired girl slept downstairs.

Interesting view of a tornado in Mullinville, June 11, 1915

Another tornado hit Ellis, Kansas that same day

Tornado damage near Great Bend

"About 10:30 that night I heard a train coming but something told me it wasn't and I got up to go downstairs. When I came to, I was standing on the edge of the Ninnescah in a cold and pouring rain wearing only a nightgown. I didn't know what happened or how I got there. [When] I made my way back to the house about two long blocks, it was gone. I remember a nail went clear through my foot. I found my mother but she wouldn't talk to me. Then I found my dad. He was groaning and badly hurt so I helped him get over some stairs. I found my little sister and couldn't do anything for her.

"Then I heard some neighbors calling us. They had me carrying a lantern while they got everybody into a big cave we used for storage. They flagged down the next train and put us in the baggage car and brought us to Wichita to the hospital.

"My mother had a crushed chest and a punctured lung and died very shortly. My Dad had a broken shoulder and internal injuries but he lived. My sister had a fractured skull but came out of that. The hired girl and Mrs. LeForce, a neighbor, were killed outright."[81]

Neighbors found the bodies of the two women several hundred feet from their home. The tornado caused extensive damage at Ellis and Derby where it killed a section hand and injured more than twenty others.

Great Bend Mill without a roof following the deadly tornado

Mrs. Gordon noted that, "Zyba was never built up again–nobody ever went back."

In Great Bend a tornado killed eleven people and did a million dollars in damages. The storm first appeared sixteen miles southwest of town, moving northeast. It struck the Moses and Clayton ranch south of town, where it killed a thousand sheep.

When the tornado reached Great Bend it was three city blocks wide. Residents said the roar sounded like a hundred locomotives. The twister destroyed the electric power and water plants; several flour mills and grain elevators, the Santa Fe Railroad passenger and freight depots, and 125 homes.[82]

The winds strewed debris from the storm for a distance of sixty miles! Someone found a personal letter and a check from Great Bend near Glasco, 85 miles to the northeast. Another person found a cancelled check from a Great Bend bank in Nebraska, where it had been dropped by the tornado. The storm also damaged buildings in Ellinwood and Hoisington.[83] Map Available: Appendix 1.

The tornado knocked a box car off the tracks near Great Bend

TORNADOES/SQUALL LINES, APRIL 19, 1916

On April 19, 1916 towns in East and Southeast Kansas were in the middle of a squall line that covered over a hundred miles. The storm killed at least two people at Fort Scott. Newspaper reports said entire families were missing. Wilson and Woodson Counties had extensive damage and a twister ruined nine farmsteads near Yates Center.

A bad storm killed one person at Hoyt and injured three others. The noise of the oncoming tornado attracted the attention of all the residents. Earl Gregg watched from his front door as the funnel took shape. At first the clouds looked like a black swirling mass, and then a terrible "tail" dropped down. Gregg noted, "It came lower and lower, swinging back and forth like a rope, then it touched the ground just in front of the house. We went inside and my brother-in-law held the door with all his weight to keep the wind from blowing it off the hinges. The wind passed around the house, picking up the barn, bringing it around in front of the house and throwing it across the road. A tent in the back yard was carried to the front."[84]

The "tail" moved all around Hoyt from one end to the other, damaging residences. When Principal Ernest Lightbody saw the clouds forming, he decided the children would be safer in the street than in school. He told them to "run west, run for your lives!" The children ran. Three minutes later the tornado struck the ground within fifteen yards of the schoolhouse. No one was injured.[85]

The wind lifted Mrs. Lucy Nagelbaugh as she attempted to run to the cellar. Rescuers later found her unconscious in the road several hundred feet away. Oddly enough, her house was spared any damage. The tornado caught Elina Whitecraft out in the open in a buggy driven by Millard Vance. It threw her from the buggy into a barbed wire fence, tearing her clothes and cutting her face. The next day someone found just two wheels from the buggy, nothing else. Elina was fortunate.[86]

At the Melton home, Mrs. Melton and her baby barely made it to the cellar before the tornado destroyed their house. Later, Mr. Melton found his favorite Sunday coat still hanging on a hook on a piece of the wall in the bedroom. The bedroom had totally disappeared. At the Munger house, the wind blew all the furniture and belongings out the windows except for the family photo album. It fell into the cellar and hit Mrs. Munger on the head, causing a severe headache.

East of Hoyt, the town of Larkinburg also reported damage. The storm injured two people and demolished several buildings. The twister hit Rock Creek and the Cedar Valley church, where it knocked over tombstones in the graveyard. A cemetery is evidently not the best place to be in a tornado.

This tornado did more severe damage when it moved into Missouri, where it killed sixteen people and injured hundreds.

ELLIS COUNTY, MAY 20, 1917

On the afternoon of May 20, 1917 a large tornado struck seventeen miles north of Hays at the C.G. Cochran ranch, where it destroyed two houses, two barns, three cattle sheds, and a corral. Two families, who were left homeless, had a loss of $10,000.

Actually there were two tornadoes. One formed two miles northwest of the ranch, the other two miles southeast, and they came together in the Saline River valley. The *Hays Free Press* noted that, "It was a mighty conflict as these storm giants met, clashed, clinched, and whirled around south of the buildings, struck the sides of a canyon, ricocheted, and passed over, round, and through the structures."[87]

The tornado only lasted about ten minutes, but during these minutes it worked overtime creating some bizarre incidents. On the Cochran ranch the twister crushed an eight-foot galvanized water tank and split the sideboard of a wagon in two, thrusting one of the pieces of the sideboard through the flattened tank. Then it carried the tank and board a half mile, where it forced one end of the board into the trunk of a tree; it left the tank dangling on the other end of the board. The tornado completely blew away a large kitchen from a house but somehow the same wind picked up a teakettle near the barn and placed it neatly where the kitchen once stood. In the bedroom a gust of wind gently moved a small aquarium containing goldfish to the center of the room without spilling a drop of water. Most of the furniture in the house was twisted, crushed, and pitched into the yard.

The tornado demolished an old rock barn, leaving nothing but a pile of jagged stones. A stand of timber near the barn took a direct hit. The funnel wrenched the trees from the ground, twisted and broke others, and completely stripped some of their leaves. The storm tore hundreds of feet of barbed wire from a fence, rolled it into a large ball and left it south of the ruined stone barn.

SOUTHERN KANSAS, MAY 25, 1917

A tornado on May 25, 1917 destroyed everything along its sixty-five mile path and killed twenty-six people. It formed in western Sedgwick County around 3:00 p.m. and swept through Andale, passing near Bentley and barely missing Sedgwick. It killed thirteen people in Andale alone. There is evidence of a second tornado near Oatville.[88]

The twister cut a swath a half mile wide between Andale and Newton, killing three more people. The sun had been shining only minutes before, and then suddenly a black cloud appeared on the horizon. Few had time to escape.

At Andale, the tornado destroyed the Missouri Pacific Railroad station and turned over six boxcars standing on the siding. It demolished the small shacks that housed the track workers.

In some areas of Andale, it was impossible to tell where the houses had been standing. At one place in the storm's path, the largest piece of board left was part of a door with the white doorknob attached.[89]

Damage in Andale, showing smashed houses

John Klein came home from work to find his house demolished. He searched frantically for his family in the debris and in the street. Finally, two blocks away, he found his wife and three children beneath some timbers crushed to death. Their little black dog, who escaped unhurt, assisted in locating the bodies. Whining pitifully, the dog refused to be coaxed away from the scene of the tragedy. Klein's brother couldn't find his baby, but that story had a happier ending–after pulling up some boards, they found the baby laughing and gurgling.

Joseph Mertes was helping his father work on a car when the tornado hit the building. Despite the fact that the older Mertes was so bruised he could hardly walk, he found his son pinned under the car with blood streaming from his head. He carried him nearly two blocks to get help. Unfortunately, Joseph died thirty minutes later.[90]

Ten people escaped injury in Gorges store due to a traveling salesman who saw the tornado coming and ran into the store yelling for everyone to take cover. Only a handful made it to the cellar before the building exploded, but those who didn't were at the backside of the store, which afforded them some protection.

Leo Hecht's house was also a scene of destruction. The large family made it to the basement in time, but not before they saw their home lifted up over their heads and the rubble fall in with them. Fortunately, the debris landed on the opposite side of the room. No one was hurt.

Although the tornado blew one car nearly a hundred yards and deposited it in Henry Rausch's parlor, another errant car saved the life of Agnes Peterson. She became frightened at the noise of the storm and crouched against the side of her home. The wind blew the car against the wall of Agnes's house where it stuck and protected her from flying debris.

More residential damage in Andale during the tornado

This tornado left behind several incredible animal anecdotes. It actually blew a kitten into a large fruit jar, and it also blew a canary out of its cage, still alive. No one ever found the cage, but the canary didn't lose a feather.

Colonel Elwood Evans, U.S. Army, and his military party were selecting sites for Army mobilization camps when they encountered the tornado near Sedgwick. They were on the inter-urban train between Hutchinson and Wichita. Evans noted, "The cloud did not have a funnel shape, but it was so black and ugly that members of the party commented on it. Then it seemed to start for us. As it came nearer we could see houses and barns demolished. It raced after us and crossed over not more than 100 yards behind us. There was a terrible roar and then we went ahead. I have heard of Kansas twisters, but this is as close as I ever want to be to one."[91]

The town of Sedgwick did not escape disaster. Rescuers found a young woman, who had been living with the William Finn family, dead several hundred yards from their home. East of Sedgwick, the storm killed Mrs. Markes, crushing her under some debris. Although William Norris was killed, his wife and children escaped by running out into an open field. The force of the wind killed one son of Pence Cable and broke the legs of another son. Neighbors found Mrs. Howard Tanner and her baby fatally injured in the rubble of their house. Elmer Corkhill died on the way to the hospital--he had a splinter blown through his head. Corkhill's daughter died two hours later from the same type of injury. Robert Blurton, caught outside on his horse, was overtaken by the tornado. Rescuers found him several hours later lying in the middle of the road with his pony's head bowed over him; they took him to the hospital where he died the next day.[92]

One of the fastest moving tornadoes on record moved from Grenola to Uniontown, passing New Albany at 5:30 p.m. and arriving at Chanute, twenty-seven miles away, at 5:45 p.m. Its speed between the two points was sixty-five miles an hour. At first someone reported it was moving at 120 miles an hour, but this estimate proved to be erroneous.[93] Map Available: Appendix 1.

COFFEYVILLE AND OTHERS, JUNE 1, 1917

Twelve people died in the tornadoes that struck Coffeyville, Morse, and Olathe on June 1, 1917. Two of the deaths and thirty-three injuries were reported at Coffeyville, where the wind demolished 150 houses. The devastated area was a strip three blocks wide, running through Coffeyville from the west to the northeast limits of town. The estimated losses were $1,000,000.

The storm struck suddenly and without warning around 5:15 p.m. and it surprised the citizens. They saw nothing out of the ordinary that day except for a small cloud in the west that shifted back and forth for an hour before approaching the town.

The tornado either demolished or badly damaged all the houses on the south side of the main street. A small shed landed in the back room of Henry Deichler's apartment, and if that wasn't enough, a car soon joined it there. Although Henry didn't have an apartment or furnishings left, he had a little of everyone else's things to make up for it. The tornado destroyed some businesses including grocery stores, a candy store, barbershop, laundry, two churches, and a greenhouse.[94]

The 5:00 p.m. bus was just leaving town when it ran into the tornado. The passengers became panic stricken when a frightened Mexican tried to force his way out of the bus by shoving other people aside. Former Sheriff Charles Paxon grappled with him, and a blow or two from the fist of the ex-sheriff soon quieted the man down. He decided to stay on board. Fortunately, the tornado passed on by and no one was hurt.

When the wind blew Reuben Evans' delivery wagon over, he was trapped in the wreckage, and his team of horses nearly trampled him to death. Just west of the schoolhouse, a brick dwelling almost became the tomb for one family, who had sought refuge in the northwest corner of the kitchen. The tornado toppled the east and south walls, and the roof, dropping bricks and debris everywhere except in the northwest corner of the kitchen. Deciding to go to any other part of the house could have cost them their lives. Outside of the storm's path, there was little wind or sound. People who lived only a few blocks away were unaware that Coffeyville had been hit by a tornado.

The squall line then moved on to O'Herin and Mound Valley, causing extensive damage. At Mound Valley, Charles Peterson's daughter was killed. The twister struck Olathe and Pomona, where its path of destruction was 150 yards wide, and three people were killed. The high winds nearly leveled the town of Morse. At this point the tornado disappeared, and the storm moved into Missouri.[95]

REGISTRATION DAY TORNADO, JUNE 5, 1917

The worst storm in Shawnee County history (prior to the 1966 tornado) was the tornado that struck on Registration Day June 5, 1917. A combination of several small tornadoes revolving around an unusually large one was accompanied by hail and rain. Fortunately, it skirted Topeka. The twisters actually affected four counties—Wabaunsee, Shawnee, Douglas, and Jefferson. In two hours it was all over.[96]

Damage near Elmont, Shawnee County

The twister began at Eskridge and raced northeast. Harold Colvin gave a graphic picture of the funnel as it roared into Eskridge:

"Just as the Santa Fe came in from the west, the storm broke over the town. There was a perfect deluge of small hailstones as big as plums, and now and then as big as hen's eggs. . . . A stiff wind accompanied the first part of the storm. These hailstones cracked windows in banks and large stores. Then there was sort of a slackening of the wind, and the large hailstones began to fall. I measured one of these larger stones. It was thirteen inches around and weighed thirteen ounces. Literally thousands of stones that size fell on the town… After the hailstorm there was a lull, and we saw the tornado approaching from the south. It was like a gigantic serpent."

The twister crossed the Kansas River about four miles west of Topeka, damaging Menoken and leveling Elmont. It also hit the railroad stops of Wanamaker and Kiro in Northern Shawnee County. In Douglas County the tornado demolished most of Clinton, and killed a small boy. From Menoken to Elmont the twister was two miles wide. Four persons died, a dozen were injured and scores were left homeless.

At Elmont the tornado swept down the face of a steep bluff that was supposed to shelter the town; it sheared off the trees growing on the slope like a giant sickle. Only four houses remained standing along with the post office and Methodist church. The wind destroyed all the other businesses.

Some witnesses reported seeing a half-dozen funnels. The clouds were so alive with electricity they seemed to be on fire. The sound of the storm was similar to a "thousand railroad engines revved up" at once. The main tornado "writhed and twisted like an elephant's trunk," and whipped leaves, limbs, and even bark from the trees, leaving them with a blasted appearance.

C.E. Layman saw the tornado coming from the railroad depot, and noting, "Instantly everything went black. It was so dark that I could not see my hand, and then everything went up and I went with it. I don't know how high the station went, but when it came down I was standing on what had been the east wall with my foot through the window. The rest of the building was all around me."[97] After leaving Elmont, the tornado split - one portion dying out just before it hit Meriden, and the other one continuing on into Douglas County.

This storm got the name "Registration Day" tornado because June 5th was registration day for World War I, and Elmont was the only town in the U.S. that didn't have its registration completed. The tornado lifted the schoolhouse where the registration was taking place over the heads of ten people without injuring any of them. The wind blew away all the records for that day.

The tornado picked up a farmhand, carried him a hundred feet, and let him down alive, but caked in mud. It blew a pane of glass from the ticket window of a railroad depot into a field and underneath a heavy weight scale without even cracking the glass. The wind drove straws into tree trunks so deep that they broke off when anyone tried to pull them out. On a shelf in the Rock Island station was a gallon of pears. Although the tornado destroyed the depot, the glass jar of pears remained intact in a pasture a hundred feet from the station.[98]

Dr. Charles Byerley of Topeka was visiting near Elmont when the storm broke. He noted, "When I first saw the storm it was directly over Martin's Hill and appeared to be about five miles away. It was shaped like a balloon that was emptied of gas. Almost instantly it was upon us. I could see telephone poles and large trees being hurled into the air from where I was standing."

Several strange incidents occurred during the storm. The twister blew a barn away, leaving only a single nest with a hen sitting calmly on it. Someone found a cook stove a half-mile from its home, buried in the mud. Rescuers found one house reduced to kindling except for the floor in one room—on the floor was a table, and on the table was an opened box of matches, all items undisturbed by the wind. The tornado blew a woman out of a buggy into a tree where she remained until morning. A group of travelers approaching Topeka saw the tornado bearing down on them. They quickly abandoned their car and tried to seek shelter in a nearby schoolhouse. After finding it locked, they ran to a small coal shed. The tornado demolished the schoolhouse and a building next to the coal shed, but the shed where the travelers took refuge was not touched. However, the wind rolled their car several hundred feet off the highway and reduced it to scrap metal.[99]

In a few years after this violent storm, the residents of Elmont rebuilt the town, but it took longer than that for them to forget the eleven people killed that day.[100] Map Available: Appendix 1.

CHAPTER FOUR: TECHNOLOGY AND UNDERSTANDING

HAYS, MAY 20, 1918

World War I was not the only event that made headlines in Central Kansas. On Monday night, May 20, 1918 a tornado as wide as a mile wrecked farms and destroyed lives from WaKeeney to Hays. Southwest of WaKeeney at the Bert Stanton farm, debris from the storm hurt Mrs. Stanton, and flying glass cut Miss Dietz' face. As the twister moved across the countryside, it killed 200 head of cattle and lifted a tractor engine, carrying it fifteen rods away. At Alex Geist's home, the tornado smashed all the buildings and killed the Geists. The wind blew Mrs. Geist, who weighed 250 pounds, through a barbed wire fence. Both bodies were naked and caked in mud.

A half-mile north of the Geist home, the storm killed three children of Adam Geist—ages ten months, two years, and five years. The force of the wind tore the youngest child from his uncle's arms, and in a field about 100 feet away, they found the baby—nearly every bone in its body broken.[1]

The tornado did not spare Codell in Rooks County. It killed two more people and six other victims had to be taken to a hospital in Hays. The tornado leveled the schoolhouse, Methodist church, hotel, and several homes. At the Bromley farm, it destroyed every building, killing Mrs. Walter Adams and her baby. On the Henry Koelling farm, the storm demolished everything and blew the furniture, belongings, and livestock all over the county.[2]

Codell has the dubious distinction of being the only community hit by tornadoes three times exactly a year apart. The first occurrence was on May

20, 1916. This storm barely touched the northeast edge of town but did extensive damage to farms outside the community. No one was injured.[3]

A year later, on May 20, 1917, another tornado struck the area just south of Codell. Again, the storm damaged some farm buildings, but no one was hurt. This last one in 1918 was the worst of all, and understandably, the townspeople were so frightened they just walked around town in a daze most of the night. After the third storm, the residents became quite apprehensive around May 20th of every year. Actually, it nearly happened a fourth time in 1919 -- there was a storm but no funnel.

Marvel Parter recounted in a 1977 interview about the storm that hit Codell in 1916:

"On Sunday evening, my parents and sisters and brothers and my fiancé' stood in the farmyard and watched the cyclone cloud go across the country. The next day, we went to the vicinity where the cyclone touched down and the most damaged farm home was owned by people we had known for years, as we had purchased apples and pears each fall from their orchard. No one was injured. Their car was wrapped two-thirds of the way around a tree. We had heard cyclones plucked chickens and we saw a few almost bare with only a few feathers around the head and ends of the legs."[4]

In 1918 Ms. Parter had another close encounter, "We were unhurt, it happened so fast, we had no time to find shelter. The Methodist parsonage was demolished and several other houses were destroyed, entirely or practically. The hotel and schoolhouse were wooden structures and were piled in heaps like pick-up-sticks. The Methodist church was made of cement blocks and the roof laid almost level to the foundation; the walls had fallen into the basement."[5]

In Ellis County the storm continued on its way. Oddly enough the year before on the exact same day, another tornado had been in the area and caused heavy damage. Previously no lives were lost, but this time five people died. At the James McIntosh house, lightning struck the house and split it in half. Then the twister came and scattered it in several directions. At the time it hit, the tornado was a mile wide.[6]

The storm carried George Balls' house a quarter mile and when it set down, the sides fell outward, leaving the family of five inside, unhurt. It killed all his cattle but left his car by the garage undamaged. On the Fulton farm, someone noticed a hen sitting on top of the chicken house, apparently asleep, but upon closer examination, they found the bird had died from a heart attack.

These tornadoes killed eight people and injured many others.

View of a tornado near Lebanon, July 1919

A second tornado passed northeast of Ellis, destroying more farms. A rural mail carrier had a narrow escape when two empty wheat tanks came rolling along the road at a high rate of speed. One passed right in front of his car, narrowly missing it. The size of this tornado was responsible for widespread damage, and due to the rural area where the storm hit; it was some time before rescuers found the survivors. Map Available: Appendix 1.

HOISINGTON, OCTOBER 8, 1919

A tornado, preceded by heavy rain and hail, formed about two miles southwest of Hoisington at 4:00 p.m. It tore a wide path through the business district and then went east into a large residential area. Three people were killed and seventy-five injured. L.M. Murney, who was on top of the Missouri Pacific powerhouse, saw the tornado approaching. He said it appeared to widen when it struck a grove of trees southwest of town and increased in intensity once it hit Main Street.[7]

Immediately after the tornado passed, people ran everywhere looking for their loved ones. The twister destroyed the first block north of the railroad depot, which included a good hall, three restaurants, a barbershop, shoe store, grocery store, drug store, second-hand stores, and the YMCA. The funnel demolished Nieden's garage and heavily damaged the cars that were stored there. The electric light plant turned upside down, a skating rink lost its roof, and the Moses Building was a wreck. The storm unroofed two banks, a tailoring shop, a laundry, the Crystal Theatre, a confectionary, and the post office. The twister totally destroyed L.J. Barrett's grain office. His office safe landed in the yard of the YMCA.[8]

Devastation in downtown Hoisington, 1919

Mrs. Tom Diggs, who was in the kitchen of their restaurant when the storm struck, claimed that a large iron kettle saved her life. The wind blew her into a corner next to the kettle, and it was so big that it kept the ceiling joists from hitting her. Falling debris critically injured Ho Me Bee, a waitress in the restaurant.[9]

Mexican laborers owned the shacks south of the railroad tracks, where the tornado dumped one on top of the other, crushing them and critically injuring several occupants. The wind blew telephone and telegraph lines down, and repairmen had to work over-time to restore these communications. The first message sent was a cry for medical assistance.

The headlines of the next *Hoisington Dispatch* summed it up: "Where yesterday were prosperous business houses and happy homes, is [now] death, suffering people, wreckage and heavy loss." The storm continued east from Hoisington to Claflin and then dissipated.

GREENSBURG, MAY 23, 1923

The 2007 tornado was not the only one to affect Greensburg. Eighty years before, the town was visited by another tornado. One person was killed and scores were injured. Mrs. Charles Minor was trapped in the twisted wreckage of her home. Sections of the home were scattered over a ten-acre lot.

Over a hundred residents were left homeless. Forty residences were demolished and the town was without lights and telephone service for a long time. Damage was estimated at over $150,000. Wichita was also impacted by the storms but no one was killed. A small town to the southwest of Wichita named Clonnel was badly damaged. A lumberyard and Catholic church were badly wrecked.

Unbelievable close-up of a tornado near Weskan on May 19, 1922

AUGUSTA, JULY 13, 1924

A tornado struck a small section of Augusta, doing considerable damage in the three blocks just north of the railroad tracks. Mrs. Robert Scott was the only person killed. The storm badly damaged the five-story Moyle Building, and the occupants stated that the entire building rocked during the high winds. It seriously injured seven people in a restaurant just across the street from this building. The tornado then swept low through the center of town, causing destruction everywhere. Businesses wrecked included the Snodgrass Building, Mecca Theater, Long-Bell Lumber Company, Schoeb Motors, the Santa Fe Station, White Eagle Oil & Refining Co., City Hall, American State Bank, the Post Office, telephone company, Augusta Glass Works, Daily Gazette Office, and the W.B. Jones Motor Company.[10] Charles Bankey was certain that there were two tornadoes—another tornado immediately followed the first one.

Harry Haberline entered Augusta after the storm and observed the following:

"When I was two miles west of Augusta the wreckage was terrible and the group of houses on the Empire Lease were wrecked. When I reached the first house, the family was just crawling out of the wreckage and had left a little six months old baby under the ruins. After lifting the board, which composed the bedroom, the infant was found in a basket without a scratch. . . . One man was placed on a 12-inch board, which was laid across the body of an automobile. The poor fellow was crushed and suffering terrible agony. When I got to Augusta, the place was in terrible condition. The people had not recovered from the shock, and there was practically no one on the streets. The stores had been pushed out into the street and a big garage was laid flat. Piles of rubbish lay in the streets and live wires were massed at every corner.

Debris where there were once buildings in Augusta.

People finally began to appear with flashlights and lanterns and searched the ruins for injured people.[11] At a lunch counter restaurant, rescuers lifted two bodies out of the debris.

"Mr. and Mrs. Karl Songer had just arrived back in Augusta after the tornado, but they could have met the storm on their way back if Mr. Songer hadn't wanted to stay for a band concert in Wichita. Mrs. Songer said, 'The wind began blowing just as we left Wichita. The first destruction we noticed was the filling station just outside of Augusta. Some men were standing in the road. Mr. Songer asked them if there was not a filling station there and they said 'Yes, 10 minutes ago." Coming on toward Augusta we found cars in the ditches and in fences where they had been blown. Several cars had been pulled out of a creek only to blow over into the fence. A house had been blown away and the occupants, a family that included seven children, were taken to the hospital. Who they were or how badly injured, we did not find out."[12]

The twister completely devastated an egg farm; it leveled everything. The employees were in shock. The workers found two people in a ditch about 800 feet from the main building. The storm and wind apparently crushed 25% of the chickens, a total of 96,000, in their cages under the debris.

Tornadoes were sighted at Clay Center, Peabody, and Lehigh. At Clay Center the tornado was traveling at thirty-five miles an hour with winds estimated at 100 miles per hour near the funnel.

There was a break in Kansas tornado activity during the mid-1920s -- enough of a break that attention was focused on other events. No longer was Kansas synonymous with tornadoes. An article in the *Topeka Capital* of March 2, 1926 stated that Texas was now the number one tornado state. Kansas had earned a well-deserved break. Map Available: Appendix 1.

CENTRAL KANSAS, MAY 7, 1927

On May 7, 1927 two, possibly three tornadoes, swept Barber, Reno, Kingman, and McPherson Counties, killing eleven, injuring a hundred and causing much property damage. The first one occurred about 7:30 p.m. in Barber County and swept northwest into Kingman County, where it killed one man. The next one occurred at 11:00 p.m. south of Hutchinson and swept northward through East Hutchinson, killing one man and injuring forty persons.

The first tornado traveled through the sand hills near Medora and Inman, where it killed two more people. The second tornado traveled the longest path of any storm on record in Kansas up to that time. This tornado originated twelve miles southwest of Aetna and ended up four miles beyond Inman -- a distance of 102 miles.[13]

When the second tornado struck the east side of Hutchinson, it demolished 200 homes as well as the boiler room of the Carey Salt Company and 31 buildings of the Solvay Process Company. It blew down a 5,000-gallon water tank that sat at the top of a 165-foot tower, crushing the water plant beneath it.[14]

Narrow escape stories were common around Hutchinson. One woman was in bed and her week old baby was in its carriage when the tornado struck. Just as she jumped up, the chimney crashed onto the bed. The carriage was hurled to the other side of the room. Where it previously stood was a mass of wreckage. Neither mother nor her baby was hurt. Mrs. John McMullen heard a "swish", and she found herself in the middle of the street and her home gone.

During its long path the storm killed eleven people, injured 300 and caused a total property loss of $1,370,000. The pressure of the wind was terrific. In Barber County there were holes a foot deep and twenty feet square torn in the soil. The force of the wind turned over a five-ton caterpillar and rolled it a hundred feet. The twister blew a span of a steel bridge near Medicine Lodge a hundred feet downstream. The width of the tornado's path ranged from half a mile to almost two miles where the destruction was the greatest. It traveled an average of thirty-four miles an hour.[15]

EASTERN KANSAS,
JULY 16, 1927

A mid-summer tornado caused eight deaths and damaged three towns in east Central Kansas: Roeland Park, Lebo, and Burlingame.

The storm struck first at Lebo. It destroyed the Thad Jones residence, catching the occupants without any warning, and killing Mrs. Jones instantly. Neighbors found her body in a cornfield stripped of all her clothing. Her son was driving home from Emporia when he saw the storm clouds approaching. He tried to outrun the tornado and reach shelter, but he arrived in his farmyard just as it hit. His car was smashed to bits with him in it, but he suffered only minor injuries. Neighbors who saw the tornado said there was a bright yellow light surrounding the cloud when it came near the ground.[16]

At Burlingame Charles Parker was cooking dinner when the storm hit. With the exception of the stove, the tornado blew everything out of the house, including Parker, and into a cornfield a hundred yards away. The storm destroyed all the buildings on the farm, but Parker somehow escaped without injury.

In Roeland Park, a suburb of Kansas City, Kansas, the storm struck again, killing four people and demolishing twenty-five houses and five businesses. The tornado hit before 5:00 p.m. and in less than five minutes, it laid waste to an area 600 feet wide and a half-mile long.[17]

At the residence of Roy Hite, the storm killed three people— Roy, Dan Hite, 12, and Mrs. James Butts. The wind carried her over 100 feet into the wreckage of another house. Mrs. Hite and three other sons were rushed to the hospital with severe injuries. The Thomas family lived upstairs above the

Burd and Blackman Store. Mr. Thomas was driving home when he saw the tornado approaching, and he reached there just when the family was having a birthday party for one of the children. As he ran up the stairs, the entire family ran into the hallway to greet him. Then the tornado hit. The wind threw them outside on the ground amid the debris and falling bricks. Although they were badly injured, they all survived. In a second story stucco building, known as the Stambaugh Confectionary Store, the storm caught eleven persons, mostly children, inside when the building collapsed. Of the eleven only one suffered serious injuries -- M.T. Stambaugh, proprietor of the store. When the storm struck, the children huddled together in a room that was left intact, and a bulky showcase sheltered the group. One of the family members was slightly injured when a car blew into the building from off the street.

J.F. Hamilton was in his garage working on his car when the wind blew the garage to pieces and deposited the car in a tree 300 feet away. Hamilton was not hurt and, with help, was able to rescue his car, but he gave up all hope of ever finding the garage.

After the tornado passed, the residents saw all kinds of livestock and plucked chickens wandering the streets of Roeland Park.[18] No one really knew exactly where they came from; they just knew they blew in from the countryside.

STRANGE OCCURRENCES,
JUNE 22, 1928

While knowledge concerning how tornadoes formed kept improving during the first two decades of the 20th century, scientists had no idea what was actually inside a whirling funnel. Finally, on June 22, 1928 a Kansas man looked straight up into a funnel—-and survived. The man was Will Keller. He told his story two years later in the journal, *Monthly Weather Review*. [19]

Between 3:00 and 4:00 p.m. on the afternoon of June 22, Keller noticed an umbrella-shaped cloud to the southwest and surmised that it could develop into a tornado. Keller also noted the air had "that peculiar oppressiveness which nearly always precedes a tornado." He continued to watch the cloud, and quickly realized he was right. He saw three funnels dropping earthward from a green-tinged black base, and one was heading in the direction of his farmhouse. He hurried home, alerted his family, and took them to a storm cellar. No rain was falling so Keller paused at the doorway to take one last look before following the others inside the shelter. What he saw was the following:

"The great shaggy end of the funnel hung directly overhead. Everything was still as death. There was a strong, gassy odor, and it seemed as though I could not breathe. There was a screaming, hissing sound coming directly from the end of the funnel. I looked up, and to my astonishment I saw right into the heart of the tornado. There was a circular opening in the center of the funnel, about fifty to one hundred feet in diameter and extending straight upward for a distance of at least half a mile, as best I could judge... the walls of this opening were composed of rotating clouds and the whole was brilliantly lighted with constant flashes of lightning, which zigzagged from side to side.

Had it not been for the lightning, I could not have seen the opening or any distance into it.[20]

"Around the rim of the great vortex small tornadoes were constantly forming and breaking away. These looked like tails as they writhed their way around the funnel. It was these that made the hissing sound. I noticed the rotation of the great whirl was counterclockwise, but some of the small twisters rotated clockwise. The opening was entirely hollow, except for something I could not exactly make out but supposed it was a detached wind cloud. This thing kept moving up and down… The tornado was not traveling at a great speed. I had plenty of time to get a good view of the whole thing, inside and out. It came from the direction of Greensburg, which is three miles west and one mile north of my place."[21]

For decades this description of the inside of a tornado remained the only account on record. Mr. Keller was lucky to live to tell about it.

On the same day, Wayne G. Neville, an air mail pilot from Dallas, Texas, crashed near Lebo, Kansas by severe weather or perhaps a tornado. A tornado was seen in the area and it may have been dangerously close to the pilot's path. The plane crashed in a pasture, where it took a nose dive and caught fire. Neville's body was found near the plane, where he was killed instantly.

ELLINWOOD, MAY 5, 1930

On May 5, 1930 two tornadoes struck Central Kansas. One hit the Ellinwood area and caused devastation for thirty miles. It did thousands of dollars in damage, but no one was killed. The storm destroyed two-dozen farmsteads and demolished most buildings on Main Street in Ellinwood.

Tornado spotted crossing Highway73 north of Oskaloosa, May 1, 1930

One family sought shelter under a small coal bin adjoining a cellar because the smaller room had a concrete roof. The force of the wind crushed the cement like an eggshell, but the three people underneath escaped without a scratch. A farmer tied two horses together in a stall in the barn. The storm carried one of the animals fifty yards, killing it, but the other one was not injured.

Herman Johanning saw the tornado coming as he was driving home. He left the car and ran into a grove of trees, but just before the wind struck, he left the trees and ran into a plum thicket. The twister uprooted all of the trees and tossed them everywhere. Johanning was not injured.

Residents of Ellinwood estimated the damage at $400,000.[22]

PRATT, JUNE 25, 1930

A "wild tornado" struck Pratt in late June, and the losses reached half a million dollars. A severe hailstorm followed the tornado and destroyed wheat nearly ready for harvest. But no one was killed, and few injuries were reported.

This house was destroyed in Pratt by the destructive power of the tornado

The twister caused a few strange occurrences. Someone found a huge snake with a splinter run through its body just back of its neck. The wind jerked the motor from an automobile owned by Dave Horton and carried it for half a mile but left the body of the car at the garage. A neighbor found a jug of vinegar undisturbed at the Scott home after the house was demolished. This was the slowest moving tornado on record; it traveled about five miles an hour![23] The day before, a tornado was spotted near Gothenburg, Kansas. Map Available: Appendix 1.

Tornado spotted near Gothenburg, Kansas, June 24, 1930

The 1930s is characterized as the "Dirty Thirties," a dry arid time with little or no rain and excessive summer heat. True to form, Kansas was spared tornado activity through the first half of the decade. However, the weather made up for it with dust storms and drought, both of which were oppressive and far more destructive.

Each year in the 1930s seemed to get hotter than the year before. In 1934 the heat was intolerable. May 29 was the first day of over a hundred degrees. During June there were twelve days over a hundred, July had twenty-nine, and August had seventeen. On July 13 the temperature reached a record 119 degrees -- the heat broke most thermometers. On many days in July, the heat ranged from 112 to 116 degrees. The nights were so hot that few people could rest without waking up in a sweat, and they often slept outdoors to take advantage of any breeze. Rivers were at record lows. The Saline River was so low people walked across it without getting their feet wet. Dust storms began to make their way from southwest to northeast -- 1935 was the most significant dust storm year.[24] A bad dust storm that appeared on March 15 scared everyone. It came all of a sudden, and everything turned pitch black. People closed off rooms in their houses so they would have a place where they could survive. Even then the black silt filtered in and made it hard to breathe. Those who were caught outdoors in the dust were helpless--they lost all sense of direction and wandered aimlessly, which only added to their fears when night came.[25]

On March 21, the *Lincoln Sentinel-Republican* made the following observation:

"The dirt was unlike any ever blown here and old-timers all agreed that they never before experienced such a storm. The wind had been blowing steadily from the south all day long, increasing as night approached. Suddenly at 9:30 p.m. the direction changed, turning to the northwest and bringing dust-laden clouds. The black soil was so fine that it found its way under the most minute cracks in window frames and for hours homes were so filled with dust that breathing was difficult.

Cloud of dust approaching an unidentified Kansas community,

October 1935

*Tractor buried in dust due to numerous dust storms,
unidentified Kansas location, July 1936*

"By daylight the wind had abated somewhat and householders arose to find their floors, walls, furniture, draperies, and clothing completely covered with dirt. Downtown businesses were equally dirty and most of Saturday was given over to 'House cleaning.'

"One woman living on the edge of town reported taking eight pounds of silt from the floor and window sills in her bedroom.

"Men who were downtown when the wind changed have many stories to tell. J.W. Dodds and F.A. Walters ran into each other behind the grocery, trying to find their way to their homes.

"Walters went as far north as the Methodist church and wandered south again. Dodd's car had stalled and he was trying to find his way to the store for a flashlight. Leo Shaffstall took two hours to get the dirt out of the Quality Shops keyhole before the key could be inserted. Saul Curtis had to resort to traveling on his hands and knees for many blocks before he could reach his residence.

"Damage to the wheat crops was disastrous. Many farmers said that their entire acreage was either blown out or completely covered by silt.[26] Meals were a struggle. Everything had to be washed, including all the surfaces in the kitchen. A week later southerly winds would bring another dust storm and with it the red soil. The color deepened as the storm grew worse, which made everything look like it was on fire. While the dust storm raged outside, people huddled in their homes cowering in fear. The wind soon changed to the west and brought black silt, which made the morning as dark as night. At noon the air cleared and visibility was fair."

Dust storms continued throughout the month but the last sixteen days of March were the worst. Every day brought dust, whirlwinds, dirt, and silt. After April 1, the winds settled down, and the dust was not quite as prevalent. Then on Palm Sunday, April 12, another severe dust storm appeared. In some places the silt piled up against fences until it covered them. It was so solid the cows could walk on top of it. Many people became depressed, which led some citizens to move west or even to commit suicide.[27]

WASHINGTON, JULY 4, 1932

A freakish Independence Day storm in 1932 took the lives of three people at Washington. The storm came late in the afternoon while many of the citizens were attending a 4th of July celebration at the county fairgrounds.

The tornado ripped through the Anderson Implement Company building and killed Alva Stimmit. Peter V. Gillett died when he was crushed by his barn. Also, a resident of Narka was buried beneath the rubble of the Frager Motor Company building, and he died instantly.[28]

Furniture store in downtown Washington after the July 4th tornado roared through town

The tornado tore through the business district and the northern section of town while 7,000 people were enjoying the festivities at the fairgrounds only a half-mile away. Oddly enough, a pilot, Robert Roberts, and his passenger, Henry Muth, saw the tornado in the air before it struck. Muth had this to say:

"It was the 4th of July and we were having a celebration. Roberts, the airman, was here with his plane, taking people up for rides, and about 5 o'clock in the afternoon, I went up with him. The sky to the west was black as the blackest night and out of it, to the northwest, was what looked like a black rope dangling down to the earth and whipping around… Out toward the southwest was another of those black, rope-like things. They looked like the trunks of elephants dropping their small ends to the earth. I knew of course that they were tornadoes, and so did Roberts who hurried to land. Don't ask me to describe the sound of that tornado as it came whirling into town… some say it was a huge roaring. Others call it a sound like thunder. There are just no words to tell the horror of it and how it filled one with fear. It was a vast, roaring, tearing, thunderous whoo-oo-oo-oo, accompanied by the sound of crashing buildings.

"The air all about me as I sat in my car was filled with wreckage flying with the speed of the wind, which some say was more than 100 miles per hour."[29]

Scenes of devastation in Washington after the Independence Day tornado

At the Burlington railroad station, the tornado derailed half a dozen boxcars and then demolished the high school and grade school. It picked up one steel freight car weighing 17,000 pounds and carried it through the air for 200 feet, hurling it against the brick wall of the schoolhouse. The twister damaged the county courthouse and city hall, and it blew the southern wing of the county jail, where nine prisoners were housed, into the street. The inmates escaped injury. The force of the wind turned the First Christian church across the street on its foundation. On the west side of the square, the tornado damaged twelve businesses.

The tornado either damaged or destroyed almost 150 homes in the northeast part of town. The death toll would have been higher except that the majority of the residents were at the fairgrounds.

When they heard the roar of the tornado, the people at the fairgrounds scattered in all directions. A ditch partly filled with water along the road served as a safe haven for hundreds, but many others hurried downtown directly into the tornado's path. George Barner was one of the first to arrive at the square. When he drove near the Frager building, the twister struck his car, and it hopped like a "bucking bronco." Then he saw the walls of the Frager building crumble. Harry Frager, who was still inside, managed to get away from the walls, but he was hit by falling timbers. Luckily he only suffered a back injury and some lacerations.

At the Lillie Lang farm, the storm tore the roof off her house and dropped a brick into a water pitcher without breaking it, but it took two men tugging on the brick to remove it from the pitcher.

Throughout the night searchers looked through the debris for the dead and injured. Farmers from the surrounding area came to town to aid the citizens in clearing the roads.

A study of this tornado by James Marshall, a consulting engineer, concluded that wind speeds of 100 to 200 miles per hour were responsible for causing all the damage in Washington.[30] Map Available: Appendix 1.

LOGAN, APRIL 26, 1933

After the dry spell broke in Western Kansas, a half dozen tornadoes appeared around Logan. Orville Mick was out in the open when he saw one of the twisters approaching. He started running for his home, but the wind threw him to the ground about sixty feet away. The twister picked up his house and carried it over the family's heads, leaving them unhurt amid the wreckage. At the Rob Lafferty farm, the barn disappeared, but the pony remained behind, unharmed. A similar incident happened at the Clarence Lappin home except that it was a Ford sedan instead of a pony. The tornadoes were followed by four inches of badly needed rain and some hail.[31]

LIBERAL, MAY 22, 1933

In Liberal on May 22nd the day began with a strong wind carrying dust and sand. By midday a typical western Kansas dust storm was in progress. At 4:00 p.m. it became so dark that everyone turned on their lights. Then the tornado struck.

The first building destroyed was the Boggs Supply Company, where cars and other vehicles were tossed around. Added to the high winds were streaks of lightning. One struck a gasoline station causing an explosion, which fatally burned Paul Amos and injured two others. The tornado flattened two blocks of business buildings, and then skipped to the residential area and demolished several homes. The storm left five dead and fifty injured.

H.L. Herring noted that, "No one could see it coming because of the dust. It lasted five minutes. I had to steer my car in and out between the house roofs and debris in the streets to get out of town."

The Liberal tornado was part of a larger outbreak that caused damage in Colorado, Nebraska, North and South Dakota, and Minnesota, and killed a total of nineteen people.[32]

INDEPENDENCE TORNADO, FEBRUARY 24, 1935

Just weeks before the worst dust storm in the history of the "dirty thirties," areas of southeast Kansas experienced another kind of destruction—heavy rains, winds, and a tornado. The tornado that struck Independence on February 24, 1935 was a little rope-like funnel, averaging 150 to 200 feet in width, and it bounced around town like a ball of fire. Before it left, however, the little twister destroyed fourteen homes and badly damaged thirty more.[33]

On Sunday a black funnel-shaped cloud approached Independence from the southwest. Reaching down to the earth like a tail of a kite, it twisted and turned, creating a path of destruction 200 feet wide and seven blocks long. The tornado lifted houses from their foundations and crushed some like they were made of cardboard. It also picked up garages, uprooted trees, and tore off porches. All this damage was complete in about two minutes.[34]

Frank Sands, editor of the *Independence Reporter*, saw the tornado coming toward his house. He barely had time to get back inside before it hit. Sands noted that most of the time the tornado remained aloft, which saved Independence from more destruction.

At the home of Ira O'Brien the storm struck quickly. His family thought the house had been hit by lightning, but when they looked outside they discovered their roof laying on the adjoining property. The tornado moved George Switzer's house eight feet off its foundation, and the Switzers sustained cuts to their heads and hands. At the Michener home, the family was popping corn when the twister hit and took away the entire front of the house, caving in the roof, and leaving the furniture exposed to the elements. Across the alley Lena Haas was writing a letter upstairs when the storm hit. Her house blew off its foundation, the second story floor collapsed and the walls caved in. Although stunned, she was able to reach a window, where neighbors assisted her to safety.

Across the street was a famous residence, the old Emmett Dalton home, occupied by Mr. Truttman and his two daughters. The tornado blew part of the old house onto the sidewalk and tore the kitchen off the rest of the house, but both his daughters were thrown free of the wreckage and received only cuts and bruises. His son had just stepped out of his car when the garage collapsed, but he held on to a telephone pole and escaped serious injury.

At the Joe Acre home, a window in the parlor blew completely out, weights, sash and all, and one weight blew across the room breaking a lamp. In a rear bedroom where another window blew out, a portion of the frame was sucked up through a hole in the attic. The wind lifted a glass top on a coffee table to another room without breaking it. The most amusing incident happened to Mr. Acre himself. He was holding a back door shut when he felt something tapping him on the top of his head. When he looked up, he found his coattail was pulled high above his head and was beating a tattoo on his scalp.[35]

The tornado blew a mirror across the room at the John Wade home and stood it up against the wall without breaking it. At the Bolick house, the porch posts were not disturbed, but the small blocks beneath each post blew away, leaving the posts hanging by the upper supports.[36]

The storm spared most of the business district except for a garage and the Independence Torpedo building. At the garage the tornado scattered twenty-two large 200-pound culvert drains all over the premises.[37]

Fortunately, no one was seriously injured in this tornado, which was the first to strike the town of Independence. Although it brought much needed rain, the price was pretty high.[38] Map Available: Appendix 1.

RAWLINS COUNTY TORNADOES, JULY 10, 1935

Rawlins County received a brief break from the hot temperatures when several small tornadoes hit the second week in July 1935. Accompanying the storm was over a half inch of precipitation. Although the rain was welcome, it did not lower temperatures— the thermometer in Atwood averaged 102 degrees each day that week.On Sunday evening, July 10, several twisters struck the county. A small one hit Atwood, destroying

A twister caught on film somewhere in Kansas, June 7, 1935

buildings and wrapping a metal grain bin around the Chicago Burlington & Quincy Railroad switch.

The squall line went north and hit the J.F. Edwards farm, where it flattened a grove of large cottonwood trees, some of which were two feet in diameter.[39]

The movie "*The Wizard of Oz*" continued the negative image of Kansas as a tornado state. That year *National Geographic* magazine printed flattering articles about individual states. Most of the complimentary descriptions brought smiles to the faces of the other state's Chamber of Commerce members. Such was not the case in Kansas! In the *Geographic's* depiction of Kansas, food production was stressed—"a big shelf in the national pantry," and a new topic was the status of the state as a national joke. Exaggerations of tornadoes, droughts, dust storms, grasshoppers, and "odd human behavior" all contributed to the merriment of the nation.[40]

SALINA, MARCH 10, 1938

A tornado struck two miles southeast of Salina, demolishing a two-story farmhouse and injuring seventeen members of the Bolby family—including fourteen children. One was a three-month-old baby. Mrs. Bolby suffered a fractured ankle, and the eleven-year-old daughter a broken shoulder. The others received cuts and bruises in addition to burns from the kitchen stove. The force of the wind lifted a cloth from the table and blew it four miles away to a farm southeast of the Bolby's.[41]

Mrs. Bolby reported, "We were upstairs trying to put a piece of cardboard in a window, which had blown out. Suddenly the top of the house began to shake… We were in the stairway when it hit. It seemed like something came down on the roof and busted it all to pieces. Something hit me on the side of the head, and then I felt something just pick me up and take me. I lit 100 yards northeast of where the house stood." [42]

TRI-STATE TORNADO, MARCH 30, 1938

Several tornadoes slashed across Kansas, Oklahoma, and Missouri on March 30, 1938, killing four people and injuring over a hundred.

The storm began around noon and the strongest tornado cut a path 400 yards wide and over two miles long through Columbus, a town of around 3,500. It demolished almost the entire town, including the Highland Grade School, where it wrecked the roof, the west wall, and all the windows. The janitor and the teachers rushed 110 children into the corridors just before the storm struck. One eyewitness, ten-year old Ted Hamlet, was quoted as saying, "I don't see how any of the boys and girls got out alive. The fire bell just missed Eddie Bradley. The wall fell in. Bricks piled against the door and we had a hard time getting out. A piece of the roof fell in just as we left the room." Nine-year-old Bruce McCall had this to say, "The windows fell in and plaster started falling on us. We ran out into the hall and everyone was coming out of their rooms screaming. We stood there for a while, not knowing what to do. Then we ran out and lay in the yard. Rain and hail fell on us and bricks rained down all around us." Most of the citizens rushed to the school to help dig the pupils out from under the debris.[43]

The tornado reduced most of the homes to rubble, and the townspeople either rushed screaming into the streets or became trapped in the wreckage. An area several blocks square was so littered with roofs, broken furniture, snapped telephone poles, and trees that the rescuers had a difficult time getting through the debris. The force of the wind blew Don Barnes' houses 75 feet before smashing it to the ground. At the E.C. Zimmerman home the refrigerator fell on Mrs. Zimmerman, and she lay there several hours unable to move. The tornado picked up Mrs. Luther Wisdom and dropped her through the roof of the Earl Tarr residence. When she fell in their midst, they asked her who she was. Mrs. Wisdom told them, but she said she didn't remember anything.

Injured people filled the city's two hospitals, in the rooms - three or four to a bed, the halls, dining rooms, chairs, cots, and one on the kitchen floor. Most of them had blood, water, and mud smeared all over them, and their clothes were either completely gone or hanging in tatters. Mothers were crying and moaning for their dead and missing babies; others were crying because their homes and everything they owned was gone.

Another tornado hit fifteen miles southwest of Columbus near Chetopa and leveled the Piety Hill Schoolhouse. The pupils were just filing out of class when one of the boys noticed the black cloud hanging overhead.

"In an instant I knew it was a twister," noted Virginia Sappington, a schoolteacher. She ordered the twenty children to run to a ditch 250 yards away. "It was dark as night. It rained hard. We all flung ourselves down in the mud and lay there clinging to the barbed wire fence. The wind roared so I couldn't hear anything else," Sappington said.[44]

The storm passed, and the schoolhouse was still standing. Their hands slashed by the barbed wire, the students headed back to the building. Inside the room was a mass of twisted desks. Then suddenly the storm struck again. Hail, gravel, and flying boards hit the children's arms, faces, and legs as they fled to a deeper ditch. "The little ones screamed with fear and pain,"

Sappington noted, "We were soaking wet and our clothes were torn. It was unbelievably cold. Farmers finally rescued the children after the twister moved on."[45]

Another tornado struck southwest of Garnett, critically injuring Mrs. Charles Sutherland, who had tried to seek shelter in a hen house; it was flattened by the wind.[46]

At Columbus the tornado twisted and crushed dozens of houses into shapeless forms. The wind tore big oak trees out by the roots, snapped telephone poles like matches, and even ripped concrete sidewalks apart. The townspeople wondered how anyone managed to escape alive. It was a miracle.[47]

CUNNINGHAM, MAY 1, 1938

A tornado struck Cunningham on May 1, 1938, killing three people and doing $25,000 in property damage. The storm began near Isabel and Nashville and moved northeast toward Penasola. At the Hartman farm the wind pushed him underneath a pile of debris, and when Mrs. Hartman found him stunned but unhurt, she dragged him to the family car and honked the horn until help arrived. When the tornado struck the John Miller farm, the force of the wind killed Mrs. Miller and their two sons, Virgil and George, and blew other family members into a wheat field, seriously injuring them. The storm scattered debris from the farm all over the area. Sadly, the next day someone found the Miller's wedding picture buried in the mud.

Since the storm struck without any warning, none of the families made it to their cellars. The Miller's cyclone cave was only fifteen feet from their house. John Drum, another farmer, stated that he had a premonition all day that something bad was about to happen. The weather made him uneasy. He stated it was a combination of something in the air or in the sky -- something that he had never felt before. His feelings were right.

Tornado caught out in the open near Stockton, Kansas sometime in 1938

The storm's narrow path followed a natural ridge in the land and cut across the divide between the Chikaskia and Ninnescah rivers. People in the area called this ridge "Cyclone Ridge," because four other tornadoes had followed that same path in recent years.[48]

LEBO, JUNE 10, 1938

A tornado caused havoc around the little town of Lebo on June 10, 1938. The residents had ample warning and saw the twister coming. At the Lynn residence a father and son ran to the basement of their house, but after finding more than a foot of water on the floor, they chose to sit on the steps. As they were sitting down, the tornado ripped the house away above them. The force of the wind tore their clothing off, making them more vulnerable to flying debris. They were hurt, but not seriously.[49]

A.H. Kellum, a trucker, was driving toward Lebo when he saw the twister approaching. He stopped his truck, shifted it into reverse, and backed away as fast as he could. The tornado passed right in front of him, only missing him by about thirty feet.[50]

Very interesting view of a winding tornado somewhere near Stockton, Kansas, 1938

BURR OAK, JUNE 14, 1939

One of the worst wind and hailstorms in this area of Kansas caused widespread damage to buildings and crops in the vicinity of Burr Oak.

The farmers lost livestock, including hundreds of young turkeys and chicks. The wind smashed a large plate glass window in the Central Barber Shop, and most of the houses in town had broken windows. Ninety mile an hour winds propelled the rain sideways and in less than two hours, five inches of rain fell. The sudden deluge washed out a dozen bridges along the White Rock River, causing farmers to travel for miles to find a bridge to cross into town. The hail was brutal. It drove corn plants, sorghum and wheat into the ground so hard that the fields had the appearance of being leveled by a mowing machine.[51]

WHITEWATER, VALLEY CENTER, JUNE 7, 1941

A tornado roared through the little farming community of Whitewater on June 7, 1941 and left a path of destruction that killed seven people, four of them in one family.

The citizens of Whitewater noticed nothing unusual late Sunday night, nothing except a severe thunderstorm. At 11:20 p.m. the power in town failed, and there were no lights in the entire area. Suddenly people living in the east and south sections of town heard a strange sound that gradually increased to a roar. It was a tornado!

Otto Penner's home was the first one hit. In the ruins of the house lay the body of Marie Penner, sister of Otto. Otto was seriously injured and rushed to the hospital. The twister demolished the Chris Thirstein home east of Whitewater, killing their small son Myron.

Gathering strength as it moved along, the tornado struck several more farms. At the home of Guy Scrivner, the funnel picked up the house and tore it away from its foundation. Not a wall was left standing. Several hundred feet east of the wreckage, rescuers found the bodies of Mrs. Scrivner, Mrs. Ralph Kruger, Margaret and Betty Scrivner, and Janet Paulson. All were killed instantly. Mr. and Mrs. Scrivner had celebrated their 23rd wedding anniversary that afternoon, and Mrs. Scrivner's birthday, so it was a happy family occasion. Within twenty-four hours, their lives were changed forever.

On the adjoining Regier farm, the tornado lifted the house from its foundation and drove a large tree through the door. A cow lay dead in the front yard. A horse had a piece of wood stuck in its shoulder, but the animal stood quietly in the barn, still alive.[52]

At Valley Center the tornado dipped down at the John Schaefer home, killing Haskell Keyes. Schaefer was badly injured, but he managed to crawl to a telephone and call an ambulance for his friend, not knowing he was already dead. In a small graveyard the storm toppled most of the tombstones. During a tornado such as this one, even the dead weren't safe.[53]

LINCOLNVILLE, AUGUST 25, 1941

A late summer tornado struck the town of Lincolnville on August 25, 1941, injuring four men and causing $50,000 in property damage. Two of the injured, Ott Haefner and Art Lewerenz, were hurt when a store wall caved in on them. Another man in a hardware store was buried when a brick wall collapsed. His wife, in a beauty salon just down the street, saw the storm approaching, but she didn't hear any noise until the storm struck. At that point, there was a deafening roar and the air was filled with debris. On the Krause farm, not a wall was left standing. Main Street in Lincolnville was a disaster area -- the tornado damaged many buildings and wrecked quite a few cars.[54]

OBERLIN, APRIL 29, 1942

A devastating tornado struck Oberlin in Northwest Kansas on April 29, 1942, killing fifteen people and injuring twenty. The air had become quite calm at midnight just before the twister hit the town.

The first signs of trouble were the hailstones, some of which weighed half a pound. Then the tornado came down full force at the Frank Urban residence, killing Norma Nicholson. She and her husband Ray had gone upstairs to investigate the storm, which was their mistake. Suddenly the windswept the house away, and Frank Urban's son, Clarence, found himself in the basement covered with plaster, but unhurt. He slipped on his father's pants and went upstairs to investigate. He found his father, who was able to go for help at a neighbor's house a mile away. Unfortunately, Norma and Mrs. Urban died before help could arrive. Despite all the devastation, a small medicine bottle was found undisturbed on the Urban's front porch.[55]

At the Dale Paddock and Gus Leinwetter homes the tornado killed all the occupants. At the Paddock's, this included Dale and his wife, their four year-old son Elvin, and Leon and Gale Railsback. All but Gail were killed instantly; she died the next day. The bodies of the Paddocks and Leon Railsback were in the creek behind the house. They were sleeping when the storm hit and they were wearing their nightclothes. Neighbors did not find little Elvin until the next morning under a pile of debris.

Rescuers found five members of the Leinwetter family strewn over a quarter mile area. They also found the body of a seven year old friend who decided to stay overnight. It was her first sleep-over. Had she stayed at home, she would have survived. The twister also killed three members of the Beneda family. Some of the bodies were horribly disfigured. One of the victims was driven head first into the ground, and another had a wooden splinter piercing his chest. Unlike many tornadoes where the survivors recount freakish stories, no one was telling any weird tales on this day. During this storm, nearly everyone was killed.[56]

Other residents in Oberlin were not aware of the destruction until after they heard the roar of the wind above the sound of the hail. Then they knew a tornado had struck. The Methodist church became a makeshift hospital; three physicians came from McCook, Nebraska to assist with the injured. Other families in Oberlin made room for the homeless. Undertakers and funeral directors worked overtime to help the bereaved bury their dead.

The path of the tornado was about 300 yards wide, and it skipped over the countryside east of town before breaking up north of Cedar Bluff near the Nebraska line. Map Available: Appendix 1.

ALLEN COUNTY, MAY 2, 1942

America was at war with Japan, Germany and Italy in 1942, but the residents of Allen County had more serious business to contend with closer to home.

The weather turned ominous late in the day at LaHarpe, and there wasn't any warning before thunderstorms and a tornado moved through the town, killing Mrs. George Dix and injuring forty others.

Two other tornadoes swept through the county. One formed four miles west of Leanna and headed northeast toward Moran, where it dissipated. However, it formed again north of town and moved on to Kincaid. The other tornado followed a northeasterly path from two miles north of Iola to six miles east of Colony. Severe lightning, blinding rain, and yes, sleet accompanied these storms. This was the worst tornado outbreak to hit the county in years.

The Dix family saw the storm coming, but when they tried to go to the storm cellar, they were unable to force the door open against the pressure of the wind. Some family members took refuge under heavy furniture, but when the house collapsed it trapped Mrs. Dix, and severely injured her.[57]

The tornado destroyed the farmhouse of the O.L. Morrison family, but they suffered only minor cuts and bruises. "Daddy saw the storm coming," one of the children told a reporter for the *Iola Register*, "and he made us lie down on the floor. We felt an awful pressure, and then the house just blew off from over us. The baby started to float off through the air and mamma grabbed it just in time."[58]

Art Nicholas was in his tool shed when he saw the tornado coming and he had to seek refuge under a threshing machine. The twister narrowly missed him, but not before sucking all the straw out the door of the shed. Another farmer tried to close the door to his house and found that the force of the wind was too strong. While he struggled with it, the roof and walls of the house blew away over his head.

"Ham" Harris of Moran was at a farm sale in Iola when the storm hit. He grabbed an iron pipe to steady himself against the strong winds just as lightning struck the building. This current went through the pipe, shocking and burning him, but his injuries weren't life threatening.[59]

The worst damage occurred between LaHarpe and Humboldt, where the tornado leveled many buildings and scattered some fences. The wind destroyed the George Klotzbach farmhouse except for a portion of one wall. The Klotzbachs were home but they weren't injured. They had only a few minutes warning. They lost some livestock, and all the chickens disappeared.

DODGE CITY, MAY 10, 1942

A small tornado damaged Dodge City's St. Mary of the Plains College, but touched nothing else!

Forty-five girls in the college narrowly averted tragedy due to the timing of their religious services at the chapel. Minutes after they left, a twister tore away part of the building and dumped tons of debris into the auditorium where they had just assembled. The only person injured was Sister Bernadetta, who was showered with brick and plaster as she knelt at the altar. She was able to walk from the wreckage unassisted.

Just as the tornado struck, four girls were entering a car at the entrance of the building, and although it hurled the car 150 yards, none of the occupants were hurt. Since the twister wrecked the dormitory at the Catholic school, the girls had to be housed at a local hospital.

Dodge City was spared. Oddly enough, no one reported any other damage from the freakish tornado.[60]

Significant tornado caught near Delphos on May 31, 1942

MULVANE, JUNE 20, 1942

A destructive tornado struck Mulvane on June 21, 1942, killing four members in one family. The funnel cloud first formed southeast of Mulvane, where it dipped to the ground several times before it stayed on the ground and traveled north. Then the cloud stalled and remained motionless in the air over one spot. The tip of the cloud formed two or three tails that whipped back and forth as they touched the ground. The storm then changed color from black to white and assumed the shape of a big pencil. After it hit Mulvane, it divided into two sections and disappeared.

The tornado first struck the farm of G. Iverson, rocking it from its foundation and tearing it to pieces. The family barely made it to the basement in time. While Mr. Iverson was investigating the damage, a large object knocked him down. That object was a cow.[61]

A Santa Fe freight train was moving down the tracks into the path of the storm. When the engineer saw the tornado coming, he commenced to stop the train. At the last minute, he changed his mind and decided to outrun it. About that time the tail of the cloud lifted and swirled to one side before reaching the tracks, and the train passed by unharmed. The engineer breathed a sigh of relief.

The twister hit the farm of C.W. Love, whose family sought shelter in some brush beside the house. They emerged unscathed. At the Howard farm, the wind demolished all the buildings. The family ran to the cellar, but the storm was so powerful it cracked the concrete ceiling and debris came raining down on them. They emerged scratched and bruised.[62]

The tornado totally destroyed the C.W. Rivers house and scattered their belongings over the fields. The Rivers family, who had just purchased the farm, had been living in the house only a month. Since none of them survived the storm, little is known about their last moments. The neighbors found the bodies of son Charles and daughter Virgalina a quarter of a mile from the farm. They found the body of Mrs. Rivers 150 yards north of her daughter. The wind lifted Mr. Rivers high in the air and dropped him head first through the roof of a shed. Searchers looked all day before finding his body wedged downward between a stock trailer and the wall of the building; he suffered a fractured spine and a broken neck. The storm stripped most of the clothing from the victim's bodies. Neighbors found Mr. River's overalls 500 yards away, and in the pockets was cash amounting to $600.

This tornado's path was different---it moved to the northwest from the southeast and ended one half mile north of Mulvane.[63]

FORT RILEY, MAY 15, 1943

On May 15, 1943 a tornado struck the Cavalry Training Center at Fort Riley and injured about 200 men, three seriously, and damaged forty-one buildings. The total cost of the damage was estimated at $200,000.

The black funnel formed over the western edge of the camp and hit some new buildings under construction. Most of the damage was to the barracks of the first squadron, second regiment, leaving those troops homeless. After twisting the buildings from their foundations, the tornado scattered broken rifles, bunks, and footlockers throughout the area.

The twister lifted two or three mess halls in the air and dropped them several hundred feet away. Sergeant Ray Hitchcock was in the process of baking a cake for a contest the next day. Unfortunately, the storm ruined his cake, but he was able to help everyone in the kitchen to safety. The unlucky Sarge said he had already survived four other tornadoes. Private Dan Gunn narrowly missed serious injury by hanging onto a telephone pole. Debris just missed his head by inches. Private John Gillespie and thirty-seven others received cuts and bruises when the tornado hit their barracks. It hurled them from one end of the building to the other. The soldiers at Fort Riley were preparing for war, not a tornado.

The funnel rose up after hitting the fort, but dipped down again several times, damaging the Alma and Belvue areas.[64]

Rare double tornado taken near Wamego on May 15, 1943

In May 1945 severe hailstorms pounded Kansas towns and ruined crops all over the state. The storms did $3,000,000 damage that month. A few tornadoes were reported, but nothing compared to the hailstorms that began on May 5 and ended on May 30.[65]

On June 26, 1945 a tornado at Liberal injured seventy people and damaged twenty-five buildings at the Liberal Army Air Field. Most of the injured were enlisted men who were in their barracks when the tornado hit. During the height of the storm, the base weather officer recorded wind velocities of eighty miles an hour. This was the second storm to hit the Air Field; the first occurred on April 10, 1944. Neither storm damaged any aircraft.[66]

During World War II, when general warnings based on synoptic maps were unavailable, military authorities recognized the necessity of a warning system for key defense installations in the Middle West, such as air bases, plane factories, and ordinance plants. They realized that warnings a few minutes in advance of a tornado or violent thunderstorm would help guard against loss of life and save the munitions of war. The time was ripe to organize a network of offices for transmitting information on violent storms moving across the country. Accordingly, the Weather Bureau, in cooperation with the military, established reporting stations that covered the region fifty to seventy-five miles west and southwest of points where warnings were most urgently needed.

Since the weather bureau chose Wichita as the main control center, officials went directly to the southwest and arranged a telephone network, which included thirty-eight towns to serve in the warning system. These were Maize, Colwich, Andale, Pretty Prairie, Penalosa, Kingman, Alameda, Murdock, Cheney, Garden Plain, Goddard, Oatville, Peck, Clearwater, Viola, Norwich, Spivey, Zenda, Nashville, Conway Springs, Riverdale, Wellington, Mayfield, Milan, Argonia, Bluff City, Danville, Harper, Attica, Sharon, Kiowa, Hazleton, Corwin, Waldron, Anthony, Caldwell, Corbin, and Perth.[67]

Reporters who were selected for these networks all served without compensation. They were patriotic citizens who could observe the sky frequently and had access to telephones. Among them were telephone operators, gas station attendants, farmers, housewives, and small town merchants. Utility companies with sub-stations and trucks equipped with short-range radios, state police, and field men of telephone and oil companies proved useful in reporting tornadoes. Radar observations in a limited number of places and pilot and control tower reports were valuable in locating storms and determining their probable paths. The Weather Bureau made arrangements to have all reports with a high priority telephoned to key destinations, and the military installations disseminated the information through the appropriate channels. They warned reporters not to send false alarms, and only report a tornado that was actually on the ground, the exact location of the tornado, the direction of movement, and the time of observation.

The government also issued a unique list of precautions for citizens to take in order to survive injury in a storm. Some precautions were common knowledge, but some were not. The list included:

- If caught out in the open, move at right angles to the tornado, and if in a car, don't try to outrun it, lie flat in the nearest depression.
- At home, the southwest corner of the basement offers the best protection. In an office building, stand against the inside wall of a lower floor to avoid flying debris and seek shelter preferably in structured steel buildings.
- Schools and factories should appoint lookouts who will keep safety officials forewarned of impending danger.

Except for the southwest corner of the basement, most of these warnings still hold true today.[68]

Warnings were to be issued to broad areas since the actual path of a tornado was hard to predict. Telephone lines were to be kept open and radio stations were to broadcast all reports of the storm. This system was so successful that it was expanded over the entire country shortly after World War II.

CHAPTER FIVE: THE MODERN ERA, 1945-1980

The time period from 1946 to 1975 was particularly active in Kansas for tornadoes. In fact, some of the worst tornadoes in the history of the state occurred during that time, such as the Udall tornado of 1955; the Ruskin Heights tornado of 1957; and the 1966 Topeka tornado, the first $100,000,000 storm. In addition, with attention focused on better forecasting, the Weather Bureau established warning systems in the major towns. The Cold War brought about civil defense alarms, which were instrumental in creating tornado-warning sirens.

In the early 1950s, the Weather Bureau made an effort to pinpoint severe weather based mainly on eyewitness reports from the field. Their goal was to alert any areas where and when tornadoes were likely to strike, but their track record through the 1950s was not very good. Some forecasters felt that an early warning system might do more harm than good by causing unnecessary panic when conditions only indicated the possibility, not the probability, of a tornado. In other words, this was the "cry wolf syndrome,"— if there were too many unsubstantiated reports of tornadoes, residents would ignore bona fide warnings of severe weather.[1]

During the late 1940s and early 1950s, the Weather Bureau expanded the number of storm warning network stations to 167 scattered in 38 states and the District of Columbia. Kansas and Oklahoma established their own networks. The Weather Bureau suggested when local stations issued storm warnings that the reporting station notified the nearest Weather Bureau so other communities in the path of the storm could be alerted.

By 1953 network observers telephoned their reports to weather bureau offices where forecasters, on duty 24 hours a day, broadcast these warnings over radio and television. When the storm scare was over, the local media broadcast an "all-clear" so the public could resume their normal routines.

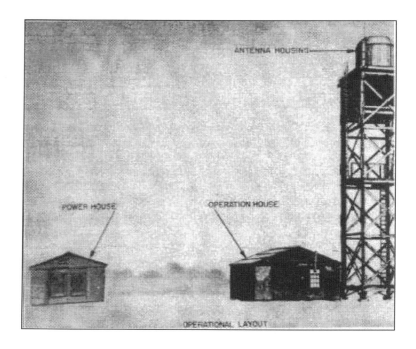

Operational Layout of a fixed radar unit, August 1945

An example of this rudimentary system was demonstrated in the Leedey, Oklahoma tornado of May 31, 1947.[2] A half hour before it struck the city, a local telephone official sighted the funnel and sounded the fire alarm, bringing all the volunteer firemen to a central point, and the townspeople out looking for the fire. The firemen announced over a loud speaker that a tornado was approaching and everyone should take cover. By the time it hit, nearly the entire population was in basements or cellars. Although the twister destroyed most of the town, only six people died. This low number was due mainly to the early warning system.[3]

Sometimes the warning system sounded unnecessarily. Warning sirens sounded in Topeka late one spring day when someone spotted a tornado thirty miles west of Emporia. Weather forecasters predicted that the tornado would reach the city in 1-½ hours, but since a tornado's time on the ground is limited, this one didn't make the eighty-mile journey to Topeka. However, it did cause the townspeople to go to their basements and cellars.

As the knowledge of tornadoes grew, the need for watches and warnings became apparent, but warnings based on the actual sighting of a tornado could not realistically be issued more than a few minutes in advance. When conditions in specific regions became favorable for tornadic activity, forecasters issued "tornado watches" to alert people to watch the skies. Intensive indoctrination was initiated so people would not misconstrue a tornado watch for a warning and be thrown into a panic.[4]

The Weather Bureau issued the first tornado watches based on synoptic conditions in advance of a series of developing storms in March 1952. A few days later destructive storms extending from Arkansas to Kentucky were also successfully forecast several hours in advance. The reaction of the public was so favorable that the Weather Bureau continued the warnings whenever conditions justified them. Originally these warnings were issued from the forecasting center in Washington D.C., but in order to insure efficiency, they became the responsibility of the weather centers located around the country. Two such sites, one at Norman, Oklahoma and the other at Topeka, were instrumental in making watches and warnings more reliable in Kansas.[5]

The broadcasting by the Weather Bureau of tornado watches and warnings was not infallible. Occasionally when they issued a watch for a particular geographic area, an adjacent region would be the recipient of severe weather. Their misjudgments of storm paths, even by less than ten miles, gave false alarms to some and inadequate warnings to others, and tornadoes would occur without any warning at all. Forecasting was an imperfect science in the early years, and sometimes even today.[6]

The Weather Bureau created a "Severe Weather Staff" in 1953, and their primary goal was to reduce false alarms and to increase accuracy through education and research. This small but elite group of forecasters developed into the National Severe Storms Forecast Center. Two researchers out of Tinker Air Force Base at Oklahoma City, Lt. Col. E.J. Fawbush and Maj. R.C. Miller, recognized that in a "perfect world" only six requirements were present in the successful forecasting of tornadoes: heat, humidity, cold and warm fronts, low barometric pressure, east winds, and clouds. However, forecasters who relied solely on these conditions found them lacking in most situations.

Two other organizations were studying severe weather at this time—the Air Force Weather Service involving the military, and the National Weather Service. They set up a hotline and teletype service between the agencies to confer on storm forecasting.

View of an early mobile radar unit, August 1945

In the late 1940s, H.L. Jones of the School of Electrical Engineering at Stillwater, Oklahoma, developed a new method for predicting tornadoes— a cathode ray oscilloscope that detected tornadoes by electrical discharges.[7] Jones determined that discharges of lightning in tornadoes are exceedingly high voltage by nature and are brighter and bluer than in other storms. Graphs of these lightning strikes as registered on the oscilloscope show they are of much greater amplitude than those from an average thunderstorm, and the top of the strike is flat and rugged, an unusual characteristic not often found in other lightning discharges. The oscilloscope successfully located tornadoes in the Norman, Oklahoma area in 1949 and 1950. This unique method of isolating tornadoes was overshadowed in the 1960s by the advent of radar systems.[8]

Radar used for weather forecasting had its origins during World War II. The first weather radar systems were the same as the ones used to track enemy aircraft. Weather forecasters were able to follow the path of a tornado in much the same way. Tornadoes develop a characteristic "hook" on radar that is quite different from any other feature of a thunderstorm. Select stations across Kansas including Wichita, Topeka, Dodge City, Goodland, and the Army Air Force at Sherman Field in Leavenworth installed radar as soon as it was feasible.[9]

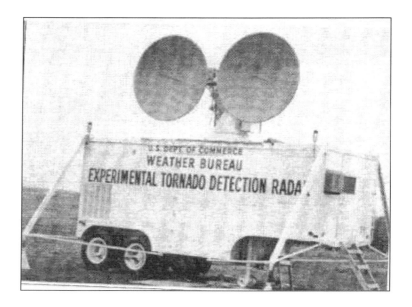

When radar was new: The Weather Bureau's first experimental Doppler radar unit, ca. 1951

In 1951 the number of weather stations dramatically increased after months of severe weather. Believing that general information on atmospheric conditions was lacking in the Kansas-Oklahoma region, the Weather Bureau established 135 stations over a wide area southwest of Kansas City, covering much of North Central and Eastern Kansas and Eastern Oklahoma.[10]

Observers at these stations were primarily part-time workers who served without pay, and the Weather Bureau equipped each one with a microbarograph, hygro-thermometers, rain gauges, and equipment for recording wind direction and speed. These people made a special effort to synchronize their clocks and other gear so that all records would coincide. In 1953 this network of stations increased to 145, including all of Kansas, Nebraska, Oklahoma, Texas, New Mexico, Colorado, and Wyoming.[11]

As commercial air flights increased during the 1950s, the pilot's fear of colliding with a tornado while airborne was a realistic one, necessitating more accurate forecasting both on the ground and in the sky. The vertical funnel cloud was a point to consider when envisioning the possibility of an airplane coming in contact with one in a line of thunderstorms. On April 3, 1950 an American Airlines pilot saw a tornado cloud at 35,000 feet, and he noted the vortex was a mile wide.[12]

On April 6, 1947, the widest tornado in history struck Woodward, Oklahoma and moved northeast to St. Leo, doing $200,000 property damage in Kansas. The path of the twister was 221 miles long, starting in White Deer, Texas. In Woodward, the tornado killed 95 persons, injured 723, and caused property losses of $6,000,000.[13] The Weather Bureau still had a big job ahead of them.

NEOSHO COUNTY, MAY 1, 1948

A tornado moved across Neosho County on May 1, 1948, killing one person and injuring three. It leveled the Bethel Church and half a dozen houses four miles north of Erie, and killed William Pemberton. The funnel then went through the Thayer area, wrecking outbuildings and killing livestock.

The same day, high winds hit Topeka and Emporia, smashing windows, uprooting trees and downing power lines.[14] This was just the beginning.

The following month, twenty-six windstorms, many with tornadoes and large hail, caused nearly $11,000,000 damage across the state. The most devastating storms swept through Cheyenne and Thomas counties on June 13, 14, and 15.[15] The losses from these storms totaled $4,450,000. The June 15 storm caused $2,175,000 damage in McPherson, Harvey, and Marion Counties. In Ness and Rush Counties on the same day, another $1,000,000 in damages occurred. A tornado on June 20 caused $191,000 damage in Cherokee, Crawford, and Bourbon counties. The next day, June 21, a tornado tore up Westport Field southwest of Wichita, injuring twelve persons and destroying several planes. On June 22, high tornadic winds did extensive damage between Horton and Leona in Northeast Kansas. Total costs from this storm came to $250,000.[16]

UNUSUAL TORNADOES, JANUARY 1949

Tornadoes began early in 1949 in Southeast Kansas. The earliest tornadoes ever recorded in the state occurred on January 3rd. They formed northeast of Altoona and struck the small town of Villas, injuring one person and destroying fifty-five buildings. Another tornado moved from Colony to Rush City, demolishing two houses. A third touched down briefly west of Ottawa. This activity was followed on January 9, 10, and 11 with a sleet and ice storm that caused $1,000,000 in damage in Southeast Kansas. The storm was especially severe in Parsons, Columbus, Independence, and Pittsburg. Due to the loss of electricity, schools closed, businesses could not open, and homes were lit by candles or kerosene lamps. A week passed before service was fully restored.[17]

ROZEL, MAY 19, 1949

On May 19, 1949 a tornado destroyed twelve houses and three businesses in this small community of 416 inhabitants. Luckily only two people were injured–Floyd Martin and Joe Patterson. The wind blew Martin out of his house. He landed twenty-five feet away and suffered a shoulder injury. Among the businesses demolished were the A.A. Seltman tractor and farm machinery store; the Union Coop Grain Company service station; the Blattner Brothers blacksmith shop; four railroad cars and the Santa Fe depot.

At Chase in Rice County, Mrs. Aaron Simmons and her four small children were in a boxcar that overturned. They suffered only minor injuries and shock. At Gorham in Russell County the high winds blew twenty-four Union Pacific freight cars off their siding, and work trains had to be sent from Salina and Ellis to clear the tracks.

This storm system was a particularly destructive one and covered a wide area.[18]

WILMORE, MAY 20, 1949

When a tornado struck the little town of Wilmore at 7:30 p.m., it lasted only five minutes, but during that time the entire business district was leveled.

M.T. Downing watched curiously but unafraid at the threatening clouds in the sky overhead.

"They seemed to be boiling," he noted, "and when they crashed together there was a roar like that of a mess of freight trains. The house began to shake and jump and it felt as if it moved. The wind jerked the roof off and my little dog Tip was sucked right through the ceiling."

The dog returned home the next day, uninjured.[19]

After the town's electric lines went down, some enterprising citizens tried heating their coffee with blowtorches. Water had to be brought in by tank cars from Coldwater. Each family poured their share in pots, pails, and washbasins.

The tornado damaged nearly every house in town and injured one person. It leveled a clothing store, some lumberyards, a gasoline station, an appliance shop, and a grocery store. The funnel lifted a large garage into the air and hurled it a hundred feet into a creek.

People came from all over the county to help clean up the debris. The Red Cross opened a stand and distributed sandwiches and coffee to anyone in need, and farmers brought in food for the workers.

This community was fortunate—no one had paid any attention to the ominous clouds approaching, yet they all escaped unhurt. The next time they might not be so lucky.[20]

Tornado near Manhattan, May 31, 1949

VIOLENT OCTOBER STORMS, 1949

Bad weather conditions in October 1949 were responsible for fifteen of seventeen storms that occurred that month. One person was killed during a tornado in Russell, and eight persons were injured in Beloit. The Beloit storm was the most destructive. It caused $250,000 in damages and demolished some structures at the Kansas State Girls Industrial School.

In Stafford County, a tornado hit the airport, wrecking several planes. In McPherson County, two tornadoes leveled windmills and oil derricks. In Pawnee and Rush Counties twisters hit Rozel and Rush Center, causing extensive destruction of property. In connection with these storms, two persons were injured in car accidents.

On October 18, tornadoes hit Marion and Chase Counties and caused damage near Florence and Cedar Point. On October 20, a twister struck Jackson County and grazed Hoyt before lifting off the ground.[21]

GREAT BEND, MAY 3, 1950

A tornado with a "blinding green flash" hit a new housing area at the Great Bend Army Air Base four miles west of Great Bend, injuring thirty people and badly damaging twenty-four buildings.

About eighty families made their homes in the subdivision known as Barton Courts. Toni Buchanan saw the twister strike the courts and she was the one who saw a blinding green flash as it snapped the electric wires. Nearby, L.B. Crawford heard the tornado coming, and when he went to the window to look, the living room wall fell away.

The Red Cross set up emergency headquarters to assist the families, and the National Guard placed roadblocks to guard against looters.[22]

McPHERSON AREA, JUNE 8, 1950

In the middle of the night on June 8, 1950 tornadoes, lightning, hail, and rain hit McPherson and Rice Counties, killing one person and injuring five others. Albert Elliott, the only fatality, was pinned in the wreckage of his home for four hours before rescuers found him.

Several strange incidents occurred. Neighbors found a tractor in Roy Kasey's yard jammed against a large tree. The wind wrapped the bark from the tree around the front axle after lifting the tractor several feet off the ground. George Morris found a good fishing rod and reel in his yard and he had no idea whose they were. Mr. and Mrs. Lindbeck were driving down the street when the tornado picked up their car, carried it a hundred feet, and threw them out. Neither one suffered serious injuries.

Electrical storms hit Abilene at 1:00 a.m. and at 3:00 a.m. Lightning struck a cattle barn and a garage, burning them to the ground. Thankfully, the barn happened to be empty at the time.[23]

WESTERN KANSAS TORNADOES, MAY 1951

Several tornadoes occurred in Western Kansas during May 1951. On May 14 two twisters straddled Elkhart, forcing the entire population to seek shelter. One tornado ripped a steel building apart and destroyed a large barn west of town. Willard Mayberry, publisher of the *Elkhart Tri-State News*, said he saw four tornadoes at one time passing over open country.

A few people reported having narrow escapes. The Lawrence Greens and their two children jumped in their car and fled from one tornado only to find themselves directly in the path of another. Fortunately, the oncoming tornado lifted and passed over the car, leaving the family unharmed.

Along with the storms came three inches of rain. Prior to the downpour, the townspeople had hired a rainmaker for $7,000 to seed the clouds with silver iodide crystals, which were supposed to make it rain. They had to tell him his services were no longer needed.

On May 19, two tornadoes caused heavy damage to Lakin, smashing huge grain bins and tossing them on the highway. Accompanying the storms came nearly eight inches of rain that caused a five-foot high wall of water to surge through town. When the newspaper office was flooded, the high water ruined files dating back to 1873.

Other towns in the area that sustained storm damage included Garden City, Holcomb, Scott City, Marienthal, Tribune, and Leoti.[24]

WAKEENEY AND OTHERS, JUNE 27, 1951

A tornado swept through WaKeeney shortly after midnight on June 27, 1951, devastating a large section of town, killing five persons and injuring a hundred more. It destroyed forty-five homes and damaged sixty others. Property losses totaled $2,080,000, which exceeded that of any tornado in the state's history.

This tornado occurred in conjunction with a widespread storm system containing hail and high winds that began at 11:10 p.m. on the 26th of June and ended at 3:00 a.m. on the 27th, extending from Gove to Saline County, a distance of 175 miles. Hail damage from the storm reached $201,000 alone.

A twister blew the walls away of one home, leaving a closet lined with clothes intact but exposed to the elements. Mrs. Marie Engleman said, "Automobiles were overturned and crushed under houses, some houses had the roofs blown off… In one block, six new brick homes only a year old were leveled.[25]

There was no warning before the storm hit. Some people who couldn't make it to their cellars had to crawl under their beds for safety. One woman pulled a mattress over her head and escaped with slight injuries. Mr. and Mrs. James Hladek died in the wreckage of their home. Dan Rohrbacker's body lay in debris in the street.[26]

This storm wasn't the only bad one that month. According to the Weather Bureau, the outbreak of severe weather in June was the worst on record up to that time. Estimated property damage came to $26,439,275. There were eight persons killed and 117 injured. On June 21, tornadoes caused $6,000,000 damage to towns and stops in Trego, Rice, Rooks, Osborne, Mitchell, Norton, and Phillips Counties.[27]

More stormy weather occurred on June 23 and extended from Kingman and Sumner Counties all the way to the Missouri border. On several occasions witnesses saw as many as five tornadoes at the same time! In Norton County another storm cloud dropped hailstones four inches in diameter; it broke one man's arm. In Stevens County a tornado hit the airport damaging three hangers and several small aircraft. Lightning also played a significant role, causing thirty-four fires and killing two people. One person died in his farmhouse near Lamont, and another in his car near Mount Hope. Supposedly it's safe to be in a car during an electrical storm, but apparently it was not safe for that man![28]   Map Available: Appendix 1.

SEVERE WEATHER, JULY 1951

Weather in July 1951 continued just as inclement as it was in June. The 1951 flood in Manhattan, Topeka, Lawrence, and Kansas City will long be remembered for the destruction along the Kansas River, but there were ten violent wind and hail storms, four tornadoes, and sixteen fires started by lightning that month. On July 4 severe winds blew down radio towers at Ulysses, tossed boxcars off their tracks at Sublette, and a tornado hit east of Bucklin. On July 7 lightning killed a team of horses and two saddle broncos in a pasture near Jennings in Decatur County. A tornado struck Palco, ripping roofs from houses. On July 8 and 9, Emporia suffered heavy damage from windstorms. Lightning destroyed two 500-gallon oil tanks. On July 10, a widespread storm system destroyed the grandstand and an exhibit building at the Cimarron fairgrounds. It caused baseball-sized hail in Mitchell and Lincoln Counties, and the lightning strikes in Crawford and Pawnee counties started several fires. On July 16 a violent windstorm raked Nemaha and Brown Counties, causing destruction in Hiawatha and Sabetha.[29] In Sherman County on July 21, a tornado picked up a 3,000-bushel grain bin and deposited it in someone's backyard. A twister hit Plainville and Zurich in Rooks County. On July 22 a tornado damaged Aurora in Cloud County. When this storm system reached Northeast Kansas, it was less severe, but the heavy rains day after day in the Kansas River valley caused flooding that left thousands homeless. North Topeka and North Lawrence never recovered economically from the devastation.[30]

LAWRENCE, BONNER SPRINGS, MAY 22, 1952

One, and possibly two, tornadoes did large-scale damage around Lawrence, DeSoto, and Bonner Springs on May 22, 1952. Eyewitnesses saw the tornado that hit Lawrence divide into two funnels before reaching Bonner Springs. The Weather Bureau was uncertain if there were two small tornadoes or one large one, but heavy damage was evident between Bonner Springs and DeSoto.

Five miles west of Bonner Springs, the storm damaged a dozen farmhouses. The Doyle Sappington family heard a loud roar three minutes before the tornado struck and managed to run to the cellar. Although the wind blew their house away, the living room floor and its linoleum covering remained intact. The Beatty family also fled to the cellar. The tornado blew their garage from its concrete footings. It rolled their Ford truck over on its top and it tore the roof from the house and crushed all the walls and ceilings. After the tornado passed, Beatty looked for his 75 chickens, as they had disappeared. On the road by his home, another truck was upside down in the ditch with its wheels spinning and its headlights on. No driver was anywhere around.

In DeSoto, Ray Ussery was slightly injured when the storm caught him unaware of approaching danger. His barn and garage fell on him. He saw his mother-in-law's house next door flattened, and when he rushed to help, he found her unconscious under some debris. She suffered shoulder and rib fractures. Ussery had numerous bumps and bruises. He claimed that the wind "blew dirt right through him."[31]

At the Mabe home, Robert had a chunk of flesh torn from his right leg by a piece of wood, and Susie had a severe cut on her head. Before they could get to shelter, the house blew away and the only thing left standing was the chimney.

The tornado leveled the C.S. Kreider home in Bonner Springs. Kreider, who was upstairs shaving when the storm struck, said, "I heard my wife scream. 'The windows are falling in,' and I started to run downstairs. Then the house seemed to fall in on top of us." The wind carried off his new truck and dropped it in a pasture a mile away.

Since the electricity in the DeSoto area was out from an earlier windstorm, the warnings broadcast on television and the radio were heard by only a few people in that locality. WDAF radio did carry seven broadcasts of the storm, including the all-clear after it passed.[32]

CENTRAL KANSAS, AUGUST 2, 1952

Tornadoes and severe thunderstorms struck a large portion of Central Kansas, including LaCrosse in August 1952. A tornado that lasted only five minutes damaged every store on the three block long Main Street. The wind picked up a 3-½ ton fuel tank and dropped it half a mile away. The storm wrecked the Shotta Lumber Company, and the debris blocked the Missouri Pacific tracks for hours.

Seven inches of rain and hail as big as goose eggs fell at Pawnee Rock. The deluge closed Highway 50 through the center of town.

At Kingman a tornado blew down a drive-in screen and destroyed the concession stand. Although the movie watchers had no safe place to go, no one was hurt. Twisters also hit Sylvan Grove, Lucas, and Vesper.

As the storm moved northeast, it destroyed an alfalfa dehydrating plant near Manhattan.[33]

ANTHONY, AUGUST 5, 1952

A heavy hail and electrical storm caused $200,000 damage in Anthony on August 5, 1952. The storm struck at 10:30 p.m. just when election clerks were working to complete the count in a primary election. Although there were no casualties, the winds had tornado-like velocities.

The storm badly damaged farm buildings and broke windows in many homes. Hail as large as golf balls came down, some weighing a pound and a half. The *Anthony Republican's* printing jobs were ruined when the front windows broke, scattering glass throughout the shop. It was just another day in the life of a newspaper publisher.[34]

MAY STORMS, 1953

During May 1953, the Topeka Weather Bureau received reports of forty-eight damaging storms. They estimated the losses at $1,453,300. There were fourteen tornadoes, fifteen hailstorms, and fifteen windstorms. Hail caused the heaviest damage, estimated at $772,500.

The most notable storms were the Udall tornadoes on May 10, which destroyed numerous outbuildings and killed hundreds of chickens. Other places hit that day were farm buildings at Caldwell and Wellington; eighty summer homes at Lake Kahola near Emporia; houses had roofs blown off at Kiowa; lightning struck one person in Belle Plaine; and a tornado damaged homes in Cottonwood Falls.[35]

On May 11 severe weather plagued Wichita in Harper County. On May 16, tornadoes hit Burdick in Morris County and Satanta in Haskell County.

On May 26, a severe storm in Mitchell County caused property damage north of town. Hail and high winds also caused problems around Perry and in the Ottawa area. Near Ottawa, one man suffered a concussion when a large hailstone struck him on the head. A widespread storm on May 27 moved through almost every section of Kansas. Observers reported damage in Ottawa, Lincoln, and Butler Counties. High winds near Brookville and Lindsborg caused farm damage. In Rawlins and Decatur Counties, a windstorm wrecked several homes. A small tornado struck Hugoton in Stevens County. On May 28, the storms continued. Wallace, Sherman, and Cheyenne Counties had hail and wind damage. In Hamilton County high winds demolished outbuildings in Coolidge and Syracuse. Farther south in Liberal a tornado destroyed a 30-unit motel and a cafeteria. On May 29 and 31 the drive-in theater screen in Ottawa blew down, and in Olathe hail two inches in diameter damaged several fighter planes at the Naval Air Station.[36]

JUNE STORMS, 1953

June 1953 was no better than May when it came to severe weather. There were 45 tornadoes; 16 hailstorms; and 13 windstorms,[37] including the following:

On June 2 a tornado hit Norton, causing widespread damage. On June 4 in Harper County, lightning struck a barn, burning a tractor, automobile, and tools of all kinds. The owner burned to death trying to save these implements. On June 5 five tornadoes hit southeast Kansas, three near Coffeyville and two near Baxter Springs.[38]

On June 7, all hail broke loose. Northwest Kansas sustained heavy hail damage. At Hill City, three tornadoes were on the ground at one time, destroying six farm homes. At Phillipsburg and Kensington more hail fell, and heavy hail damage occurred near Council Grove and Abilene. The storm moved as far east as Kansas City, where high winds wrecked planes at the Fairfax Airport.

This severe weather gave credence to a widespread belief that atomic bomb tests in Nevada were causing an unusual outbreak of storms in Kansas that spring. On June 18 the U.S. Weather Bureau, at the request of the Atomic Energy Commission, issued an announcement regarding these allegations. The report stated that there was no relationship between the transport of radioactive debris from atomic bomb sites and the occurrence of excessive rains and bad storms in Kansas.[39]

On June 19 another storm system hit many areas of Kansas. A tornado in Sumner County destroyed houses and farms near Conway Springs. Another took the roofs off homes near Albert, Hoisington, and Great Bend. In Ramona, when workers building a grain elevator saw a tornado bearing down on them, they dashed to shelter just before the walls of the elevator collapsed. On June 21, tornadoes hit Cloud County, where hailstones piled two feet deep near Miltonvale. Hailstones three inches in diameter fell around McPherson. A funnel destroyed two homes and twenty-five barns between Winfield and

New Salem. Observers saw hail the size of golf balls at Dexter. West of White City hail covered the ground to a depth of two inches.[40]

On June 24 there were reports of more wind and hail damage in Kingman County and Marshall County. A small tornado blew over two drive-in theater screens, one in Kingman and the other in Marysville. Severe storms on June 16 and June 25 hit Overland Park. Lightning killed one man. On June 28 the wind blew down another drive-in screen in Plainville.

All in all June was a bad month to be in Kansas.

WICHITA, JUNE 21, 1953

On June 21, 1953 a small tornado dipped down in Central Wichita about 5:30 p.m., killing one man and injuring 94 others. This storm was one of the most destructive hail and windstorms to date, causing $9,000,000 damage. Later the same evening, a second storm followed the first. Officially it was not called a tornado, but one witness saw a funnel dip from the cloud and hit East Wichita, where heavy hail and high winds broke thousands of windows. In addition, the wind blew in storefronts and downed power lines and trees.

Just how wild can the weather be in Kansas? On March 18, 1954, snow reduced the visibility to near zero in Goodland. Dust cut the visibility to less than fifty feet in Dodge City, and winds up to 75 miles an hour swept through Garden City. At the same time there were heavy rains in Eastern Kansas, thunderstorms along the Kansas-Missouri border and tornadoes in several places in Central Kansas, and hail between Salina and Topeka. Temperatures of 67 degrees in the afternoon at Chanute went down to 31 degrees at Goodland. There were two funnels near Wakarusa and Herington and a tornado at the Horton City Airport that wrecked two airplanes.[41]

Hutchinson residents reported the worst dust storm in the area since the "dirty thirties." It was so dusty that motorists going west had to return to town, as they couldn't see the road ahead of them.

The old saying in Kansas, "If you don't like the weather, wait five minutes," definitely described conditions on March 18, 1954.

TOPEKA, MARCH 18, 1954

Early in the afternoon of March 18 several small tornadoes dipped down around Topeka, causing widespread damage. No one was injured. At various times that day, Topeka had rain, high winds, sleet, hail, tornadoes, and dust.

Weather Bureau officials stated the tornado that caused the most damage was one that demolished the William Jacobs farm three miles south of 21st and Gage. It tore the porch off the Topeka Country Club and damaged buildings at 18th and Kansas Avenue. Weather Bureau employees in East Topeka spotted the twister as it dropped down into the Kansas River, picking up sand. Hail and sleet accompanied the storm, and Forbes Air Base reported wind gusts to 80 miles an hour. The temperature dropped to 43 degrees at 2:30 p.m., and then shot up to 63 degrees by 3:30 p.m.

It was definitely a weird weather day. There hasn't been one quite like it since.[42]

MAY STORMS, 1954

Violent storms caused nearly a million dollars in damage in May 1954. Although observers reported seeing seven tornadoes, no one was killed or injured. Tornadoes caused $149,000 damage, but hail caused an estimated $786,000. There were two bad storms, one at Syracuse and the other in Neosho and Bourbon Counties.

On May 1st, a major storm system caused damage near Hutchinson and Independence. At Independence, a tornado destroyed buildings along a five mile path just east of town. In Labette County the storm damaged farms near Altamont. The wind picked up a man and set him down on a woodpile 100 yards away, uninjured.[43]

On May 17 witnesses saw seven large tornadoes aloft in a thirty-mile radius of Sublette. On May 26 a tornado damaged nineteen homes in a residential area of Syracuse. On May 27 there was tornado damage reported from Decatur County to Johnson County. On May 28 hail severely dented several places at the Salina airport, and lightning knocked a man unconscious for several hours.

THE "PERFECT STORM"

UDALL, MAY 25, 1955

The dubious honor of being struck by the most violent tornado in the history of Kansas may go to Udall, for what was the "perfect storm," with regard to catastrophic damage and horrific deaths.

A series of tornadoes on May 25, 1955 killed 115 people and injured over 800 in a four-state area. In the town of Udall alone 76 people died and more than 200 were hurt. The surviving Udall residents abandoned the town for weeks because not a single building remained intact. Some of the dead were still unidentified two days later, and a few people were never found.[44]

At 10:10 p.m., "a loud whistle like an old tin horn," was the last thing 76 people heard— fifteen seconds later a huge tornado struck the town and left a mass of twisted debris. The only living thing the first rescuer found was a little black dog moaning on a pile of rocks. There was not a tree or building left standing.[45]

Bad experiences and close calls were numerous. Jean Foote, who worked at the Boeing Plant in Wichita, rushed home to Udall when word of the tornado reached him. He found his wife and children safe. They had crawled under a bed, and the mattress saved them when a wall collapsed.

Bird's Eye View of Udall, Kansas after the tornado, showing the extent of the massive devastation

G.J. Walton was lucky— his home escaped complete destruction. He ran next door to his mother-in-law's house and pulled her from the wreckage, but she died while he was carrying her out. He stated that the winds "seemed to come from every direction."

Charles Booth said the tornado struck without any warning, catching most people asleep. The twister leveled the south half of the town, including the high school. It destroyed three elderly care homes nearby. Three businesses remained standing: the bank, the post office, and the Odd Fellows Hall. The only house that survived unscathed was the Barry Holmes residence. The tornado demolished all three Udall churches, and a rescuer found the body of an eight-year old boy lying on the highest section of one of the churches.

Oliver Stone found a two-year old girl lying in the street in the pouring rain. He gave her first aid, but she died on the way to the hospital. Roy Harris of the Sumner County Sheriff's office said the devastation "is the worst I ever want to see. There were no lights. It was raining. In the darkness— dark as the inside of your hat— you could hear people screaming, moaning, and calling for their families. My God, my God, it was terrible."[46]

Udall's mayor, Earl Rowe, spoke of the gruesome job ahead of him. "I counted seven bodies around my home. They're still digging out the dead and injured. They'll be lucky if they get them out by tomorrow... I was standing at the front door in my boots. There was lightning and just a little rain. Then it hit. My house just floated away. I don't know where it is. My wife and children were in the house— they lived, but one of the boys had a big gash. I had two cars in the driveway. Nobody's found them yet. I was knocked out— got an eight-penny nail driven through my leg. There's nothing left. It's just heartbreaking."

"I thought the night would never end," Mrs. Augustine Smith said. She and her husband were in bed, and their two young daughters were in the room next to them. "There was no warning," she said, "the roof caved in and pinned me and my husband. I crawled through the wreckage to make sure my babies were all right. Then we started to look for shelter." The Smiths went to an area that can best be described as resembling a war zone. Dead babies lay in the street. Screams of injured men, women, and children could be heard above the noise of the wind and rain. The Smiths lived near the Shady Rest Home for the elderly. "I don't know how many were killed. We heard the awful screaming coming from the place where I thought the building was," Mrs. Smith said.[47]

The tornado killed Mr. and Mrs. Warren Nash in their bed, buried beneath the wreckage of their home. A man covered by eight feet of rubble emerged alive, and a small girl with a piece of lumber driven through her thigh, survived.[48]

A group of rescue workers strained to lift the side of a house off the ground. From beneath the twisted framework cries of agony could be heard. With renewed vigor the men lifted the side higher and saw to their horror the broken bodies of two women and a man. A doctor feverishly administered drugs to the injured group as the workmen freed them one by one from the wreckage and put them in an ambulance.

Staring straight ahead as if in a trance, a man stumbled along a street strewn with debris carrying the limp body of his small boy in his arms. Holding the child close to his chest the man allowed workers to lead him to an ambulance where he reluctantly relinquished his hold on the lifeless boy.[49]

Deep in a storm shelter a group of fifteen women, children and one man sat with blankets wrapped around their shoulders. The man stared with unseeing eyes until one of the women explained that he went into shock as he stumbled down the steps into the shelter. One woman told a reporter, "We didn't have any warning. I listened to the radio weather news and the announcer forecast only small showers. The next thing I knew my house began tumbling down around us."[50]

Outside the shelter medical personnel frantically worked to stem the flow of blood pouring from the leg of a small girl. The child's left foot was almost severed from her leg and blood flowed from a deep gash on the right side of her head— but she was alive.

At one intersection the bodies of six elderly women lay broken and torn in the rain-filled ditches. Rescue workers, who had to pass by the dead for several hours, tried to save the living. When they unearthed the heavy switchboard at the telephone office, crushed beneath it was Mary Taylor, the only telephone operator most Udall residents had ever known. Mary's stepson also died in the storm.

The LeForce family lost two of the six patients in their rest homes, including Mrs. LeForce's mother, the other four were seriously hurt.

They also told about a family of six who actually appeared out of the air and landed in the LeForce kitchen. "They lived a block away," Mrs. LeForce said, "and they have no idea how they got to our house." The flying family had only minor injuries.[51]

Gaylord Gann snatched his 13-month old daughter from her crib when the wind began to blow and started from the bedroom to the kitchen. "The wind was so strong, I couldn't get through the door," Gann said. He added, "The wind took the door off a closet in the bedroom and blew it right out the door. The door bounced around the dining room, off the walls, and then the wind blew it back into the bedroom again."[52]

The tornado ripped the city water tower open, and two persons in a car drowned when the water gushed down on them. Udall residents had just recently watched the dedication and opening of their new rural high school. Within minutes the twister demolished the school building, and rescuers carried the bodies of seven victims from the wreckage. A shiny red fire truck stood motionless in the debris on Main Street. On the doors of the truck bright gold letters proudly proclaimed "Udall Fire Department," but its service to the community ended that day.

Days after the storm some citizens complained that the forecasters gave insufficient warnings to the community. However, the Weather Bureau in Kansas City stated that they issued a tornado watch about two hours before it struck for areas in Oklahoma, Missouri, and Kansas, including Udall. A tornado watch had been issued at 1:40 p.m. earlier that day, and another forecast issued at 4:30 p.m. warned of possible tornadoes in Oklahoma and Kansas. This watch area, however, missed Udall by ten miles. A third warning issued at 10:08 p.m. included Udall. A Wichita newspaper quoted a survivor of the Udall store as saying he heard the warnings on the radio but ignored them, assuming that if any tornadoes were in the area they would be someplace else; they always were in the past.

Tornadoes struck other towns in Kansas that night. At Oxford the twister killed five out of ten children of the Raymond King family when a funnel hit their home. Mrs. King later recounted the horrible night when the storm wiped out half her family, "It was raining heavily and there were thunderstorms and lightning all around when we got ready to go to bed. One of my little girls laughed and said, 'I like to go to sleep in weather like this, Mommie.' Later, I woke up when a window blew out. I got up to try to fix it. Then the walls of the house began to shake. I tried to get all of the children together in the living room. I missed Nancy and Ronnie, but finally we were all together. All of a sudden the whole house began to cave in on us."[53]

Mrs. King stated the next thing she remembered she was lying under a tree, near the family car. Two of her children were with her. They managed to crawl into the car, where they sat for hours as the long night passed, until finally one of the other children got in with them. When searchers arrived and assisted Mrs. King and her youngsters, they were still huddled in the car. The rescuers checked the wreckage of the King home and pulled out the remains of the five children. One other child was still alive, but seriously hurt.

In East Central Kansas, the storm hit Osage City at 12:30 in the morning. Marshal Darrell Noble stated that he was driving his car east over the Santa Fe tracks when the twister struck and lifted his car three feet off the ground and carried it down an alley, setting it down undamaged. In the southeast part of town, the tornado damaged several houses and blew out the plate glass windows of the *Osage City Journal-Free Press* building. The tornado was a mile wide as it swept across twenty-five miles of the county.[54]

The next day Henry Harvey of the *Topeka Capital* summed it up, "It was the stillness that got you. Where there had been the roar of a tornado there was only stillness. But the quiet lasted only briefly." The wailing of sirens and the cries of the wounded broke the silence. In his last paragraph, he stated, "The continuing moans of the yet-to-be discovered injured drummed through my head. It was the worst sight of my life. I shall not forget it."

The one good objective derived from the storms of May 25 was that it led to each community installing its own tornado warning system. Although nothing could make up for the lives lost, at least the installation of weather radar, sirens, and volunteer storm watchers was a positive outcome for all Kansans.[55] Map Available: Appendix 1.

STORMS, MAY 27-31, 1955

The Udall tornado was not the only bad storm in May 1955. On May 27, a tornado struck Anthony, moving across the southeast edge of town. Although there were no injuries, the hotel, other business buildings, and several residences had damage. This time the weather bureau issued adequate warnings, and everyone was safe in their shelters. Tornadoes also hit near Manhattan, Osawatomie, Hillsdale, Wichita, Dodge City, and Hutchinson. A storm that struck Arnold in Ness County piled hailstones six inches deep on the streets. The Weather Bureau in Dodge City reported this system was the largest one tracked over the central and southern sections of the state. The residents in these communities were nervous after hearing about the devastation two days before in Udall and promptly heeded the weather warnings. On May 31 another storm system moved over the eastern third of the state. West of Topeka a windstorm damaged a hangar and aircraft at the Allen airport. Tornadoes also hit in Anderson and Johnson Counties, and the towns of Stark, Thayer, and Fort Scott. No injuries were reported.[56]

WESTERN KANSAS, JUNE 4, 1955

On June 4, 1955 at least a dozen tornadoes hop scotched across Western Kansas. There were, however, no reports of injuries. In Pawnee County, a tornado hit Garfield where a fire alarm siren sounded, warning the residents to seek shelter. When the menacing cloud approached Larned, the fire alarm sounded there too, thus giving citizens time to find a place of safety. A siren blew before the storm struck Mankato, where the wind unroofed the Seymour Packing Company, knocked out the electric power plant, and demolished a schoolhouse. Tornadoes also hit near Lewis and Osborne, and four more tornadoes were on the ground near Sharon Springs and Oakley.[57]

*View of tornado outside Great Bend,
June 4, 1955*

TORNADOES, APRIL 1, 2, 1956

On April 1st and 2nd, 1956 more than a dozen tornadoes churned across the state, causing two deaths and a few injuries. A squall line extended from Arkansas City to eighty miles past Toronto. A funnel dipped down and struck a farmhouse near Grenola, killing Ethel Whited. Near Toronto a tornado cut a swath four miles long, leveling several houses. It demolished the home of E.E. Reek, killing him and injuring his wife and daughter. The next morning another tornado roared through Baxter Springs and wrecked several buildings. A twister struck the Lake Kahola area near Emporia, destroying nine cabins.

The storm demolished homes in Maple City and Otto, stripping trees and damaging houses "as completely as anything."

On April 2 a small tornado hit Southwest Topeka around 21st and Gage, where several homes were badly damaged. The wind blew the porch off Hank Griffin's home and crushed his aluminum boat. Hank said that it was "pitch-black" outside, and when he opened the door, the wind blew him back inside.

On Atwood Street, one block east of Gage, lightning struck John Misum's house. "I heard the tornado warning on T.V.," he said, "and I went to bed about 10:30. Then I got up before midnight when it was raining and there was a strong wind. I heard a whistling noise. There were a lot of flying lightning bolts and tree limbs. We have a basement, but we were so excited we didn't even think of going down there."

At the J.K. Ellis home, he noted that, "I saw a black cloud full of lightning. The wind was blowing very hard. We were scared but it was all over in a minute. Like most of the houses around here, we don't have a basement, so there was nothing we could do."[58]

View of tornado damage near Claflin, including damaged silos and grain bins

Damage was excessive downtown. The wind blew out all the windows on the west side of the Hotel Kansan and at the State Printing Plant— almost 500 windows total. Hail, rain, and water damaged all the floors of the Printing Plant. A drainpipe broke on the third floor, sending water gushing through the lower floors. Several months elapsed before this building could be occupied again.[59]

For many years an old Indian legend, believed by nearly every citizen, foretold that Topeka would never be hit by a tornado. The town was supposed to be protected by a high hill to the southwest known as "Burnett's Mound." Unfortunately, this tornado and the one to follow in 1966 completely dispelled that belief.[60]

In the late 1950s a new method of forecasting a tornado became popular. Norman Weller developed a "pseudo-scientific" way of detecting tornadoes while at home, and it involves, of all things, the television set![61] Weller claimed it worked in the following manner:

1. Turn on the television set.

2. Turn to Channel 13. Using the brightness control, darken the screen to dim.

3. Turn to Channel 2. Do not reset the brightness.

4. Lightning will appear on the screen as horizontal streaks or flashes. As long as the screen does not have a steady glow, the approaching storm does not contain a tornado.

5. The sign of a tornado in the vicinity is when the television screen glows with a steady, bright, white light. Or, if there is a station on Channel 2 and the darkened picture becomes visible and remains visible, a tornado is in the area.

6. Seek shelter. Do not become absorbed in watching the screen and forget to take cover---fast.[62]

Channel 2 is a megacycle band and the closest television channel to the electromagnetic frequency pulse of a tornado. Some scientists think tornadoes emit electromagnetic energy in different wavelengths from those in a normal thunderstorm, but this theory is open to conjecture. If this were true, several theories on tornadoes and electricity paralleling each other would have some merit. Sorry, this method does not work on cable television.[63]

SPRING HILL, OTTAWA, MAY 20, 1957

Most residents of Kansas City remember the tornado that hit Ruskin Heights and Martin City, Missouri in May 1957. It destroyed scores of homes and businesses and killed more than thirty people. However, this same tornado was almost as destructive to the Spring Hill and Ottawa communities in Kansas.

For those interested in reading a good book about the Ruskin Heights tornado be sure to read *Caught in the Path* by Carolyn Glenn Brewer.[64]

The tornado struck Ottawa and Spring Hill between 7:00 and 8:00 p.m. and hopscotched between the two communities before heading into Missouri. Storm spotters sighted at least nineteen tornadoes in Kansas as the squall line moved across the state. Some towns affected were Kanorado, Bird City, Downs, Phillipsburg, Beloit, Burr Oak, Concordia, and Madison.

The storm took no lives until it reached Ottawa in Franklin County. Mr. and Mrs. J.A. Marsh were the victims. Mrs. Marsh died beside her wrecked house. Her husband died in an Ottawa hospital. At Spring Hill the tornado killed Barbara Davis, a thirty-one year old mother of two, and destroyed her farm home.[65]

View of the famous Ruskin Heights tornado approaching
Spring Hill, May 21, 1957

When an Ottawa policeman saw the tornado form, he stated there were two funnels at first, but they joined together and became one massive tornado. South of Ottawa the twister leveled Bob's Truck Stop on Highway 50 and smashed a twelve-unit motel, gas station, and restaurant. A waitress at the restaurant lost her car in the storm because she couldn't find her keys. When she, along with other patrons, saw the tornado coming, they ran out of the café and jumped into their cars. Since she couldn't find her car keys, she fled the scene with her friends. Later she returned only to find her car a quarter mile away, flattened to two feet high![66]

Roland Hind tried to outrun the tornado in his semi-trailer truck. At first he was able to keep away from the funnel, but then it changed course and came straight at him. When he saw what was happening, he stopped the truck, jumped out, dashed to the other side of the highway and lay down in a ditch. The tornado sucked his glasses off his face, debris hit him in the head and back, and an agitator from a washing machine fell on his leg. After the storm passed, he found the cab of his truck just west of the highway and the trailer a half-mile away in a field. The next day another truck driver was hunting the trailer to his truck. It had disappeared without a trace and was never found.

A farmer in the Rantoul area, who saw his home smashed by the tornado, had difficulty describing the scene the next day. "It was terrible, just terrible," he mumbled over and over. Another farmer was just walking aimlessly in his field. He said he was looking for his combine. It, too, was never found.[67]

The citizens of Kansas City have been lucky. The Ruskin Heights tornado was the only major storm to hit the metropolitan area between 1957 and 2003. Considering the size of the city, they are fortunate to have missed severe weather so many years. Map Available: Appendix 1.

EL DORADO, JUNE 10, 1958

About 5:45 p.m. on June 10, 1958 a tornado developed on the backside of a huge black cloud that threatened El Dorado for over an hour before striking the town. Vaughn Seiver, who saw the funnel forming said, "It seemed to dissipate, but came up again maybe ten minutes later about two miles northwest of here."[68]

The twister dipped to the ground near Oil Hill, damaging several houses and a school building, then hit the American Legion golf course on the west side of El Dorado. From there it moved into the new Towanda addition, raising briefly into the air and dropping again in another housing area southwest of town. The funnel damaged some homes, and others just simply disappeared. Debris littered a forty-block area, and fallen trees and wires were everywhere. The hailstones accompanying this storm were as large as small oranges, and when they hit they struck with a numbing force.

The tornado moved past the south city limits and lifted after crossing Highway 77. The swiftness of this storm astonished everyone.

It tore its way through southwest El Dorado in almost two minutes, trapping residents in their homes. Rescuers found bodies in the debris, but they also found others outside where the tornado had picked them up and dropped them to the ground. This was the second worst tornado of the 1950s, Udall being the first. This twister killed thirteen people and injured sixty. It damaged or destroyed over 200 homes.[69]

View of damaged cars and machinery after the El Dorado tornado

Ken Jenkins had a terrifying experience as he was approaching the El Dorado turnpike exchange, "When I saw the tornado in my direction, I realized it would be safer to get out of the car. Another car was occupied by the Gordon James family, and they also pulled on the shoulder and together we decided to climb the embankment and take shelter under the first overpass… When the wind passed us the suction was so great it tore Mrs. Gordon loose. I grabbed her arm and managed to hold on but her head struck one of the girders. Both cars were shattered like paper boxes. I don't know what happened to the Gordon family—I was too stunned and dazed after that."[70]

When the wind began to increase, Mrs. Ernest Hall went to her front door and stood beside it while the ceiling dropped around her. Then the roof disappeared. The tornado left the walls of the house standing and a piano unscathed in the center of one room. At the C.O. Catrell home, fifteen people sought refuge in their basement. Jane Stevenson, who was one of them, was planning to be married in a month. However, the tornado destroyed her new mobile home and the only thing she salvaged was her wedding gown.

Rollin Robertson was just turning into the driveway of his home when the tornado pushed his car through the garage door and out the back wall. He was not injured. The wind lifted another automobile off the street and tossed it into the attic of Amos Ott's house.[71]

Mrs. Charlotte Offen wrote the following article about the disaster for the *El Dorado Times*:

"What's it like being in a tornado? One minute you're happy peeling potatoes for dinner. The next, you hear a roaring noise resembling a rushing freight train. You continue working, and suddenly there is a loud cracking and popping. Then your husband is yelling, 'Come to the basement!' Window glass is breaking and flying all around you. The big window on the north is gone. The new knotty pine wall falls in. As you run down the basement steps, glass from the porch windows falls all about you and you wonder if some of it will cut your throat. In the basement you find a window nearest the southwest corner open. You close it. Then you realize the one on the east is open. You run through the darkness stumbling over things. But when you reach the window and look up, you see the black, swirling cloud is just sweeping across your nearest neighbor's back yard. A million objects are swirling around in the dust and wind. Who knows what? Kitchen articles, wearing apparel, boards, parts of huge trailers that once stood on the corner of Towanda and Skelly Road.

"You both rush upstairs to find the north wall leaning halfway to the floor, lamps upset, pictures lying on the floor, your drapes flying out the picture window. Then you rush to the porch and look south. There stands your neighbor's roofless house across the street. The once beautiful living room is in ruin, the floor heaved up in the middle but no sign of life except the little white dog, "Butch," standing there whining. You try the bedroom door but it refuses to open. You rush outside and see the neighbors standing inside their garage, numb with shock.

"You look across Towanda Street southward and what were pretty little homes is now a leveled expanse of broken timber, crushed cars, and scattered furniture.

"'Come,' you shout, 'many of them must be hurt.'" The first house you reach reveals no sign of life. Live electric wires lie all about you. A woman and man approach from the street. "Is this your home?" we ask. "Yes," the woman replied flatly. She was barefoot. "Where were you?" we ask. "In the car,'" she said.

"We think of friends in the west and run as fast as we dare through the nail-littered area. The first house, one that had a fine basement, is leveled. Your husband says, "Here's a body; do you know who it is?" But a quick look tells us identity is impossible. At first we think it is an elderly woman. We think of the dear soul just across the street whose house is now gone. But a later glimpse of a small dainty foot tells us it is a young woman, stripped of all clothing.

"We look about for the dead or injured, but find none. We go south heedless of the rain and wind. We find a home standing, at least the walls are. Two young men run over, one white and speechless. The other asks, "Where are they?" "They're all right. The little girl has a cut above her eye."

"Nowhere was there hysteria. Everyone walked about or ran in a dazed sort of way, not quite believing what they saw. The beautiful homes were gone… There was only death, and grief, and the injured--and approaching darkness… The young broken body we had seen could never be repaired, nor life returned to it."[72] Map Available: Appendix 1.

MERIDEN AND ELMONT, MAY 19, 1960

A storm of enormous proportions struck northeast Kansas on May 19, 1960 destroying 150 houses and killing one person. The counties of Pottawatomie, Shawnee, Jefferson, Jackson, Wabaunsee, Leavenworth, and Miami all suffered damage, but the tornado was particularly destructive in the small town of Meriden in Jefferson County. Elmont in northern Shawnee County was hit, as was Wamego, Rossville, Silver Lake, North Topeka, Oskaloosa, Ozawkie, and Leavenworth.[73]

No one in town sighted a funnel cloud, but the high winds demolished the depot and heavily damaged business buildings in downtown Meriden. Some of the structures were still cracking and caving in hours after the storm passed. In the eastern section of town, the storm either demolished or damaged 75 homes.

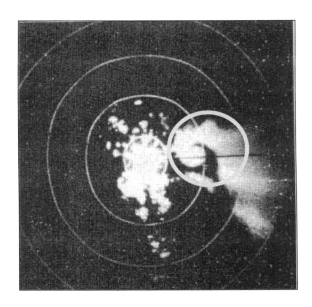

View of a tornado "hook echo" on radar, Meriden tornado

Although the storm didn't strike Meriden until 6:30 p.m., electric service was disrupted a half hour earlier. Then darkness descended on the town. The residents had no outside contact so the ambulances and highway patrol didn't arrive until after 8:30. Trees and debris blocked the main highway, forcing evacuation workers and rescuers to find alternate routes. These people found the body of Mildred Huntley, operator of a Meriden café, under a heavy rock in the wreckage of a nearby tavern.

In Elmont the tornado blew the Hollis home away, and no one could find the family. They had started for the basement when their youngest son became frightened and ran from the house. They immediately ran after him. The family was all accounted for the next day, but for a while everyone was concerned.

Aerial view of tornado damage in Meriden, May 1960

Outside Elmont a twister more than half a mile wide destroyed eight farmhouses. Several families saw the huge black cloud rolling in from the southwest and escaped by driving south and out of its path. Charles Edward's wife didn't see the storm until the last minute, and as she gathered her three children and a nephew to go to the basement, the wind flattened the house. Later they found the nephew under the kitchen stove with a head injury. All the others survived unhurt.

Rossville barely missed destruction. After the tornado lifted up over the town, it dropped back down, destroying the home of H.P. Stockman. Mrs. Stockman remarked, "It sounded like the heavens were coming down on us. A big beam fell across my lap and just brushed the back of Henry's head." The tornado swept away the walls of the house and dumped the roof down on the foundation. The storm destroyed the Richard Cantillan home, smashing the house down to basement level. No one was home at the time.

Tornado recovery and salvage in Meriden, May 1960

Farther east, a small tornado skimmed Northeast Topeka, causing slight damage as it moved across a truck lot on the highway, demolishing a concrete block storage shed and overturning several semi-trailer trucks.[74]

At Oskaloosa the sheriff had to be hospitalized after the wind turned his patrol car over on him while he was standing behind it. The top floor of the Jefferson County Courthouse caught only the tail end of the tornado, but it tore away most of the roof. Elsewhere in town, trees, lights, and telephone wires littered the streets.[75]

On the west edge of Leavenworth, the twister destroyed seventeen houses. The sheriff's patrol, first on the scene, found several children wandering in a daze near the ruins of their homes, unable to find their parents.

All total, there were thirty-four persons injured. One of them was a Topeka woman caught in her car while driving north of town. The tornado spun her car around and splattered it with mud. She quickly abandoned the car and lay face down in a ditch, holding on to a hedge tree; she escaped with only scratches and bruises. W.F. Critchfield was driving a station wagon eight miles north of Topeka when he saw a funnel bearing down on him. He drove into the yard of the nearest farmhouse and ran inside to the basement. The storm only lasted a few minutes, but when he came out, his station wagon was gone. His 1959 Ford was never seen again.[76] Map Available: Appendix 1.

HUTCHINSON, NEWTON, MAY 24, 1962

Mid-afternoon on May 24, 1962 a humid, windy day gave way to thunderstorms in south central Kansas when the temperature reached ninety degrees. The first tornado activity developed in the Abbyville-Nickerson area, and two hours later spotters saw another tornado on the ground four miles south of Halstead. A twister struck the small town of Burrton, demolishing the Kinsley Appliance store and several trailer homes.[77]

At Hutchinson, policemen observed a tornado aloft about three miles southwest of the city and sounded the sirens at 4:30 p.m. Storm spotters reported two more small funnels dangling from the clouds west of town but they dissipated in about fifteen minutes.

The hail and windstorm that battered Hutchinson was one of the most destructive in the city's history. Hailstones ranging up to grapefruit size damaged cars, stripped trees, ripped awnings, and shattered windows. Surface winds gusting to ninety miles per hour tore porches off and unroofed a 32-lane bowling alley.

This storm injured two people. Rodney Peterson was climbing a ladder outside his home to survey roof damage when the wind toppled his ladder and threw him to the ground, knocking him unconscious. Connie Wilson suffered a broken finger when a hailstone hit her hand.

High winds tossed the roof of a house on Huxman Avenue into the street and extensively damaged five others in the same area. At the Carey Salt plant, the roof caved in, and the roof of the Bankers Life and Casualty Company landed in the street. The Hutchinson Floral Company's greenhouse lost all its windows, and the Baker Hotel and Grace Hospital had a total of 138 windows broken. At Clown Town Kiddieland, large hailstones killed a Shetland pony named "Little Orphan Annie."[78]

The city held an impromptu contest trying to find the largest hailstone. The sizes ranged up to thirteen inches in circumference. At the W.D. Yates home, an eleven-inch stone crashed through a storm window and slid across the floor, damaging a table.

At 6:35 p.m. a ham radio operator at Hesston informed the Weather Bureau that a tornado was on the ground demolishing farm buildings and heading toward Newton. C.E. Patterson, Newton Police Chief, said he saw four or five funnels in the air at the same time. One man claimed he saw a tornado dip down to tree-top height over the northeast section of town.

Tornado sirens blew and residents took cover as strong winds buffeted the city. Wiley Ward, a service station attendant, watched as a giant billboard hit the ground and several pumps and signs blew over. He said it looked like a dust cloud almost a half mile wide, and the wind in the cloud kept changing directions.[79]

At the Countryview Nursing Home, W.M. George said he saw the same twister three times. He stated, "It came from the west and it tore apart a windmill. It seemed to dip down about a hundred yards from the [nursing] home. And it came back from the north and came again from the southwest."[80] The residents waited out the storm in the recreation room. "A two by six came through the window," George said, "and Al Matthews was sitting just four feet away. All he said was 'Well, I guess it's time to move.'"[81]

The next morning the townspeople began digging out from under the debris left by the storm. Their beautiful tree-lined streets were a jungle of fallen leaves and broken limbs.

TOPEKA, MAY 26, 1962

On May 26, 1962 just two days after the Hutchinson storm, tornadoes hit the Topeka area. The storm was similar in several ways— it contained heavy rain, large hail, strong winds, and tornadoes, seven of them.

When the spotters sighted three funnels south of the city, they sounded the new Civil Defense sirens. One tornado touched down at 57th and Burlingame Road, destroying a house, barn, and garage owned by the Stuver family, who were not at home. When they returned, all they found was a mass of twisted boards and a large picture window on the east side of the house.

Neighbors came to help them salvage frozen food from their freezer, which was sitting in their driveway. Other neighbors tried to help by loading clothes and household goods and looking for their pick-up truck buried under the wreckage.

Around 29th and Arnold Streets, a funnel briefly touched down and receded back into the clouds. The Weather Bureau also reported a funnel over Forbes Air Force Base but no damage to the aircraft. Spotters reported prolonged winds of 40-60 miles per hour around the city.

Eight major car accidents occurred during the storm as residents raced for shelter. Many pulled under bridges and overpasses to escape the large hail. About thirty-five people spent more than an hour in the basement of Allen's Drive In at 35th and Topeka Avenue. The management served hamburgers, French fries, and cokes "on the house." A woman and her child were injured running for cover when they fell down an embankment near the Smith Trailer Court.

After the storm passed, Robert Jones, Civil Defense Director, asked the citizens to organize tornado shelters in their own neighborhoods to prevent this dangerous last minute dash for safety.[82]

HOLTON, AUGUST 6, 1962

The city of Holton barely missed being destroyed when a tornado tore through the center of Jackson County, cutting a path fifteen miles long. Shortly after 5:40 p.m. on August 6, 1962 the city's civil defense sirens sounded, warning residents of an approaching severe storm.

As the townspeople watched, a long, white funnel formed and appeared to be moving directly for the city. However, the twister hesitated, and then resumed motion several times, dipping up and down. Then, suddenly it changed direction.

View of the tornado aloft in Hoyt, August 6, 1962

Clarence and David Schirmer were bailing hay when they first saw the tornado and quickly took cover. When they returned to the field, not a hay bale was in sight. The tornado then hit the Holton cemetery, where it knocked down trees and headstones. Next was the bulk plant of the B & P Gas Company south of town, where the twister scattered gas tanks in all directions. At a nearby farm, Don Newman found a dead horse in his silo. Strangely enough, the horse did not belong to him, and no one ever claimed ownership of the animal. The funnel destroyed the brick Grange building and a brick schoolhouse—the oldest school in the county.[83]

The storm moved southeast and hit near the town of Birmingham. At the Clair Gunther home the tornado blew away the house and all outbuildings. Gunther found his new car upside down in a field 200 yards from the house with a carpet draped over its front end. One person injured in the storm was Charles Lewis. The wind blew him 200 yards from his house, and he survived with only cuts and bruises.

Holton residents saw the funnel and heard the ominous hissing sound it made, but they were lucky - they escaped a direct hit.[84]   Map Available: Appendix 1.

The Cold War and the space program had one secondary but important side effect - the release of weather satellites. These satellites provided photographs of an entire hemisphere to users in the United States within thirty minutes of scanned time. The U.S. Weather Bureau could monitor the intensity and development of weather systems by combining sequential photos into motion picture loops. In addition, infrared data allowed the display of cloud systems at night and indications of both temperature and water vapor both day and night.

Satellite photos revealed components of storm systems heretofore inaccessible. For example, frontal boundaries could be located precisely, since sharp cloud lines accompany fronts.

The location and configuration of jet streams were identified through analysis of cirrus cloud streaks. The Weather Service tracked low-level moisture via low clouds moving from the Gulf of Mexico into the Central Plains in advance of severe storm and tornado outbreaks. Satellite technology effectively monitored both hurricanes and severe thunderstorms.[85]

GARNETT, APRIL 12, 1964

On April 12, 1964 tornadoes, high winds, rain, and hail pounded Eastern Kansas and Western Missouri, killing five people and injuring at least thirty-five. The storm was especially destructive in Anderson, Douglas, and Leavenworth Counties.

When the tornado roared across Highway 59-169 near Garnett, it shoved six cars and two trucks off the road, killing three people. Welcome Stanton, a newsman from Iola, saw a car blown into the timber 500 feet from the highway. He reported, "I saw parts of cars and clothing, apparently from luggage, hanging in the trees." The dead were Mr. and Mrs. Warren Kenyon and Mrs. Jack Wilson.[86]

Another tornado hit southwest of Lawrence, where it damaged fourteen homes and a trailer house, injuring three people. Robert Jones, a student at the University of Kansas, watched the tornado pass west of the campus. At first he thought the funnel was heading straight for the college, but it veered to the north.

At Leavenworth high winds damaged seventy-five houses and injured ten persons. Citizens said the storm sounded like a big freight train. The cloud was so close to the ground there was no visible funnel. After leaving Leavenworth, the tornado lifted back into the clouds and headed into Missouri.[87] The storm system continued on a rampage for several more hours, but the devastation was confined primarily to Kansas.

GEUDA SPRINGS, MARCH 16, 1965

Survivors called the tornado on March 16, 1965 the "instant tornado" because they said it came from out of nowhere. It hit Oklahoma the hardest, but Sumner and Cowley Counties in Kansas suffered extensive damage. No one reported any serious injuries, just stories of miraculous escapes.

D.R. Sheets of Winfield was outside doing chores. When he saw the tornado in an adjoining field, he rushed to the house, grabbed his wife, shoved her in a pickup truck and hurried out of the yard. They managed to outrun the funnel by driving in circles around a square mile area. All the while, boards and other debris hammered the truck. Mrs. Sheets said the tornado looked like a big, white billowing cloud on the ground.

At Geuda Springs the tornado took the roof off a concrete block building, setting it down sideways against the walls. A truck driver reported the twister blew a horse across the road in front of his vehicle, killing the animal. Ernest Bilyeu of South Haven luckily escaped with minor injuries when the tornado piled his barn on top of him.

Unaware there was a tornado in the area, the Vernon McCord family of Winfield heard the sound of it approaching and tried to go to a shelter, but suction from the passing funnel pulled them from the entrance and knocked them to the ground. They suffered minor injuries.

The "instant tornado" left as quickly as it came.[88]

WICHITA, MAY 13, 1965

The first of two tornadoes hit Wichita on May 13, 1965. It struck the city's west side, injuring one and leaving heavy damage in its wake. Barney

Lambdin was the only serious injury. Rescuers found him pinned under a mobile home.

Spotters first reported the tornado on the ground at Belle Plaine, nineteen miles west of Wichita, around 9:25 p.m. The Weather Bureau, tracking the storm as it moved toward Wichita, noticed it heading for their office. Twenty-five minutes later, they were vacating the premises and taking cover. The tornado passed directly overhead, knocking out the radar.

Police officers on U.S. 54 and Tyler Road reported another tornado coming toward them. This radio transmission reported: "Traffic One, we're at the Big Ditch—we are in it—there it goes!" Those officers said the twister skipped over them and across the west side of town at tree top level.[89]

Officers John Gillock and Phil Beurskens saw the funnel dip down. "It looked like it was 50 or 60 feet off the ground and was about a block wide," Gillock noted. Then damage reports came in—several homes demolished, the Starkey School destroyed, and light poles down everywhere.

Twenty minutes after losing radar, the Weather Bureau was back in operation and had the tornado in their scope twenty miles northwest of their office heading for Halstead. No further damage was reported.[90]

WICHITA, SEPTEMBER 3, 1965

During a late summer thunderstorm over Wichita, the worst possible scenario occurred— a tornado appeared unexpectedly, injuring twenty-seven people. It was a miracle no one was killed, as the storm hit without warning when everyone was at home.

A pilot on a TWA flight saw three separate thunderstorms near the city before he landed about 8:00 p.m. These storms merged into one, and as he was taking off from the airport, he reported seeing a funnel in the northeast section of the city.

Lieutenant George Greenly, weather forecaster at McConnell Air Force Base, was at a drive-in theater when he saw the tornado forming. He stated there was a distinct funnel, light gray in color and accompanied by greenish lightning. The initial vortex pulled back into the clouds, and then two thin rope-like funnels dipped down to the ground again.[91]

The twister struck the Prairie Village Shopping Center in the northeastern part of town, destroying a supermarket, clothing store, drug store, flower shop, hardware store, toy shop, and several other businesses. At the Cowboy Cleaners, Patty Weniger ran to the front window just as it shattered, hitting her with pieces of glass. Don Preston, alone in a liquor store, tried to shut the door when the wind blew it open, but he decided it was too late and jumped behind a counter. The liquor bottles exploded, showering him with glass.

Flying glass cut several employees and customers in the Colonial Fountain and Grill. The Candle Club cooks, John Bonfiglio, stood by the back door looking at the clouds when he saw the roof rise up, fly over him, and crush several cars in the parking lot. He yelled at people to "hit the deck!" Some rushed into the walk-in refrigerator.

Dr. and Mrs. William Nelson were in their vehicle at an intersection when the tornado lifted the station wagon from the ground, turned it over and set it up right again. As the car rolled, it threw little David Nelson, 2, out and hurled him against the pavement. All the glass blew out of the car as the vehicle spun in the air. David escaped with minor injuries.[92]

Mrs. Hubert Davis and friend were eating ice cream at the Colonial Fountain. They sat at a front row table watching the rain, hail and intensity of the storm, when suddenly, across the street, the wind bent several light poles all the way to the ground. This was their cue to dive under the table. Just as they did, the front window exploded, filling Mrs. David's mouth with glass. She said, "I heard an awful whistling sound, and the roof collapsed. Everything around the store seemed to be swirling around. It went dark. The manager yelled out for everyone not to panic. He told us we should all get down to the basement. We had to hold on to one another, hand-in-hand in a line, to get down the basement stairs. We stayed there awhile and then came up. The place was ruined."

In the excitement, Mrs. Davis lost her shoes, but an employee gave her another pair so she wouldn't cut her feet. She thought her car would be gone; it was still there full of debris.[93]

During the first hour after the storm, everyone was confused. Damage was bad, but how bad, no one knew. Men yelled back and forth and police radios crackled with reports of injuries and of destruction. Ambulances and fire trucks with sirens blaring streamed in and out of the area all night.

At the shopping center, broken glass lay everywhere—from slabs as big as a door to slivers too tiny to see. A river of whiskey poured into the street from the hundreds of shattered bottles at the liquor store. Workers stayed all night boarding up open storefronts and salvaging what they could from the businesses.

West of the center in every direction, there were flattened and crumbled homes. People stood in the streets, shocked and confused, telling each other where they were when the tornado hit. Police officers went door to door searching for dead bodies. Fortunately, they found none.

After the storm, a few citizens found some humor in the disaster. At the flower shop, someone covered the front window with a board, decorated it with flowers and a message that read, "Remodeling."[94]

EASTERN KANSAS, MAY 12, 1966

The spring of 1966 was wet and ushered in by severe thunderstorms and a particularly destructive tornado outbreak beginning on May 12. Twisters destroyed three homes, damaged two-dozen others, demolished two school buildings, and wrecked barns, garages, and cars.

The first tornado dropped down in Washington County early that May afternoon, and did serious damage at Linn, destroying two homes, damaging ten others, and wrecking two schools. At the Linn High School the students rushed to safety in the basement before the storm struck and unroofed the structure, sucking an entire classroom out of the agriculture building.

"It all began happening about 1:30 p.m.--that was when the town was alerted for the tornado," Mayor Ed Doupnik of Linn said. The Weather Bureau's alarm gave the town time to get the children to a safe place.[95]

Near Linn the tornado destroyed several more homes. The wind drove shingles from one house several inches into the ground. A camper tent blew away, but under the tent, two pieces of garden equipment only moved two inches. The twister hurled a 55-gallon drum more than half a mile away, where it smashed a neighbor's garage door.[96]

About two hours later, another tornado hit near Elmont in northern Shawnee County, following the same path as the storm of May 19, 1960. This time the tornado lifted just short of Meriden and Ozawkie. Mrs. Willard White remarked, "We saw the funnel coming and ran for the cave. I think the children grabbed us instead of us grabbing them. We didn't hear the tornado because we were in the cave but we could feel the cave shake."

At the Henry Kahle home, disaster struck twice. The tornado flattened the home and scattered the rubble over a nearby field. The home had just been rebuilt after a tornado destroyed it six years before. The family huddled in the basement unhurt. Hazel Kahle remarked, "We had been sitting in the living room watching it (the tornado). We prayed it would go up in the clouds this time. We all just went to the basement. There was nothing else that we could do." The tornado in 1960 was a mile wide at Elmont; this one fortunately was smaller.

Another storm hit the city of Pittsburg about 150 miles away, injuring one person.

THE FIRST $100,000,000 TORNADO

TOPEKA, JUNE 8, 1966

The tornado that struck Udall in 1955 was the most destructive storm to hit a Kansas community in the 20th century. Despite their comparative size, urban areas such as Wichita, Topeka, and Kansas City more or less escaped major tornado damage. On June 8, 1966 all that changed. Topeka was the target of the first tornado in the nation's history to exceed $100,000,000 in property damage.

In the past, Topeka barely missed being hit by twisters. An oft-repeated legend recounted that Chief Abram Burnett, a whiskey drinking, horse-trading 400-pound Indian, once stated that as long as no one built anything on his beloved mound, the town would be safe from a tornado.

First view of the famous Topeka tornado of June 8, 1966, as it approaches Burnett's Mound in Southwest Topeka.

Tornado rolling over Burnett's Mound and heading for the city

In the early 1960s the city built housing developments to the southwest, nearly to the top of "Burnett's Mound." A few years later, the tornado descended, and that was the end of the legend of Chief Burnett. [97]

Homes that are moments from destruction and disaster, Southwest Topeka

June 8th began as a typical spring day in Kansas— warm, windy, and humid. By noon the Weather Bureau forecast the possibility of severe storms later in the day. Nothing unusual, spring had already been wet and stormy. As the day progressed, the mixture of sun and humidity led to increased cloudiness and thunder heads, causing the Weather Bureau to dispatch tornado spotters to various locations, including Burnett's Mound. [98]

A large thunderstorm moving northeast from Emporia grew in intensity as it approached the Topeka area. Between the towns of Dover and Auburn to the southwest, a tornado touched down, killing two people. Now the twister was heading directly for Topeka, and Burnett's Mound. By the time spotters on the Mound sighted the funnel, it was a half-mile wide, filling most of the skyline. The Weather Bureau sounded the sirens at 7:15 p.m., which gave the citizens about ten minutes to take cover.

Aftermath and destruction, June 8, 1966

Weather spotters Rick Douglass and Officer Dave Hathaway, stationed on Burnett's Mound, were the first to see the huge funnel. It was bearing down directly on top of them! Douglass radioed, "I can see the funnel cloud, and it's coming up behind me. I've got to get out of here!"[99] But he stood there as long as he dared. As the twister came closer, he made one last broadcast for residents to take cover, and then he dashed for his car. The tornado smashed into his vehicle and rolled Douglass on the ground, covering him with mud. Officer Hathaway radioed for the last time that night, "Those houses at 29th and (unintelligible) are gone— they're just gone, all gone!" The fact that both men survived was a miracle.[100]

At this point, residents in southwest Topeka saw the tornado as it surged down Burnett's Mound, heading for the new homes and apartments on the edge of the mound. Now the funnel was three-fourths of a mile wide and contained wind in excess of 300 miles an hour. It flattened the first homes it struck like they were made of paper, and then it destroyed a new brick apartment complex, heaving cars in all directions. One ended up in the swimming pool.

Entire blocks reduced to splinters and broken glass

At the WIBW television studio, the weathermen and news anchors began warning the city of the impending danger. One of these men was a young broadcaster named Bill Kurtis. As he listened to the reports of devastation, he was overcome with fear at what was happening, but he kept his composure, went to the microphone and warned Topekans, as calmly as he could, "For God's sake, take cover!!" Thankfully, most of his listeners did just that.

After leaving the Burnett's Mound area, the tornado headed for the Veterans Administration Hospital, but at the last minute it veered south, missing the VA by six blocks. Next in line lay Washburn University. The twister did not miss, and the college took a direct hit. The funnel destroyed nearly every building on campus, including some stone and brick buildings over eighty years old. It wrecked dorms, sucked furniture out of classrooms, and it destroyed the observatory. Nearby homes in the College Hill neighborhood, both old and new, disappeared in the path of the tornado.

Downtown Topeka lay directly in the tornado's path. It eased by the Capitol building, breaking some windows and tearing siding off the dome. The State Printing Plant, the National Reserve Building near the Capitol, and the bus barn all took a direct hit. It tore off roofs, broke all windows, and flattened the buses. For years after the tornado, the National Reserve Building stood unrepaired as a grim reminder; an old painted sign on the south side of the building read, "A Refuge in Time of Storm."[101]

After the twister left the southern area of downtown in shambles, staffers of the *Topeka Capital-Journal* waited for what seemed like an eternity for the storm to hit. Editor Bert Carlyle reported:

"You could hear the roar now. Rain was coming down, not in drops, but in great sheets of water. The roar grew louder— like a thousand freight trains passing over us. Suddenly there was a deathly stillness--no wind, no rain, nothing. Then all hell broke loose. The tornado was just south of us. We could see the debris whirling and dashing to the ground.

Injuries know no boundaries—a small child hurt on an old door

"As the funnel cloud passed, the sky grew bright with a white light that was almost blinding. And then it was gone. Driving down Kansas Avenue, it looked like the aftermath of an A-Bomb strike. . . . We went first into a residential area, and found cut and bleeding people walking around, dazed, not knowing what had happened to them— not fully realizing the impact of the fact their homes were gone. Walking around, taking pictures, we would go up to a house and call out, "Anybody here— everybody all right?" Sometimes there was an answer, more often not."[102]

Still, the tornado stayed on the ground. It rotated through some older housing areas in Oakland and East Topeka, leveling homes and smashing cars. The twister's next "victims" were the Billard Municipal Airport northeast of town and the Weather Bureau. These people tracked the tornado from the beginning, and now they were its target. As the funnel roared overhead, the staff dove for the floor. It missed them, but not the airport. The wind tossed planes around like toys, causing thousands of dollars in damage.

The tornado rumbled on, crossing the Kansas River, sucking up water as it disappeared from sight, leaving behind seventeen dead and 600 injured.

Throughout the night, the city was lit up with emergency vehicles trying desperately to help those trapped in buildings or hurt by flying glass and debris. Hospitals were overrun with people who were cut and bruised, or those with head wounds, broken limbs, and internal injuries. The tornado demolished the southwest side of Topeka, and no one seemed to know what to do next.

Carlyle noted, "Luxury apartment homes, built without basements or storm shelters, were leveled. People were being dragged out, injured, dead and nearly dead." In the downtown area, looting became a problem, and sightseers jammed the already busy streets, blocking police cars, ambulances, and other officials.

The statistics were grim. Besides the 17 dead and 600 injured, the tornado damaged over 3,000 homes and completely destroyed 1,000; it also leveled 250 business buildings.

For Topeka, this was the tornado to "end all tornadoes."[103]

Topekans were still picking up the pieces from the 1966 tornado when Meteorologist Joe Eagleman appeared on the scene, attempting to find out what made tornadoes such an enigma. He continued his study through the 1970s by following the destructive paths left by tornadoes in Texas, Missouri, Ohio, and Mississippi. Eagleman not only studied the destruction left by those tornadoes but he also created miniature ones— ten feet tall and a few inches wide— in his laboratory at the University of Kansas. What he discovered rewrote the rules on tornado safety.[104]

Eagleman reported that the Weather Bureau radar detected only about thirty percent of all tornadoes, and that the most accurate information came from weather spotters and from the public. In the 1960s, weather forecasters were batting about .500 as only half of all tornadoes actually occurred within a watch area, which caused some residents to have little or no warning.

In Topeka, Eagleman studied the tornado damage to about ninety houses. Four months after reviewing his findings, he discovered that the northeast corner of the house or basement was the safest place to take cover. For years people were told to take shelter in the southwest corner, probably because any falling debris should blow over them. However, most of the damage to a structure is on the southwest side, causing the rubble to collapse into the basement. Eagleman also noted that a house usually shifted on its foundation in the direction the tornado rotated, which caused debris to fall in the southwest part of a basement.

Further findings revealed that the opening of windows before a tornado struck made no difference in the destruction. Also, steep roofs seemed to fare better than slightly slanted or flat ones. Smaller rooms, including closets, on the northeast side of the house were the safest places, other than a basement, during a tornado.

In 1974 other professors in the field of Meteorology defended Eagleman's findings.[105] Map Available: Appendix 1.

GARDEN CITY, JUNE 25, 1967

On June 23, 1967 six tornadoes pummeled the Garden City area, killing one person and injuring thirty others. The storm had the potential of becoming more destructive than the 1966 Topeka tornado, at least in size and ferocity.

The National Weather Service nicknamed the funnels "pups," describing the fingers reaching down out of a swirling black cloud. They "bopped" along, dipping down, lifting back, and then dipping down again.

After threatening clouds appeared northwest of Garden City, residents listened to their radios and watched television for any warnings, but they heard none. Later the media said there wasn't time to give an alarm before the storm knocked the stations off the air. The twisters formed north of town and no one saw them until it was too late. What really saved lives was the distinctive menacing clouds hanging over the city that the citizens found hard to ignore.

A band was playing that night at Stevens Park, and scores of people attended until the dark clouds forced them to leave early. The Gillan family arrived home from the concert just as the tornado struck their house. They sought refuge in the garage, where a wall and the roof crashed down around them, but they were not injured.[106]

The tornado totally destroyed the Kansas State University Agricultural Experiment Station. It was a tangled mass of wreckage. The wind battered seven homes occupied by the station employees. Total damage estimates were $250,000. The building housing the station records sustained less serious damage, which saved the old records dating back to 1907.

The only death was Mamie Largent. Her son found her in the basement of her demolished home. Medical personnel treated thirty others for lesser injuries. The tornado destroyed 125 houses and damaged a nursing home, two grade schools, a high school stadium, the Flamingo Hotel, a furniture store, and a tractor showroom.

Damage estimates to farm buildings in Finney County was $750,000. Additional losses occurred in Gray and Kearny Counties, where a tornado formed between Lakin and Leoti, scattering dozens of steel grain bins, trees, and irrigation pipe for miles.

The tornado continued east of Garden City, destroying the Brinkmeyer and Largent farmhouses. The storm surged on for a few miles, and then dissipated.[107]

CENTRAL KANSAS, JUNE 21, 1969

This storm was known as the ten million dollar tornado that hit Salina on June 21. Although the tornado didn't kill anyone, it bounced all over the city, injuring sixty persons. The only casualty was Theodore Nelson, who died of a heart attack while cleaning up debris.

The tornado began its path of destruction at Ellsworth, and then moved through Saline, McPherson, Morris, and Dickinson Counties. Farmers in all five counties reported heavy property damage after high winds and heavy rain flattened homes, barns, and wheat fields. The storm came late at night, hitting the area around 11:30 p.m.

In Salina alone, the twister destroyed 26 homes and 7 businesses, and damaged 650 houses and 21 businesses. The heaviest destruction occurred at the Salina Airport, where the wind demolished several buildings occupied by Beech Aircraft, formerly Schilling Air Force Base. The tornado tore the roof off a large round top hanger used for the assembly of missile target drones, destroyed nine aircraft and damaged sixteen others. It deposited a light plane on the roped-off lawn at Rapid Air, the airport's fixed base operator, and moved a Kansas National Guard plane along the ramp into a parking stall between two parked cars. The damage carried over into an adjacent housing development known as Indian Village, where 500 houses were ruined beyond repair.[108]

Larry Johnson, one of the victims, bought his new home on June 17th. Five days later the tornado demolished it. The Johnson family was camping at Kanopolis Reservoir when the storm hit and it threatened to blow their tent away. They decided to return home around 4:00 p.m. only to find their house gone and their belongings scattered everywhere. Across the street, their neighbors sought shelter from the storm in their bathroom, which was the only room left standing. The Robert Mermis family lost the roof to their house. Three years earlier, they lost their roof in another storm. James Bagley was in the kitchen and his wife was in bed when the storm hit. He never heard a thing until a 2 x 4 came crashing through the window. The tornado struck without a sound.

Hundreds of people were camping at Lake Kanopolis that night, and the damage was extensive. The wind overturned campers and trailers, tore boats loose from their moorings, demolished several bathhouses, and blew pieces of trailers two miles away. The tornado knocked the yacht club building off the floating pier and twisted trailers off their hitches. Mr. and Mrs. Ernest Berg found themselves trapped when two trees fell on their camper and two more fell on their car. Berg had to smash a back window with a frying pan in order to escape.

Other towns in the area suffered damage. The storm wrecked barns and outbuildings around Brookville, and at Gypsum the wind blew out all the storefronts on the east side of Main Street. At Lindsborg the tornado shattered most of the windows at the high school, and the roof of Deere Hall on Bethany College Campus caved in when two trees smashed it.

This storm outbreak was considered the worst and most widespread of any to hit Kansas during the 1960s.[109]

REGIONAL TORNADOES, JUNE 23, 1969

Two days after the Salina storm, tornadoes struck again. A series of storms moved across the state around 5:30 p.m., and a tornado dipped down near Goddard, where it destroyed the Thome farm, injuring the residents. On the far, the tornado killed half of the 10,000 turkeys in Thome's flock. His children had been left home alone while the parents were out in the field harvesting wheat. When they saw the storm approaching, they ran to the neighbors for shelter, which probably saved their lives.

William Kramer was driving down the highway in his pickup truck, when the wind tore it in half and threw it 300 yards into a ditch. Kramer suffered chest, hip, rib, and leg injuries but managed to survive.

Several tornadoes in the Wichita area caused residents to take cover. Although the town escaped a direct hit, the storm disrupted power to a large portion of the city. Lightning strikes sent several people to the hospital. One of the injured was checking wind damage to his house from the top of an aluminum ladder.[110]

PRAIRIE VIEW, MARCH 13, 1973

Early in 1973 two tornadoes did extensive damage to the Prairie View community five miles east of Arkansas City. The tornadoes moved in a hopscotch fashion across the area. They ripped off metal roofs and destroyed outbuildings. The high winds and heavy rains came too fast for most residents to seek shelter.

Curtis Dixon was sitting in his living room when the tornado hit. The perceptive man stated, "I knew something was wrong when the living room window blew out." The wind damaged his home and blew his pickup truck about 75 feet into a ditch. The tornado destroyed the outbuildings on Earnest Healson's farm and shoved a boat and trailer 200 feet into a pigpen.[111]

Residents saw two twisters west of Silverdale, and they moved on to do damage in Burden and Atlanta. A tornado hit Plainville, destroying twenty mobile homes at the Short Mobile Home plant. The National Weather Service first reported the storm as a tornado, but later they determined it was straight winds of a hundred miles an hour or more.

At Ness City the wind tore the roof off the high school gymnasium, and students at a Vo-Tech School in Goodland escaped serious injury when high winds knocked over a block wall, breaking a pipe on a gas meter.

At Bogue a gust of wind toppled a grain elevator across the railroad tracks. At Hays a man was injured when the wind blew his mobile home over on its side.

NORTH CENTRAL KANSAS, SEPTEMBER 25, 1973

During the 1970s one of the worst tornado outbreaks in Kansas history occurred on September 23, 1973, killing five people and injuring forty.

Residents first sighted several tornadoes near Salina at 5:03 p.m., one of which leveled the Sundowner East Mobile Home Park southeast of town, causing four injuries. The funnel went up and down until it was within a mile of the mobile homes, and then it stayed on the ground. Observers called it "a huge black funnel." After the sheriff hurried through the area warning tenants, most of the ninety-five occupants were in the shelter when the storm struck.

As he stood watching the clouds, Bob Cochrane worried about what the hail might do to his car, but then he noticed several of his neighbors looking west and pointing. When he turned around, he saw a giant funnel heading in his direction. He quickly grabbed his wife and ran to the shelter house. This was just in the nick of time. When they came out, they had to climb over a truck covering the shelter house door. Cochrane was shocked to find a large pile of debris lying where his trailer house and car once stood.

Cary Tanner received a warning call from her mother-in-law in Salina, where the sirens were already sounding. She had twenty minutes to escape to the shelter house before the tornado hit. She lost her trailer but found most of her personal belongings piled in one place. She said the tornado sounded like a huge vacuum cleaner when it went over the court.

When Larry Hilding returned to his trailer, it was gone. He found a crumpled tape player and a wedding picture. Everything else had disappeared. Jeff Lawrence said his wife lost all but a $25 guitar and case.

Jerry Garwood and his wife rode out the storm in his pickup. They escaped injury, but they could hear glass breaking everywhere. When the storm passed, their trailer was still standing. Tom Kohn, a resident, stated, "All we have left is the Bible and our bodies."[112]

After the tornado smashed through the park, pieces of forty-seven mobile homes were scattered for half a mile. When everyone came out of the shelter, the sheriff ordered them to meet in one place for a head count; he also warned them that more storms were on the way.[113]

At about 6:30 p.m. the tornado surged on through Niles in Ottawa County, flattening the south side of town, destroying the grain elevator, and killing Marie Bell by hurling a grain bin into the café where she had taken refuge. Only two of the fifteen grain bins remained standing. The wind wrapped sheet metal from some of the bins around telephone poles. Outside of town the tornado destroyed the Blue Ridge Hunting Club and killed about $35,000 worth of pheasants and quail.[114]

At Bennington a tornado struck another café, injuring four people. Two were burned due to the ignition of a butane tank where they sought shelter. In New Cambria a twister injured two people and demolished an elevator, garage, fire station, and several homes.

The storms moved on to Clay County. Here the sky seethed with tornadic activity as Sheriff Bill Gonser sped through the torrential downpour north of Oak Hill about 5:30 p.m. The twister just missed the little town and was moving in the direction of Clay Center. Gonser radioed ahead that the tornado was coming, but when he reached the top of a hill, he met the funnel head-on. It struck the car broadside and hurled it 150 yards into a pasture, causing Gonser to suffer broken ribs, bruises, and internal injuries.

Meanwhile in Clay Center, the tornado sirens sounded. Thankfully this tornado veered to the west of town, and everyone exited from their cellars breathing a sigh of relief. Life went on. Shortly after 8:00 p.m., Commissioner Buck Reed sighted another tornado a few miles south of Clay Center heading straight for the outskirts. "It's in the city!" Reed yelled into his microphone. This was his last warning before the lights went out. The twister struck from the south, ripping a two block wide swath up 6th Street. Although the funnel appeared to be two blocks wide, heavy damage was reported for several blocks on either side of its path.[115]

Police officer Lorin Kasper hurried across town to 6th Street and turned south. "I got to the A & W Drive-In and saw it coming up the street. It was a big white twirling mass and I saw the Co-op Elevator go. I grabbed my mike and yelled, 'It's here!' and dropped the mike and laid down in the front seat. I thought I was gone. I felt the thing pick up my car, and it moved in the air about ten feet and smashed into a big pole and fell upright to the ground. All the glass shattered in the car. I held onto the steering wheel tight as hell. I got bounced around then cut up a little. It lasted about thirty seconds. That was the longest thirty seconds of my life."[116]

It was impossible for officials to get any idea of the damage after dark. Most of the city's main streets were strewn with wreckage. The storm smashed the Episcopal Church, wrecked a Thriftway Store, flattened other businesses, shops, and service stations, and heavily damaged two hundred homes. Cars and trucks lay bent, wrinkled, and crushed, as though a gigantic man had stepped on his toys.[117]

Hospital Administrator Charles Gray said although the tornado didn't injure the patients, it destroyed the lobby and front office. An employee nearly lost his arm when the wind slammed a door shut on him while he was helping to move a patient to the basement. Twenty-nine persons were injured, but there were no fatalities.

At 11:00 p.m. storm spotters south of town reported sighting another funnel heading for Clay Center. The sirens sounded again. Men roamed the streets in cars with loudspeakers blaring warnings. Everyone headed for their basements. Hospital employees moved patients again to places of safety. In one corner of the darkened hospital, Mrs. Lena Green gave birth to a healthy baby girl. By midnight the storm system passed without producing any new twisters for the ravaged city.

The storm continued to move to the northeast. At Hanover a tornado derailed a Union Pacific train, knocking twenty-three cars off the tracks. In the northeast part of town, a low rent housing unit, Highland Haven, lost its roof. The wind toppled the steeple of the Zion Lutheran Church, leaving debris scattered everywhere. Fortunately, there were no deaths or serious injuries reported.[118]

Such was not the case in other areas of Washington County. Near the little city of Linn, a tornado inflicted heavy damage to the town. Most of the residents knew nothing about the approaching storm, and no sirens sounded. Only a few people heard the warning on television and radio broadcasts.

A tornado struck the town at 7:05 p.m., entering on the southeast edge and leaving homes and businesses either completely destroyed or badly damaged. The funnel blew the Missouri Pacific depot off its foundation, which blocked the streets with debris. It gutted the *Linn Enterprise* newspaper building, twisting heavy steel beams as it tore the roof and walls away. The wind destroyed a creamery and wrecked the Rice-Johntz Lumber Company. The school suffered roof and window damage. Eight years earlier another smaller tornado pounded the same schoolhouse. The twister destroyed a car lot, post office, state bank, and feed store. While residents were coming out of cellars and assisting the injured, another storm appeared on the horizon, but this one went south of town.[119]

Another tornado dipped down from this storm system and headed straight for Greenleaf, where it killed two little girls, Angie Buhr and Harmylin Buhr. The family was in their basement when the house collapsed on top of them, and it took two hours for rescuers to find the bodies in the debris.

Tornado near Pomona, 1973

The tornado damaged or destroyed most of the town of Greenleaf. An ammonia tank ruptured, causing gas to escape, which forced the evacuation of the town until the leak could be repaired. The twister destroyed the new Greenleaf State Bank as well as numerous other businesses. It started north of the swimming pool and went straight north through town. The Co-op elevators were not touched, but the funnel twisted the adjoining buildings into distorted shapes. A gift shop, grocery store, beauty shop, lumberyard, funeral home, car dealership, garage, and motel became nothing more than a pile of bricks. The beauty shop was open less than two weeks. The Masonic Lodge was roofless, and several grain tanks at Greenleaf Grain and Feed were gone. The wind scattered debris all over the countryside and tossed pieces of tin around the cemetery.

This was one of the worst tornado outbreaks in North Central Kansas up to this time. Greenleaf had to be rebuilt, and the town chose a mall type concept for rebuilding the downtown area. [120]

The *Greenleaf Sentinel* remarked after the storm that, "We are sorry we're a day late, but due to the tornado, it was impossible to go to press any sooner."

HUTCHINSON, MAY 13, 1974

The people of Hutchinson realized they were lucky the night of May 13, 1974 when Reno County sheriff Jim Fountain retraced the path of the tornadoes. They made a two-mile swath from the Arkansas River to a point northeast of town.

A tornado struck four mobile homes at Victory Village, injuring five persons. Reverend Bill Cowell, the director of Victory Village, stated there were at least seventeen people inside four trailers when the storm hit. He said he did not actually see a tornado, but the force of the wind tossed one trailer up in the air.

High winds damaged buildings and trailers near the KTVH tower. One family's trailer disappeared. They suspected the tornado blew it into a deep farm pond located nearby. A tornado also struck the Municipal Airport, where it blew a Douglas DC-3 three-fourths of a mile down the runway and into a ditch. The air traffic controllers abandoned the control tower due to the high winds and their fear of window glass breakage.

At Partridge and Moundridge, residents reported high winds and funnel clouds aloft. South of Moundridge two tornadoes hit at different times— one around 6:00 p.m., and the second at 8:52 p.m. Their paths were extremely close. One neighbor was assisting another whose home had been destroyed, when the second tornado struck and demolished the home of the neighbor providing assistance.[121]

Sheriff Fountain, who saw at least a dozen tornadoes, said the whole system was moving in a circular direction.

EMPORIA, JUNE 8, 1974

On June 8, 1974 a tornado slammed into a shopping center, a mobile home park, and a residential area in Emporia, killing seven people and injuring eighty. Apparently the warning sirens sounded at the same time the tornado struck.

City Manager V.A. Basgall stated, "There just wasn't enough time." Five of the seven victims were residents of the Lincoln Village Trailer Park, and rescuers found another one in the debris of the Flint Hills Shopping Center.[122]

At the shopping center, the tornado unroofed the Woolworth Department Store and gutted the inside of the building, littering the mall with glass and rubble. In the pet department, the animals escaped from their cages and scurried around in what was left of the building. Mrs. Richard Gibbs was just leaving Woolworth's when she saw the twister. She immediately ran back inside the mall, yelling for everyone to take cover, but by then it was too late. A lathe fell on her, pinning her down on the floor.[123]

Eyewitnesses claimed there was no warning. Steve Saylor, manager of Walgreen's Drug Store on the mall, had just enough time to throw himself to the floor. He noted that, "There were people screaming and yelling with nothing to do." Most of the customers said they had only two or three seconds to react.

Milton Hinrich barely escaped injury when the wind blew him down the mall hallway. He ran inside a shoe store and jumped behind a counter for safety. Clothing flew over him, which he grabbed for protection.

People were wandering around the shopping center bleeding and crying, without any means of communication or transportation. The wind destroyed dozens of cars in the parking lot. Some were piled one on top of the other. About that time, the police ordered everyone out of the mall. One storeowner attempted to cart his cash registers out the door, but he was stopped and questioned before they would let him pass. Although rescuers did not find any bodies, one person dragged a mannequin from the debris, thinking it was a victim.

Across the street from the mall, the twister shook the Dolly Madison bakery plant, blowing away part of the roof and overturning the bakery trucks. The force of the wind literally sucked the cakes and cookies out the door. The tornado moved on through Jones Recreational Park and destroyed the West Side Baptist Church.

At the Lincoln Village Trailer Court, dubbed "Emporia's Finest," only one of the trailers was left intact. One of the residents stated, "I looked out the window when I heard it. I was in the bathroom and I took out running for the rec. center. There was no warning. There was just this big cloud."[124]

From her window, Ethel Cunningham saw the tornado coming. It was traveling an amazing speed of a hundred miles an hour. The air was full of debris. When she turned and opened the door of her mobile home, she was sucked outside and down behind the front step, which helped shield her from serious injury. Pieces of glass and metal pelted her arms and back. When it was over, the tornado had taken everything from her but her life. Margaret Martin also saw the tornado approaching and decided to make a run for the river. She barely made it. The death count at the mobile home park might have been higher, but it was Saturday night and few people were home.[125]

Just across the interstate from the mobile home park was the exclusive Country Club Heights neighborhood. The tornado hit a row of houses there, demolishing three and damaging many others. Tom and Anita Wright, who lost their home, said that first the wind blew hard from one direction, and then turned and blew even harder from another direction. Then the tornado struck. Fortunately they had enough time to go to the basement. After the tornado passed, they said the warning sirens sounded.

Dr. Melvin Dietrich was at home asleep in his easy chair when the tornado hit. He awoke when the front door shattered, and he escaped injury by crouching next to the fireplace. The wind blew Mrs. Dietrich down the basement steps. She landed on her head and shoulders. The storm lifted up the roof of their house, sucked out all their belongings, and then dropped the roof back down again. The Herschel Shepherd family had barely enough time to run for the basement when the tornado struck. Just as they hit the steps, the upstairs recreation room fell into the basement with them.

Outside a damaged house someone had raised an American flag. Its red, white and blue colors waved in the wind over broken glass and a red Volkswagen, which had been pushed into the side of the house.[126]

The twister knocked large holes into the sides of the Flint Hills Manor Nursing Home, breaking all the windows and seriously injuring several of the patients. Inside, glass and other debris littered the floor everywhere.

The tornado moved on to the Quesada Apartments. Dixie Wolfe saw the storm coming, so she ran to the bottom of the stairs and crouched in the corner. Then she tried to get into the building's crawl space, but it was locked, and she was pelted with glass and other debris. The wind blew one tenant's car into another tenant's living room. The whole apartment complex was badly damaged.

While initial cleanup efforts were underway, another tornado alert sounded. A storm spotter sighted a twister five miles southwest of Emporia. Fortunately, it lifted before hitting the community.

During the next few days, rescue and cleanup attempts were chaotic and curious onlookers hampered these efforts. Town leaders were not equipped to cope with the aftermath of such a destructive tornado. Within a few years after this storm, however, a group of volunteers composed of law enforcement officers and medical personnel organized into an efficient emergency preparedness group. When the next tornado struck in 1990, residents of Emporia were better prepared.

Some local legend foretold that any city located between two rivers would be spared tornado destruction. Using Emporia as an example, nothing could be further from the truth.[127]

One of the leading tornado experts to emerge in the last thirty years is Dr. T. Theodore Fujita. He is responsible for developing the tornado scale of intensity used by meteorologists today. Tornadoes vary in power and destructiveness. His scale goes from an F1 tornado—the least powerful, to an F5—a tornado whose destruction and power is devastating.

Only a few F5 tornadoes have occurred in Kansas, but the Andover tornado of 1991 was one of them. For a short time the Hesston tornado of 1990 was thought to be another one and it was considered the most powerful Kansas tornado of the 20th century. Since then, however, it has been downgraded to an F4.

Dr. Fujita did most of his research at the University of Chicago. He claims that tornadoes follow a 45-year cycle. In Kansas it tends to follow that pattern. He published his paper on the "cycle pattern" in 1975, and in it he suggests that tornado activity rotates clockwise throughout the country, with particular regions experiencing strong tornado outbreaks for six or seven years. Dr. Fujita later downplayed this cycle theory when there appeared to be too many variations to this pattern.[128] Map Available: Appendix 1.

MORTON, STEVENS COUNTIES, MAY 18, 1977

At least two tornadoes did extensive damage by destroying several farms in rural areas of Morton and Stevens Counties on May 18, 1977.

The twisters caught Kenny Sullivan out in his pickup truck, which the wind lifted up and dumped down on the road. Kenny jumped out of the vehicle and took refuge in a ditch. Nearby the tornado hurled his trailer house in the air and tossed it around a parked car. It split his furniture apart including the backs, sides, and drawers from an old antique dresser, a family heirloom.

An unusual incident occurred at the Wesley Schmidt farm. Earlier that day, the Schmidt's home caught fire, and although the blaze was brought under control in a matter of minutes, the place was a mess. Wesley moved his household goods to a trailer standing beside the house. Late that night when a tornado came through, it skipped over the burned out home and destroyed the trailer containing his salvaged belongings! This happened within fifteen minutes after he had transferred the last article. The only item left in the trailer in one piece was a toilet stool. Another tornado moved in a straight line from twelve miles south of Ulysses to Hickok seven miles east. Although at least thirty-five weather spotters were in the area at the time, no one sounded the warning sirens.

At Garden City spotters saw seven tornadoes and sounded the sirens at 8:15 p.m., but the "all-clear" was not heard until 10:45 p.m., over two hours later. Fortunately none of the funnels stayed on the ground for more than fifteen minutes, but there were quite a few of them, and they were everywhere. Several observers saw funnels form, dip for the ground, but not quite make it all the way down.

The storm system did not change as it moved east. Spotters saw several tornadoes dipping back and forth east of Topeka. A large tornado that could be seen for miles did significant damage near Lawrence.[129]

JACKSON COUNTY, MAY 31, 1978

A destructive tornado hit Jackson County late in the afternoon of May 31, 1978. A funnel was first sighted north of Louisville in Pottawatomie County, then near Emmett moving northeast towards Holton.

Three deaths occurred southwest of Holton when the twister demolished Edgar Larrison's mobile home. Larrison and his family had no warning of the storm, and they lived too far from town to hear the sirens. The family had just finished eating dinner when large hail began to fall. Then the trailer just blew apart. In Holton, the sale barn southeast of town suffered the most damage.

This tornado was part of a storm system that covered most of Northeast Kansas. One funnel injured several people and left a path of destruction twenty miles long and a half mile wide. This same storm derailed sixteen Union Pacific freight cars near Marysville. When the train's crew spotted the tornado heading for them, they stopped the train and ran for cover. The twister struck the 129 cars, tossing them in all directions.

A helicopter carrying a news crew from a Kansas City television station crashed near Onaga after filming scenes of the damage in the Holton and Marysville areas. The four persons on board were lucky, as they escaped with only minor cuts and bruises.[130]

THE MOST BIZARRE KANSAS TORNADO DISASTER

THE WHIPPOORWILL, JUNE 16, 1978

The passengers never saw it coming... or did they? That's the story behind the most bizarre of Kansas tornado disasters. The outcome was tragic—sixteen people died when the Whippoorwill took its last dinner cruise on

Pomona Reservoir. The 65-foot boat was loaded with forty-six passengers and thirteen crewmen intent upon enjoying dinner and a show. The cruiser just left the main cove and was heading for the deep channel when the passengers sat down to dinner and iced tea. "Dames at Sea," the musical comedy presentation, hadn't started yet, and the performers, known as the Vassar Players, were not in their costumes.

One passenger stated that he saw a tornado descend over the boat from the southwest at 7:10 p.m. Another witness said he saw three tornadoes. One was a large waterspout that formed just ahead of the boat, but it hung over the lake for some time before descending. The crew, who apparently spotted the funnel, tried to turn the boat around before it hit, but by then it was too late.

The boat capsized, knocking the passengers into the water. Flying debris and pieces of the hull injured them. Bill Shelton managed to hold on to the side of the boat and keep his head above water. His girlfriend, Barbara Hilmer, nearly drowned before pulling herself on top of the flat-bottomed craft, which was now bottom-side up. Only about three feet of the hull was actually out of the water. These two helped pull others to safety.

Two passengers, Lindsey and Viola Pherigo, could not remember whether anyone screamed, or how he and his wife got out of the boat. Viola stated that she was trapped underwater briefly when the boat capsized, but she fought her way free and up on top of the water.

Reverend Milton Vogel, his wife and four family members were on board celebrating the Vogel's 40th wedding anniversary. Of this group, only three survived. One, a nine-year-old-girl, was missing for twenty-four hours. Also on deck were Mike and Judy Patterson, who were celebrating their 5th wedding anniversary. Judy, who was eight months pregnant, drowned when the boat capsized. Four Emporia State University faculty members were also on board. Three of them drowned. Most of the people who died were seated on the upper deck, which meant they fell into the water first and were under the boat when it turned upside down.

Immediately after the disaster, boats from all over the lake came to assist in rescuing the passengers. Many were seriously injured and several were unconscious. Two more tornadoes appeared while rescue efforts were underway, but this did not dissuade anyone from helping the survivors. Underwater teams searched the capsized boat for bodies as some rescuers thought they heard voices coming from the hull. Later the teams gathered at the lake marina and made an attempt to compare the people they found to the passenger list, but some of the survivors who had made it to shore, ran for their cars and headed home. This made identification difficult.

Eventually the rescuers called tow trucks to the scene to pull the craft out of the water, which was a lengthy task that was accomplished slowly. With the help of a large flotilla of boats and dump trucks lashed to another row of trucks, they gradually brought the Whippoorwill back to shore.

Since that fateful and tragic evening, there has never been another "Show Boat" on Lake Pomona.[131] Map Available: Appendix 1.

CLAY COUNTY, OCTOBER 18, 1979

Before an autumn thunderstorm struck Clay County, the air was warm and heavy, like an August day, and the sky was a peculiar greenish color. That afternoon a small funnel formed near Idana, and then developed over the Clay Center Country Club, where three small tornadoes merged to become one large twister.

The most serious damage occurred at the Key Milling Company Egg Farm two miles east of Clay Center, where a tornado destroyed a two-story house, leveled five sheet-metal chicken houses, and injured four employees, one critically. Police officer Alan Longren arrived soon after the storm hit and learned that some of the frightened employees actually ran into the center of the tornado while trying to escape. The last person out of the mill was Christine Reed, who jumped into a culvert by a mailbox. Two farm workers described the twister as "big and black" and by this time the funnel was a quarter of a mile wide. The storm killed an estimated 100,000 chickens and demolished most of the farmstead.[132]

Virtus Haws described the tornado, "it was moving extremely fast," he said, "Dirt was going everywhere. It kept getting bigger and bigger, and darker and darker." A mobile home owned by Don Martin virtually disappeared. Ironically, members of the Martin family were all in the hospital following an automobile accident and escaped the destruction of the storm.

The tornado moved east to the Manhattan area, where it injured fifteen people and caused $1,000,000 in property damage. A furrowing house collapsed on a farm near Louisville, injuring four persons. Three tornadoes formed in the area of Leonardville, dropped to the ground and then lifted back into the clouds. The residents saw five other funnels aloft. The lightning was so intense that observers said it resembled an aerial bombardment. Lightning struck and burned a hay barn at Kansas State University. A direct hit by lightning at the Jeffrey Energy Center shut the generator down for two hours.

In Jackson County near Holton, the sound of the storm was deafening. According to Mrs. Gerald Lierz, the noise was so loud, "I had to hold my hands over my ears. You couldn't breathe." On the outskirts of town a twister damaged an airplane and a hanger, an implement store, the construction site of BMB, and the Holton Livestock Exchange Barn. The wind ripped the roof off the Fireside Lanes bowling alley and the Jolly Troll restaurant south of the city.

Again, people complained, especially in Holton, that they had no warning. The civil defense directors said they relied on the weather spotters who were out but didn't see the funnel until it was too late. Thus, the siren never sounded.[133]

CHAPTER SIX: RECENT EVENTS, 1980-2008

The decade of the 1980s was a stark contrast to the previous three decades, which were characterized by mild weather and above average precipitation. With the eruption of the Mt. St. Helens volcano in 1980, the climate dramatically changed to one that was warmer and drier than normal. In fact the 1980s could be described as hot and arid, resulting in fewer storms, especially severe storms. As late as 1988 and 1989, the number of tornadoes seen in Kansas fell far below the average. Unfortunately, this trend did not last. By 1990 and throughout the decade of the '90s, the climate took several strange twists that resulted in more severe weather, including two notable tornadoes that brought an end to a period of relatively quiet climatic conditions. As t-shirts proclaimed after the tornado that destroyed much of Hesston, "Gee Toto, I think we're back in Kansas."

The first four years of the 1990s threatened to break all weather records. Just through June, eighty-five tornadoes were sighted in Kansas, a figure more than double the average. By late August temperatures were as high as 110 degrees, and it was so dry that water rationing occurred in Wichita.

The severe weather changes that occurred in 1990 could be blamed on sun spots as solar activity fluctuates in cycles every eleven years, or on El Nino, which is a sharp increase in ocean temperatures off the coast of Chile that correlates with the way the jet stream moves, or the greenhouse effect. All three could be blamed. The changes were also in time with Dr. Fujita's "cycle effect."[1]

Weather forecasting had many new technological breakthroughs in the 1990s. However, severe weather was difficult to forecast more than twenty-four hours in advance with any degree of accuracy, and skillful forecasts were necessary to cover large areas, i.e. parts of Kansas, Oklahoma, and North Texas. The broadcasting of tornado watches became more menacing in their descriptions. For example, the National Weather Service predicted the 1991 tornado that hit Andover would be bad; verbiage that day indicated that "this is an especially dangerous situation with the potential to cause very damaging tornadoes."[2]

Doppler radar, an elaborate radar system used to measure the relative velocity of a storm and the radar target, made its appearance during the last twenty years. The operation of radar is based on the Doppler frequency shift in the target echo and is proportionate to the radial component of target velocity.[3]

LAWRENCE, JUNE 19, 1981

A potentially devastating tornado struck Lawrence on June 19, 1981, when a funnel descended without warning and moved through southwest Lawrence, killing one person and injuring thirty-three others.

The twister demolished the south end of K-Mart on Iowa Street. About a hundred customers and workers were in the store at the time. Stanley Pittman, a K.U. computer assistant working in the store, died when falling debris crushed him. The manager told everyone to move to the back of the store, but only a few made it. The rest fell to the floor when the tornado hit. The storm only lasted thirty seconds.

The Jim Clark Motor Company suffered $500,000 in business and vehicle losses when the twister picked up the sales office and dumped it on the other side of the street.

The tornado struck the Prairie Meadows residential area and the Gaslight Village Mobile Home Park, injuring twenty-nine people. The residents had no warning. The spotter who first saw the funnel was flipped over in his car as he was reporting it. The total occupancy of the mobile home court was around 1,200, but many of them were away at the time. Sue Ann Magana was in her trailer when the storm hit, "I saw it start blowing and knew things were bad. I didn't know what to do. I knew it wasn't safe outside, but I didn't think it was safe inside either. I took my daughter and we hid in the hall under a heavy piece of furniture."[4]

Gene Schimmel said the storm sounded like a low-pitched siren and his trailer started twitching like "a train going through a tunnel," then shifted off its foundation. Trent Booth was caught by surprise and took refuge under a pine tree during the storm, barely escaping injury. All five of the Mike Reese family crouched in spaces that afforded little protection, but when the trailer split apart and disintegrated, none of them were hurt.

Jim Schwada and Rick Hessmeyer barely escaped from Kuehn's Liquor Store, where they were working. They stated they had no warning at all and had two seconds to get out of the building. They crouched behind a brick wall and stayed there until the storm abated. Collin Hermreck, a clerk at the Commerce Plaza Gas and Mini-Mart, ran to a cooler in the back of the store just as the building collapsed. After the tornado passed, he and four customers were trapped in the debris for about thirty minutes; otherwise they were unhurt.

Three of the seriously injured were from two families who sought shelter outdoors when the storm struck. Kate Stires, her son Kelly, and Pam Studebacker were injured when they fled from their car during the storm. Kate, who became separated from her son, was buried under some debris.

The high wind blew her son into some rubble. Both had cuts and abrasions but were not seriously hurt.

Many people criticized the meteorologists for not sounding the sirens ahead of time, but the storm intensified too quickly for them to react. Large hail also hit all over town, causing extensive damage and power outages. The storm moved towards Eudora but lost its intensity as it went east.

It was some time before folks in South Lawrence recovered from this storm.[5]

SHAWNEE COUNTY, JULY 19, 1981

A tornado the National Weather Service said shouldn't have developed ripped the roofs off two houses six miles north of Topeka on July 19, 1981. No one was killed, but nine people were injured.

Radar showed a heavy thunderstorm in the area. Rich McNulty, meteorologist, said, "Initially, it sounded like strong winds (caused damage) . . . but we've concluded it must have been a tornado. It came down and just hit those houses and went back up into the clouds very quickly. It came down far enough to lift the roofs. Whether it touched the ground is questionable."

The Larry Repp family and four visitors were sitting at the dining room table drinking coffee, when the ceiling fell in on them, covering them with insulation. "We heard a loud swoosh and the roof fell in," Larry said.

Ronald and Kathy Sheley were still in bed when the tornado knocked down a garage wall and ripped the roof from their house. The oldest son, Andy, was in the living room and stated he watched as ceiling insulation dropped, coating the sliding glass door, followed by a loud boom. Sheley said the family was alert enough to dash for the basement, but the tornado was gone by the time they reached safety. "It took five seconds and it was over," he said.[6]

SOUTHEAST KANSAS, MARCH 15, 1982

More than a dozen tornadoes cut a deadly swath through Southeast Kansas on March 15, 1982, killing three people and causing $100,000 damage.

The worst twister surged into Mulberry, killing Judith James and leaving the town looking "like a war zone." Crawford County Sheriff Lynn Fields said, "I've been here since '55 and this is the worst one I've ever seen. It was a big son of a gun. Looking at it, you couldn't see anything but it. It sounded like a freight train."

In the Cherokee County town of Hallowell, Ruby Hamlin died. County authorities said the tornado destroyed three houses and left six other people injured.

At Mulberry, Eddie Beard was watching television with his family when the program was interrupted by a weather bulletin that may have saved their lives. A tornado warning prompted Beard and his family to take a blanket and a flashlight and huddle under a kitchen table until the storm passed. The twister that ripped through the town picked up Beard's house and dropped it in the street. "God protected my family," he said.

A tornado roared through Tyro eleven miles west of Coffeyville, killing Carl Thomison. The storm destroyed or damaged a dozen buildings before heading out of town.

Another tornado skipped along the east edge of Woodson County through northwest Allen County and on into Anderson County just before dusk. Most of the damage centered on Piqua, where a funnel swept down out of an ominous black cloud and bent the cross on top of St. Martin's Catholic Church parallel with the ground. The Knights of Columbus Hall sustained significant damage from parts of buildings, chunks of tin, and other debris that the twister picked up and slammed into the building. Kenny Small, employee of Farmers Co-op, said the wind pulled tin loose from the elevator and tore bricks from the top of the old Piqua bank building, caving in one wall. Small said, "It's strange some of the things that happen in a storm. A transformer held up by a double set of poles was knocked down. Trees right beside it weren't damaged at all.

Near Iola a tornado caused severe damage at the Don Kessinger farmstead. Miles Kessinger said, "We didn't have a minute's warning. It came with a roar like a freight train and the next thing we knew the living room was full of sparks and smoke." When the chimney fell, wind roared down the stack, forcing smoke and burning wood into the room.

A violent storm swept through Woodson County producing tornadic winds that left a path of destruction a half mile wide near Yates Center. The storm was part of the same system that swept an eleven county area in Southeast Kansas and spawned thirteen tornado sightings.

A tornado blew across the southeast corner of Greenwood County damaging twenty to twenty-five cabins and mobile homes in Vaughn's Acres, a settlement on the northwest edge of Fall River Reservoir. It cut a strip two blocks wide and a mile long through the settlement before dissipating.

Eddie Beard of Mulberry observed, "Just be thankful for what you've got and realize it is possible for this to happen to anyone."[7]

SILVER LAKE, EFFINGHAM, APRIL 26, 1984

There were some close calls at Silver Lake when a tornado touched down one mile west of town, scattering a house for a mile and injuring two children.

Jim Thomas was watching television and his two children were asleep, when Thomas heard a noise at the back of the house. He went to check, and the tornado stopped him right in his tracks. Suddenly the house, teetering on its foundation, collapsed around him. Something had torn away his shirt and punctured his back. He began to search for the children and kicked open their bedroom door, but "There was nothing there. All that was there was the floor." About twenty feet from the house he found his daughter, but he still couldn't find his son.

The desperate search for the boy lasted for nearly an hour. Finally, as Jim ran into the field yelling for him, he heard a reply. The boy was lying in debris about a quarter of a mile east of the demolished house. "He was just covered up with mud," Jim said. "All you could see were the whites of his eyes."

The night was still not over. On the way to the hospital, Jim and the children were involved in a car accident. Medical personnel treated the family for numerous lacerations and released them. Not only did Jim lose a home, but he also lost a pickup, a Mercury Cougar, and a camping trailer.

Jack and Peggy Gregert were lucky. He had just finished a shower while she worried about all the wind and the rattling of the back door. When Jack emerged, he walked through the kitchen and into an enclosed back porch. Just as he put his hand on the doorknob, the tornado wrecked the porch. "It happened so fast— just boom, and I hit the floor and it was over with," Jack said. "It was like a great big blast, like you had opened a door and it hit you." He escaped with painful cuts on his head and hands.

Jack Metz, sheriff's deputy, said the Silver Lake tornado arrived without warning. "One of the guys out here said, "It hit so fast we didn't have a chance to go anywhere."

About 9:30 p.m., residents of Hoyt saw a funnel dip from the clouds, causing damage to homes and businesses. The worst damage occurred in the center of town where at least five of the city's businesses lost storefronts.

Rob McManus said that although the tornado sirens sounded, he and his family "stayed upstairs in their home and watched for tornadoes, although it was too dark to see anything." He said when the winds "gusted up", they headed for the basement. Several minutes later they emerged to find their house was gone.

Wade Hinman said he was listening to the severe storm warnings on television, and when he looked out a back window, he saw water being sucked out of the pond not far from the house. By the time Hinman gathered his three children together, the windows were already breaking. With no time to run to the storm shelter, he put the children on the bedroom floor, lay on top of them and waited. Within minutes, the storm slammed into the farmhouse. "We finally looked around and the whole north wall was gone and part of the east wall. There wasn't any great amount of sound. It was just the wind."

In Hoyt approximately a third of the homes sustained damage. The mayor, who credited the city's storm spotters for preventing further injuries, said the sirens had completed their cycle by the time the tornado passed through town. "They (the storm spotters) said definitely two and possibly three funnels were in the Hoyt area."

The storm system continued moving northeast until it struck Effingham in Atchison County, injuring Dale Gaddis, his daughter Dawn, and demolishing their mobile home. Rescuers found Dawn underneath a clothes dryer in the middle of the street thirty feet from her home.

The tornado cut a two-block wide path through the west half of town and the business district, damaging nearly every building. It destroyed eight mobile homes, damaged thirteen houses, six businesses, the high school, the Effingham Middle School, and the grade school.

Don Kloepper was among forty people at the Corner Bar downtown when the tornado struck. "The front door was open. You could hear the wind and the hail. Someone said, 'She's coming.' People got under the counters at the back of the tavern and four of us got under the pool table before the tornado hit."

The town's electronically controlled warning system didn't sound because the power was knocked out before anyone saw the tornado.

That night Jim Thomas of Silver Lake watched as lightning lit the northeastern sky and the storm moved away. Good riddance, he thought.[8]

WICHITA, APRIL 29, 1984

In the same week as the Silver Lake storms, tornadoes and violent winds whipped through Sedgwick County, causing scattered property damage. Storm spotters saw seven tornadoes on the ground and at least twenty funnel clouds in the air. "We can only guess how many we had, but it was easily more than twenty," weather service forecaster Frank Hanson stated. "Even where they weren't seen, there are numerous places where there was damage from down bursts of wind."

Meteorologist Larry Schultz said Sedgwick County was hit by two waves of tornadoes that originated in Oklahoma. "This is typical for this time of year," Schultz said. "It was probably a little unusual in the sense of getting so many sightings." Tornadoes were on the ground in four separate places in Wichita in the morning. In the afternoon, spotters saw them four miles southeast of Haysville, at Rose Hill, and at Cook Field where high winds blew the roofs off hangers.

The most serious damage occurred at the Pleasant Valley Mobile Home Park. Jackie Pepper heard a sound "like a jet was going to land on top of my house. I looked out the kitchen window and the cloud was black on top, and underneath it was red, like a sunset. The radio announcer said 'Take cover. We're not kidding.' I picked up my two dogs and dove into the bathtub." Pepper said her home shook "like a roller coaster. All I could think of was, Dear God, let this thing lift! I feel like I'm awful fortunate. Believe me, awful fortunate."

The whine of the tornado sirens began just as the Rev. James Murray started his Sunday morning sermon. As the skies darkened, the eighty people in the church strained to look out the stained glass windows. After telling the worshipers they could move to shelter, Murray kept on preaching, saying later he "felt like the captain who wouldn't leave the ship." He said, "They weren't really listening but at least they didn't sleep through the sermon."[9]

Reverend Murray said a few people immediately moved to the church basement. As the storm worsened, others, including the choir, went downstairs. Without the choir, Murray had to give up the final hymn, which was "May Faith Looks Up to Thee O Lord." "We didn't get that far," said Murray.

CARBONDALE, OCTOBER 31, 1984

A tornado on Halloween night struck just north of Carbondale, killing five people and injuring ten. The National Weather Service did not sound the sirens because they didn't see the tornado on radar and they had no report of one before it struck.

The twister first caused damage near Scranton, and then it skipped across the county, striking the Mineral Springs Trailer Court. Norman DeForest was crushed when he ran from his mobile home to find cover in a shed, which collapsed on him. Edith Rogers was in her home across the highway from the court when the tornado struck. An emergency worker on the scene said the house "looked like a bomb" had hit it. Rescuers found Edith's body in a ditch 150 yards from her home.

A young couple survived unscathed when their mobile home rolled over and flew to pieces. Ray Barnes and Tanya Pearson said they had not installed anchors to the foundation because they thought the tornado season was over. Barnes managed to crawl under a bed when the tornado struck; he wound up atop the debris. Pearson held onto a couch before landing out on the grass.

Three miles north of the trailer court the storm wrecked the residence of Robert and Deanna Renyer. Deanna said when she tried to shut the front door she discovered that she could not because of the suction. On her third attempt, the wind blew her ten feet back into the room and off her feet. Since she was near a table, she crawled underneath and waited. "I didn't even know we were in a tornado watch," she said.

Meanwhile Renyer took shelter under a truck in one of the garages that lost its windows and doors. The second garage was "lifted up off the foundation and thrown north into the pasture. When it dropped, it must have just exploded," he said. Despite the damage, Deanna said, "It didn't seem to me like the wind was blowing that hard. I don't think the tornado actually came down. I think we just got the suction from it. I wasn't scared. I didn't panic. I just tried to get out of the way of the glass."

Three members of a Topeka engineering firm were killed when the small plane they were in crashed in a farm field a mile north of Carbondale. That brought to five the number of people killed during the storm. Sheriff Robert Masters said, "As far as we're concerned the crash was storm-related. We can't see that it's anything else."

Richard Billings, who lived near Carbondale, "heard a big noise. I thought a car had wrecked in my yard. It sounded like a car rolling. I heard the loud thuds," Billings said. "I couldn't find it. I stepped outside, saw a tornado coming and said 'To hell with it.'" He sought shelter. "The tornado's tail was whipping back and forth. It was loud. There was a freight train coming with it," he said, referring to the storm.

The next morning Billings located the plane wreckage and reported it to the Osage County Sheriff's Department.[10] Map Available: Appendix 1.

NORTH CENTRAL KANSAS, MAY 10, 1985

A "super thunderstorm cell" spawned sixteen tornadoes as it marched its way across four counties. Classified by the National Weather Service as "the biggest storm in this area in 24 years," monstrous clouds tumbled ominously along a sixty-five mile path. Touching down, spinning back into the air, a tornado hedgehopped its way across county after county. The first funnel was reported near Cedar Bluff Reservoir in Ness County and then reappeared west of Ellis. The storm moved to southwest Rooks County and then hit the Phillips County line.

In Stockton a tornado alert sounded for the first time. The people who had basements or storm cellars took cover, but most of the others just stood around waiting for the storm to hit. The authorities at nearby Webster Lake alerted the campers to clear the area and go into Stockton to the courthouse shelter. Some did and some didn't, and those who did were dismayed to find the keys to the shelter were not available. There was no damage at the lake area and the closest the tornado came to Stockton was ten miles away.

Before the storm dissipated, it crossed Highway 36 and overturned monuments and uprooted trees in the old Dixon Cemetery north of Gretna. The tornado reformed eight miles north of Agra and completely devastated a four mile area nearly a mile wide. Homes were flattened, outbuildings torn apart, machinery scattered, and cattle turned into statues covered with mud.

Sheriff LeRoy Stephen said, "There were at least 15 tornadoes on the ground in the space of an hour… It was fortunate that none of the towns were hit, or the disaster would have been much worse."

The storm reached its peak at the Molzahn and Rathert farms north of Agra. Louis Molzahn decided to stay in his mobile home unless the storm increased in intensity, but when the skirting on his trailer blew off, he knew he had waited too long. "I felt it tremble and begin to rise, but I don't remember anything else until some men helped me into a car," he said. The wind pushed him into the ditch at the side of the road where rescuers found him standing up, plastered with mud, holding a 2 x 4 for a crutch.

The tornado completely demolished the Kenneth Molzahn place. He just finished an improvement program. "I have been expanding my operations, and my buildings were all complete. Now they are gone. I'm back to square one," he said. Kenneth, his wife and son James took refuge in the basement. "I put James on the floor and laid down on him. He didn't make a sound. Janet pulled sleeping bags over us. It seemed like the storm just kept churning forever."

The tornado ripped the roof off the Harvey Rathert home, dropped the chimney into the bedroom, and caused damage to such an extent that it is beyond repair. "I'm not sure what we will do at our age (85)," he said. At the Errol Rathert home, the tornado left only the foundation. The family lost all their clothes, furniture, and personal possessions, these items were "rolled up in a ball at the base of a tree" on the other side of the road. "We went to the basement when the storm came," Errol said, but a neighbor disagreed. "They were standing by the side of the road when we came along, he was holding their dog in his arms, but as far as we could tell, they had nothing else left."

The storm system moved into Nebraska where it lost its severity and dissipated.[11]

BUTLER COUNTY, JULY 5, 1987

A violent thunderstorm packing 100 mile per hour winds howled through Central Kansas, spawning tornadoes that smashed buildings in Douglass and tossed 130 camping trailers and boats around El Dorado Lake. About twenty-five campers suffered bumps and bruises.

Two tornadoes struck in Butler County, damaging at least twelve buildings in Douglass and three houses in Rose Hill. Cheryl Moore, a clerk at a Kwik-Mart in Douglass said, "The electricity went off, my ears started popping, and I could see insulation flying around. I hit the floor where I was at, and the roof just left. It just took off!"

Neighbors rescued Chad Stover, who lived behind the store, after the tornado trapped him in his home. Chad said, "I saw the one little twister with the fire going around in it. It's just like you hear people say: it sounds just like a train… It just happened so fast. Everything was everywhere."

At El Dorado Lake, winds snapped the steel cables that anchored a 200-boat dock at Shady Creek Marina. Fourth of July campers sought cover as high winds hit the water, causing what some campers described as a hurricane. When the rain came, you couldn't see a thing, just a solid wall of water," said Dave Piper. "After it kind of let up, we looked over and saw trailers on their ends and on their sides."

A widespread storm system caused damage near Ottawa, Great Bend, Winfield, and Junction City where lightning struck the old St. Joseph Catholic Church's bell tower, damaging the limestone structure.

Meteorologist Mike Smith described the storm as the worst in South Central Kansas since 1981.[12]

THE SOUND AND FURY

TORNADOES IN THE SPRING OF 1990

Reminiscent of the storm outbreaks of the late 1940s and early 1950s, the year 1990 can best be described as terrifying. Spotters reported seeing twenty-two tornadoes through March 13th. The first sighting was in Reno County on March 11. On March 12, the National Weather Service recorded seventeen reports of hail and windstorms in northeast Kansas.

When a tornado struck Topeka just before midnight on the 12th, Stan and Patty Grewing were asleep. Stan remarked, "I woke up as the house was coming apart. I was trying to run to the kid's rooms when the house just exploded." Patty fell through the floor into the garage below. In fact, Patty and the waterbed both ended up on top of the family car. The twister destroyed three homes and damaged twenty-five others in Shawnee County.

The tornado wrecked the Shawnee Heights United Methodist Church and the administration building for the Shawnee Heights School District. The media also reported damage in McLouth, where the path of this tornado was a hundred yards wide. The twister was about eight feet off the ground when it removed the roof from a school supply warehouse. The next morning residents of the Shawnee Heights area and McLouth surveyed the damage. Little did they know then what havoc the afternoon would unleash on other Kansans!

Later that day the Hesston tornado struck and caused wide-scale devastation.[13]

HESSTON, MARCH 13, 1990

On Tuesday, March 13th, the day started out windy, humid and unseasonably warm. At 9:30 a.m. the National Weather Service issued a tornado watch for Central Kansas, an unusually early time for a tornado watch, which was in effect from 10:00 a.m. to 10:00 p.m.

The first sighting that day was at 4:14 p.m., when a tornado touched down in Reno County two miles from Pretty Prairie, advancing northeast at forty miles an hour. The funnel was moving so fast it caught Bill Rogers by surprise. Having no time to reach his storm cellar, he stood in the hallway of his house. After the storm passed, he surveyed the damage and discovered his machine shed, barn, grain bins, and outbuildings were completely gone. At another farm Henry Berndsen not only saw his house disappear, but also his garage and the vehicles inside.

Hesston tornado roaring through town

The tornado moved rapidly from Pretty Prairie to a point between Yoder and Haven, damaging farms and outbuildings. Then the twister struck the town of Burrton, killing Lucas Fisher, 6 years old. A chimney collapsed on him, breaking his neck. The house just fell apart, trapping the Fisher family in the basement.

The Bontrager family decided to outrun the tornado instead of going to the basement. This decision saved their lives. When they returned, their house had disappeared and a trailer was upside down in their basement.

Caroline Haines jumped out of her truck near Yoder when she saw the tornado heading directly towards her. She took refuge in a ditch and watched as two funnels whipped down out of the clouds, just missing her by a hundred feet.

Near Yoder, Polly Fry noticed a big dark cloud to the southwest, but decided to go on with her evening chores. When the siren sounded, she saw the black cloud was only about a half mile away. "It sounded like a freight train," Fry noted, "and stuff was boiling around in it. I was going to get in the southwest corner of the basement, but I didn't want the shelves of canned fruit to fall on me… I felt like my head was going to explode, and I can't describe the sound. It was just awful! I heard a pop— and then it got so dusty I could hardly breathe. I think that's probably when the house was lifted and set back down."[14]

Enormous Hesston tornado roaring down the highway

Dean Eales said although he had seen many tornadoes, he was overwhelmed by the Hesston storm. "This one never made any attempt to raise or get off the ground. It looked like it was a shy half-mile wide. It was ungodly."

It only took Toby and Wilma Royer a few minutes to get the family to the basement, where they knelt down and covered their children with their bodies. Although the tornado destroyed their house and plastered mud on everything around them, they weren't hurt. Lynn and Kathy Geffert thought the storm looked like just a rain cloud. However, when they heard the sound of a freight train they realized it was a tornado. Lynn was convinced the twister was going to miss them until a blast of wind blew out the windows. The first wind gust was followed by a few seconds of relative calm, and then came a second and much stronger gust. When the Geffers crawled out of the wreckage, they found the entire house swept away.[15]

This photo shows how enormous the Hesston, Kansas tornado really was.

The tornado was enormous when it moved into Harvey County. It was not your typical funnel. It was not narrow at the bottom and not pointed at the bottom of the vortex. It was a huge cloud hugging the ground generating 200 mile per hour winds. At the Kenneth Stucky farm, a twister destroyed the house and garage for the third time. The first was in 1942 and the second in 1974. Both times the tornado spared the house, but this time it did not.

At 5:00 p.m. when the National Weather Service predicted the tornado was headed for Hesston, the city sounded the sirens. This tornado was the first major Kansas twister covered extensively by amateur photographers with camcorders. Townspeople took pictures of the storm from every angle. By 5:25 p.m., when the tornado came roaring through town, the people with video cameras stopped filming. Now it was time to take cover.

At 5:30 p.m. the tornado cut a wide swath across the city, injuring thirteen people. Hesston looked like a war zone. Cars were scattered and wrecked, and all that was left of houses were concrete slabs and basements. Fortunately, the funnel missed a nursing home, retirement center, trailer court, and Hesston College. Within fifteen minutes, the twister damaged half of Hesston, killing one person and leaving at least 300 people homeless.

City Councilman Bob Davis and his family sought refuge in their basement and survived. His daughter Melissa noted that, "there was a brief calming, and then the wind came up suddenly. Parts of our ceiling were falling, and one part even hit me on the back. I tried to close my ears with my fingers and screamed really bad. Then a sound like dynamite filled the air, and our windows blew out."[16]

After the tornado passed, people emerged one by one from the rubble. Fifteen people poured out of the Pizza Hut, where they had found shelter in the walk-in cooler. The employees continued to make pizzas up to the last minute. At the Heritage Inn Hotel, twelve people huddled together in the hallway, which saved their lives.

The immensity of this storm took many residents awhile to comprehend. Despite the warnings and the changing weather conditions, the tornado caught them by surprise. They believed it was just another false alarm. Mildred Martens was shocked when she suddenly realized she was walking over broken glass and splintered wood in her bare feet. Martens noted, "I looked down and said, 'I don't have any shoes.'"[17] Within minutes a neighbor gave her the pair of shoes she would wear for the next two weeks.

Shortly after the tornado swept through the city, emergency crews were on the scene. The Mennonite Disaster Service helped tremendously— the Whitestone Mennonite Church in Hesston founded the organization. Other volunteers, trained to help in natural disasters, arrived by the busload from as far away as Pennsylvania and Canada. Governor Mike Hayden toured the region and declared eight counties disaster areas, clearing the way for federal assistance. Nearly $25,000,000 damage was done in Harvey County. Of this amount $22,000,000 was in the city of Hesston.

J. Pat Kearney, who took pictures of the storm as it passed through town, put his best photo on a T-shirt with the slogan, "Toto, we're back in Kansas." Kearney sold the popular shirts and donated part of the profits to the relief effort.[18]

As usual the tornado revealed certain oddities. Milt Miller found a pair of trousers hanging from a tree, still encased nicely in a cleaner bag. Kirk Alliman emerged from the ruins of his home to hear the sound of a ringing telephone. His mother was calling to find out if he was all right. Someone discovered a Hesston street sign in Riley County, some sixty miles away.

As the storm left Hesston, two small funnels merged to become a massive F5 tornado, striking the home of Isaac and Esther Ratzlaff. The family ran to the basement when they heard the howl of the wind and the sound of breaking glass. The twister claimed another farmhouse and the Ratzlaff's never rebuilt. They retired to Goessel.[19]

The tornado approached Goessel, where the tragic story of Harold and Ruth Voth unfolds. When Ruth visited her husband at the Newton Medical Center that afternoon, they talked about life and death. Harold was recovering from cancer surgery and he wanted to prepare Ruth for widowhood in case the surgery was unsuccessful. When Ruth went home to Goessel late that afternoon, she evidently didn't see the gigantic cloud headed in her direction before she died. Rescuers found Ruth's body along the road, surrounded by many of the things she and Harold owned. The home they had shared for thirty years was gone. After Harold was released from the hospital, he put a mobile home on the foundation of their house, but his stay there was limited. Six months later he passed away.

Ernest and Agnes Bina, who lived a mile northeast of Pilsen, heard the tornado warnings, but dismissed them as just another storm. A half hour later, the twister bore down on them, demolishing their house and damaging most of their possessions, except for the wall full of family photos it left untouched. Ernest was seriously ill with cancer. He died exactly three months after the tornado.

Mark Strand was fishing at Herington Reservoir when a 2 x 4 splashed into the water beside him. Looking up, he saw shingles, insulation, popcorn sacks, and other junk fall into the lake. When he returned the next day, he found a bank deposit slip from Burrton and a photograph of a woman and her child. Strand said the shower of odds and ends descended twenty minutes ahead of the storm.

Residents at Tampa, southwest of Herington, reported seeing debris falling to the ground for several days. Pat Vogt remembered a piece of tablecloth and other household items descending from the sky just as the radio reported that the tornado was in Hesston. A church paper containing Ruth Voth's name and address ended up at Helen Schwartzman's home in Tampa. Some items belonging to a business in Hesston landed on the hospital and airport grounds at Manhattan.[20]

The tornado missed Herington by a few miles, which was fortunate because their sirens were not working. A tornado passed near White City, tearing up fences and power lines, and it damaged several homes near Dwight. Another twister that day touched down in Wamego at 8:00 p.m. At that time, there were fifty other tornadoes on the ground in Texas, Oklahoma, Nebraska, Missouri, and Iowa. This was an incredible tornado outbreak.

The Hesston tornado was on the ground for two and a half hours, and it stayed there for more than a hundred miles. Its average width was three-fourths of a mile. The two deaths recorded in March were the earliest in the year on record for Kansas. The previous date for early deaths was March 15th. Meteorologist Mike Smith of Weather Data, Inc. noted that the F5 Hesston tornado may have been the most intense tornado ever recorded in Kansas.[21]

Another tornado that night hit the Burrton-McPherson area, destroying several homes. This one zigzagged, thus sparing some houses and demolishing others. Many residents were home that evening watching on TV the horrifying events at Hesston, and they weren't aware that the same chaos was about to descend on them. Since there was no warning, they had only a few seconds to seek shelter. Marla and Bret Gillmore had just enough time to take cover under a stairwell in the basement, which was a smart move. Nothing was left of the house but the stairwell. Several people found Marla's wedding pictures, ripped from an album, and returned them from various parts of the county. Nine families lost their homes in McPherson that night. This F3 twister was about one-fourth mile wide and contained winds in excess of 200 miles per hour. It dissipated a few miles south of McPherson, but its path extended for about fifteen miles.

So, little loss of life in Hesston was due to an advanced warning system. Emergency sirens sounded three times, and storm spotters in the area kept the public informed. After the tornado passed, the ham radio operators kept busy coordinating assistance. For days afterwards, the Mennonites, whose aid was invaluable, helped the people stricken and left homeless. They also provided financial support to the victims.[22] Map Available: Appendix 1.

ELLIS COUNTY, APRIL 25, 1990

At 6:30 p.m. on April 25, 1990, residents of Ellis County faced down a large tornado that destroyed a dozen farms in the area. Although the twister formed in northern Ness County, most of the damage occurred from Dodge City to Smith Center. The National Weather Service reported four funnels on the ground at the same time; their combined path was over 120 miles long.

Some people heard the sound of a freight train. Others only heard the sound of breaking glass. The David Seibel family sought refuge in the basement while the tornado ripped the roof off the house, overturned their trucks, and uprooted trees. Dennis and Sharon Bittel lost everything when a funnel destroyed their house. The next day they spent hours scouring nearby fields for their belongings. Their friends, who had a metal detector, successfully located Sharon's wedding rings. In Phillips County, eighty miles away, someone found a few of their favorite photographs, which had been blown there by the wind.

Frank Slaughter, whose residence was slightly damaged, found truckloads of other people's possessions in his wheat field— including dishwashers, refrigerators, furniture, and bicycles. The tornado twisted these things like pretzels, and some were barely recognizable. The only item he found in one piece was a shoe.[23]

CENTRAL KANSAS, MAY 24, 1990

A huge thunderstorm in Barton County on the evening of May 24, 1990, caused the formation of a half dozen tornadoes that damaged forty farms in six counties. Spotters sighted the first tornado two miles northeast of Hoisington. It then moved through Ellsworth, Rice, and McPherson Counties, causing $6,000,000 in damage. Fortunately no large towns were affected by the storm, and the only injuries were to a Claflin woman and four oil field workers.

Ida Gasaway hid in a closet from the storm, but she suffered a broken foot when the tornado blew her out in the yard. The high winds ripped all the carpeting off the floors and carried a bathtub a half-mile away. No one ever found Ida's refrigerator. A mile from her home, the tornado derailed 87 freight cars on a train headed westward. The engineer and conductor, who saw the storm coming but didn't see the twister, were confident that the wind couldn't derail the train. They were wrong.

Debbie and Mike Urban were in a cemetery mowing grass when the sky turned dark and threatening. They decided to outrun the storm in their trucks, but when the high winds hit, they tried to jump out of their vehicles. The wind tore the doors off Debbie's truck and sucked her out of the cab. Later, she remembered being airborne and running, but not touching the ground. Mike attempted to reach Debbie, but he blacked out. When he regained consciousness, he was shielding her body with his own. As they lay in the ditch watching the debris fly over their heads, a deer sailed by four feet off the ground. After the storm, they found their pickups half a mile down the road.

Between Bushton and Holyrood the tornado lifted the Frees house off its foundation. Karma Frees later remarked, "The first big sound I remember was the stairs. We're sitting under the stairs, and I heard this big creaking, and the stairs just went, just rose up. I could see them leave, and at that point the kids started screaming. I thought we were gone at that point."[24]

Four oil workers north of Bushton spotted the tornado and tried to out run it. That was a mistake; rescuers had to cut them out of their wrecked car.

Another tornado traveled a path on the river road between Marquette and Lindsborg. The sirens sounded at Marquette when spotters saw the twister southwest of town. Both towns survived without any damage, but the storm destroyed several farmhouses in the area. The tornado then passed north of Marion Lake and demolished the home of Dean and Pat Bina east of Pilsen. Their parents, coincidentally, lost their home during the March 13th tornado at Hesston.[25]

EMPORIA, JUNE 7, 1990

Twenty-one people were injured when a tornado whipped through west Emporia on June 7, 1990, cutting a path from south to north. The tornado, one of four sighted on the ground that evening, caused extensive property damage. According to the Red Cross, 9 homes and 8 businesses were destroyed, and 35 homes and 40 businesses sustained heavy damage. Authorities sounded the sirens two minutes before the storm struck.

Doug Main and his three-year-old daughter were seriously injured. He suffered a broken neck and the girl had a broken arm and a head injury. Doug was carrying her in a car seat to the home of his brother Kenneth, who remarked, "They had just opened my front door when they were sucked out of the house." He said the wind tossed his brother against a garage wall and pulled the little girl from her father's arms. They found her, still strapped in the seat, in a vacant lot north of the house.

Law officers followed the slow deadly tornado as it churned its way across town. Under-sheriff Randy Thomas said, "The power lines by me started sparking, and debris was flying, and I started hollering, 'It's headed right for the high school!'" Instead, the tornado skipped over the school and came down again in the West Ridge housing development. "I watched this housing district explode," Randy said. "I was about two blocks behind it. We were lucky it wasn't a big one."[26]

Businesses leveled included the Ineeda Uniforms Service and several car dealerships. "Oh, my God, look at the cars! The cars!" exclaimed an employee at John North Ford. A semi-trailer truck was on top of several vehicles, and the tornado picked up at least sixty cars, dropping them like toys. In front of the demolished Ineeda Uniform Service, Leon Bazil pointed to the smashed delivery truck and joked, "I don't think there will be any deliveries today."

Although the twister damaged the roof and back of the building at the Cowboy Palace, it hit with more force next door at Herm's Body Shop. Gladys Herman, the owner, said the wind strewed car parts hundreds of feet from the building. "We spent the night here last night. I felt we needed to stay. Everything we have is here." Activity at the shop was disorderly as people ran in and out of the office and in the chaos, someone stole her purse.

Many people in the West Ridge housing area were homeless and in shock. Jim and Joyce Cress took shelter in a small closet, covering themselves with blankets. "Both our children were gone at the time. We got a hold of them later and told them we didn't have a home anymore," Joyce said. She said only a few items in the house were left untouched. "The guns in the cabinet were still intact, and a key that we kept on top of the cabinet didn't move at all… In the kitchen… the table and all four chairs did not move. Even the salt and pepper shakers on the table didn't budge."

Leslie and Joyce David took cover in the basement just minutes before the tornado hit. "We heard an awful sound and knew the house was being hit. When we came upstairs… it was really shocking. I think I am still in shock."

Police officer Mark Locke observed that, "It was a relatively small tornado, a real light tan color--almost white. It wasn't very wide, maybe the width of a street." The force of the tornado kicked up a wide swath of debris. He said, "I saw it hit Norton Oil. All I could see was debris."

Cindy Willis said the storm hit businesses near her home. "I stood in the doorway of my basement and watched it come in. I just couldn't believe it. And tomorrow (June 8) is our anniversary of the last one." A tornado hit Emporia on June 8, 1974.

Jeff Hayes said he is going to be out of town when the next tornado comes. Most of the people in Emporia echo his sentiments, especially those who survived both storms.[27]

INLAND HURRICANE, JUNE 19, 1990

The term "inland hurricane" is often used to describe a widespread wind-shear storm that does damage similar to a hurricane. People who live on the East Coast or the Gulf Coast tend to scoff at such comparisons, and there is an element of truth to their disdain. This particular storm system, however, deserves the title of an "inland hurricane."

This storm swept from southwest to south-central Kansas, leaving property damage of $50,000,000 in its wake. Meteorologists called this outbreak one of the worst of the 20th century.

The six-hour storm formed and intensified near Pratt, where wind gusts reached 67 to 100 miles per hour. From Pratt, the storm moved towards Kingman, where 100 mile an hour winds uprooted trees, downed power lines, and ripped off roofs. Traveling northeast, it blew across Cheney Reservoir into western Sedgwick County and hit Wichita, where it left 20,000 residents without power for days.

There were several confirmed tornado sightings, but even without the tornadoes, the storm had wind speeds of more than 80 miles an hour. Later that night a second wave of storms hit Sedgwick, Harvey, Butler, and Reno Counties, and wind gusts of 70 miles an hour were recorded before the gauges ceased to function.

At Wichita, tornado sirens sounded three times during the night, and sustained winds of 100 miles an hour destroyed businesses, blew houses off foundations, snapped utility poles, and tossed cars into ditches. Damage was extensive around the Towne East Shopping Center, and at the Marriott Hotel, where all the windows exploded outward and shattered. The wind blew out car windows in the hotel parking lot. The Jabara Airport reported severe damage to thirteen aircraft.

Other towns in the area had hurricane force winds combined with rain, large hail, thunder and lightning. At Andale, the wind blew away the grain elevator, and at Mt. Hope a tornado did extensive damage to residences. At Bentley Corner several businesses sustained structural damage. A falling tree split a mobile home in half. In Valley Center straight-line winds clocked at 114 miles an hour destroyed the high school, a church, and several grain elevators. The mobile home of the Jim McPheeters family turned over with them inside, but miraculously they escaped serious injury. One mobile home rolled across two lots and landed on top of a car. Meteorologists estimated the straight-line winds at Valley Center comparable to an F3 tornado.

At Sedgwick, the high winds caused more destruction. Police Chief Bob Crawford was on storm watch that night when a wall of dust, high winds, and rain pushed him into the ditch. Winds clocked at 115 miles per hour destroyed the Sedgwick Grade School and band building. At Park City, the Chisholm Creek Manor mobile home park sustained damage of more than $1,000,000. At Furley, fifteen miles northeast of Wichita, the wind shear knocked down three miles of power lines and destroyed the grain elevator. From there the storm's path paralleled the Kansas Turnpike, but by that time the wind's velocity had decreased.

Assistance after the storm came from the Mennonite Emergency Assistance organization, the Kansas State Guard, and the Salvation Army, who were all instrumental in clearing the thousands of downed power lines and trees and in helping the people who lost their homes.

Arguments among authorities persisted that the storm was not a straight-line wind, but a tornado. However, thorough surface investigations finally concluded that powerful straight winds caused most of the damage. All in all, it was one of the most devastating storms to hit Kansas during the 1990s.[28]

CENTRAL, EASTERN KANSAS, MARCH 26, 1991

The first major storm of 1991 occurred a month before the Andover tornado. Thunderstorms rolling across the state in March produced a dozen twisters, severe hail, and high winds in Pratt and Reno Counties.

In Hutchinson a tornado hit the 1920s suburb of Willowbrook especially hard. This area was once a part of the country estate of Emerson Carey, founder of the Carey Salt Company. Witnesses saw as many as three tornadoes on the ground headed for Willowbrook, where they leveled seven of the thirty-six homes and damaged twenty more.

The tornado carried the Ron and Carol Heironimus family seventy feet from their house. They were battered, bruised, and cut, but they were alive. At first their son Rob did not appear to be breathing as he lay in a field covered with debris. A daughter Tracy was also badly injured, but both children survived.

The greatest damage in Lawrence was caused by golf ball-sized hail and high winds that blew out 200 windows in several buildings on the University of Kansas campus. The storm and heavy hail wrecked 300 vehicles at Laird Noller Motors. In some places the hail was so deep that it had to be shoveled away. In all, $22,000,000 damage was caused by the hail. Straight winds gusting to eighty miles an hour caused $1,500,000 damage.[29]

WICHITA AND ANDOVER, APRIL 26, 1991

The most violent weather outbreak in recent years was the Wichita and Andover tornadoes of April 26, 1991. An exceptional book written shortly after the storm, *Like the Devil*, recounts the complete story of those deadly tornadoes.

Within hours after the storm system passed, these huge tornadoes had affected the lives of thousands of residents, killing twenty people, including two babies, destroying 1,120 homes in 11 counties and damaging another 571. The total damage was $222,000,000, not including business, utility, or uninsured losses, and in addition, the U.S. Air Force estimated a loss of $72,000,000 at McConnell Air Force Base.[30]

Severe weather was expected that April day. Early in the afternoon, a powerful cold front towering eleven miles into the atmosphere worked its way south into the warm, unstable air from the gulf. Above this moist air, the speed of the jet stream exceeded 110 knots. Wichita's Weather Data, Inc., a private forecasting firm, predicted severe weather with possible tornadoes. Meteorologist Rick Dittman stated it was "a rare, rare day, weather-wise," and Dick Elder, meteorologist at the National Weather Service in Wichita said, "It was an explosive day."[31]

At 4:00 a.m. the National Severe Storms Forecast Center in Kansas City issued an unusual alert, a warning that included the eastern half of Kansas as a target for severe weather. Extra staff was called in to help man the Wichita weather service office and the station at McConnell Air Force Base. On that day, fifty-six tornadoes swept the Great Plains from Texas to Nebraska; twenty were in Kansas.

A single tornado was first spotted on the ground seven miles northeast of Anthony. It touched down again outside Clearwater, clipped the northwest corner of Haysville, and then roared through southeast Wichita.

At Clearwater, Deanna Mills lived in a mobile home with her nine sons. When she heard a tornado was headed her way, they ran to a well house and huddled together. The tornado wrecked their mobile home and sucked two of the boys out of the well house. They were scared but unhurt. Neighbor Glenn Collins noted that "it danced like the devil. It was big and ugly and black. It looked mean. It made me feel cold all over."[32]

At Haysville, Jack McCreery barely made it to the basement before all of his property disappeared—-combines, a barn, trucks, tractors, his house, everything. Policeman John Coleman, who was cruising through town, heard about the tornado sighting on his radio. The Chief ordered him to drive out of town and, if possible, locate the tornado. Once outside the city limits, he found it, but he couldn't tell where the funnel left off and the sky began. He followed it as it moved through Haysville, taking pictures along the way.[33]

The tornado, packing winds of 206 miles an hour, hit the Timberlane Addition first. At Donna and Tony Tobler's house the heavy rain and hail that had been falling suddenly stopped and then, dead silence. When they looked out the window, they saw debris flying in the air. The tornado was only two blocks away. Each grabbed a child and dashed to the basement just as it hit. All of them survived.

The forecasters at the National Weather Service in Wichita were frustrated. Still using an old radar system scheduled to be replaced, they were unable to get a clear picture of the weather to the south, and tornado activity too close to the radar wasn't visible on the scope. This situation forced the weathermen to rely on the storm spotters.[34]

By this time the tornado sirens were wailing in Wichita. The tornado's path was not in a straight line. It zigzagged, unsure of which direction it wanted to go. The color of the vortex changed from black to purple. At 57th Street South and Broadway, the tornado destroyed twenty-eight mobile homes and injured seven people. At the Levernez house, the children were picking up their toys before their father came home, and as Linda turned on the television to see the weather report, the sirens sounded. She grabbed the kids and ducked into a closet, using pillows for a shield. Everything outside became deadly quiet. The television blinked on and off and went blank. Then they were surrounded by a roar that kept getting louder and louder— so loud they couldn't talk to each other. Linda's ears were popping from the pressure. Suddenly the door to the closet flew open, and she could see the tornado pass by in the yard next to hers. After it was over, Linda went outside to look and all the houses to the west were gone, but shining above all the devastation, she saw a rainbow.[35]

The tornado raced on, hitting a neighborhood near the Kansas Turnpike, where it damaged twenty-five homes. Glenn Collins, who was watching the tornado at this point, stated that, "It got bigger and blacker and was spitting out stuff everywhere. Big pieces of debris. Everything was covered with dirt and it was raining out of the sky." Then it destroyed Meyer's Garden Spot Nursery and Greenhouse where Collins worked. The sirens only gave employees at the nursery a few minutes warning, but it was enough. Gloria Hardesty led the workers to an old storm cellar. "It was just like in the movies," Gloria said, "We were running as fast as we could. . . . The wind was blowing faster and faster. Debris was all over our faces. It was dirty and dark. We were pulling, trying to get the door closed and the wind was sucking it open. No one was saying a word. The tornado was loud as thunder. Then all at once it was perfectly quiet. We came out and everything had been turned upside down or blown away. Huge chunks of concrete from the office were everywhere."[36]

The residents in the River Oaks Mobile Home Park had only a few minutes to take cover before the tornado struck. When they climbed out of their shelters, they found the storm had demolished many of their trailers. One man had a board run through his stomach, but if more people had been at home, the casualty rate would have been higher.

The tornado moved through another mobile home park at 53rd and Hydraulic Ave., leaving a hundred homes damaged. Then it crossed the Santa Fe tracks just south of Boeing Wichita. As the tornado passed, 3,200 Boeing employees moved to this assigned shelters.[37]

At McConnell Air Force Base, Sgts. Mike Snell and Jim Williams were working in the airport control tower. When Snell spotted the funnel several miles away, it was partially hidden by the Boeing Plant. He jumped onto a window ledge for a better view and watched as the tornado surged across the runways. It was pure white. The men were so fascinated by its appearance, and they had such a feeling of helplessness, they couldn't move. As it roared toward the weather station, the men dove for cover under their desks. The tornado passed within 200 yards of the building, just missing the flight line where 84 jets and two B-1 bombers stood, loaded with nuclear warheads. Had those planes been hit and exploded, the radioactive plutonium leakage would have been devastating.

The tornado destroyed the base hospital, gymnasium, NCO club, and 104 housing units. Sgt. Jay Taylor took shelter in a storm culvert rather than stay in the barracks. Although flying debris hit him where he lay, he had a "front row seat" and saw all the devastation, an experience he would never forget.

The twister intensified and grew wider. Mike and Patti Lamb and their three boys lived across from McConnell. They were shocked when they looked out their upstairs window and saw a huge black funnel moving across the base, leading in their direction. The Lamb's had no basement, so they grabbed pillows and blankets and raced to a downstairs bathroom. They felt their ears popping, then heard crashing sounds. In a few seconds, it was all over. Their house was a wreck, but they all survived.[38]

Tornado approaching McConnell Air Force Base and Andover

The tornado moved through an area near Pawnee at 143rd and Kellogg, wrecking entire blocks of homes and killing four people. The twister caught Charlene Montgomery, her daughter Keri, and nieces Anna Marie and Susan Elizabeth out in the open when they attempted to run to a neighbor's basement. The tornado literally blew them away. Charlene died on the way to the hospital, Anna and Susan were killed instantly. The force of the wind threw Keri across the street into a tree, breaking her back.

While Paula and Herb Bruce were rounding up their cats, the funnel suddenly came through a line of trees and was upon them instantly. Paul later remarked, "It was like a big jet flying into us at full power. We felt the air pressure drop and our ears filled and crackled. When we heard a noise like a freight train going over a wooden trestle, we knew it was right on top of us. Everything started shaking, including our knees." In twenty seconds, it was over. The tornado caught Mathilda Behout, who lived two blocks from the Bruces, outside and killed her instantly.

Irene and Claude Irwin had seen firsthand the destruction caused by the Udall tornado in 1955. Unfortunately, a twister destroyed their home again. In Udall, they rode out the storm under a bed; this time they hid in a closet in the basement.[39]

The television stations did an excellent job informing residents of the storm, but the tornado moved so fast that one minute the sky was clear and the next, the tornado appeared. Its immense fury was so frightening that some people just froze in their tracks.

Although Lance Darling owned a house near Pawnee and Greenwich streets, he watched the tornado from his place of business downtown, the Marriott Hotel. After it passed he hurried to see if the storm had hit his house. Within three blocks of home, debris in the street stopped his car, and he had to start running on foot. He actually ran past his house and didn't recognize it; there was nothing left. Oddly enough, that morning when he tried to put his dog out in the backyard, the dog refused to go. Lance had to force him outside. Is this another sign of an animal's keen sensibility to the weather? The dog did not survive. Lance found his body later that night under some tree limbs in the yard.[40]

Tornado approaching Andover

Sharon Williamson was driving east on 162nd Street, and when she and her passengers saw the tornado, they abandoned the car and jumped into a ditch. Williamson had to blink her eyes in disbelief as she watched her daughter Brook Ibara riding on a broken branch through the air. Although Brook suffered a collapsed lung, broken shoulder blade, and several cracked vertebrae, she survived. From where Williamson lay, she could smell smoke from downed power lines and saw an engine from a John Deere tractor setting just two feet from her. By now the tornadic winds were 318 miles an hour. The funnel was a half-mile wide, and it kept growing blacker as it approached Andover from the southwest. In town, city officials ordered the sounding of the warning sirens, and a dispatcher pressed the siren's radio-controlled trigger. Nothing happened. The dispatcher pressed again, and again nothing happened. He pressed the trigger four times, but the siren would not respond. The officials had to send emergency vehicles with sirens into the streets to warn the residents of the oncoming storm.[41]

Andover Police Sgt. Paul Troy See drove to the Golden Spur Mobile Home Park with his lights and siren on. Fire trucks with horns blaring circulated all around town. One drove to the Pizza Hut. There the fireman announced, "Run for your life! Get out!" At the nearby Livingston's restaurant, employees and customers ran to the Pizza Hut's basement, a prearranged agreement in case of a storm.

The Rockstad and Hartman families didn't see the tornado coming across the golf course right at them. When they did, they rushed for the basement. Even then they couldn't believe it was a tornado. It just looked too big, too much like a massive cloud. After the storm passed, Tollie Hartman found half of her home still standing. "I had walls where I had stairs," she said later. Her house was the only one for blocks that wasn't completely destroyed.

Suzie Storrer was in a business meeting when the sirens sounded. When she learned the predicted path of the tornado, she hurried for home. Her two daughters were alone at their residence in the Countryside Third Addition. She could only drive within a few blocks of home, so she took off her high heels and ran the rest of the way. Fortunately, the girls were safe, but the tornado had flattened their house. Suzie lost $200,000 worth of uninsured antiques. Out of forty Aladdin lamps, only one survived, and out of twenty-five antique cabinets, none withstood the wind.

In the same addition, Janet Kiser's family had only minutes before the storm hit to go to the basement. Afterwards, they walked upstairs to find no ceiling and trash everywhere. Once outside, the family looked east. "We could see the whole trailer park," Janet remembered. "There was nothing . . . all those homes were leveled. No dogs barking. No birds flying around. I kept thinking, I'm not really here."

Sgt. See was watching as the tornado approached from the southwest, and he thought the Golden Spur Mobile Home Park looked nearly deserted, but he drove around it until finally he had to seek refuge himself. There was a tornado shelter in the center of the park where 200 to 300 of the residents had taken cover. "We were packed in there like sardines," said Karen McCrary who, along with her daughter, made it to the shelter just minutes before the tornado hit. Her husband Tony was already there. Screams and moans of the residents could be heard as the funnel bore down on them. The lights went out, andABC the only sounds heard then were the roar of the tornado, the screech and groan of grinding steel and aluminum, and the terrified cries of the people.[42]

The tornado destroyed all but a few trailers. It killed eleven people, including a son and his father who died shielding his dead wife; and a Good

Samaritan and the two elderly neighbors she attempted to lead to safety. The twister crushed two others to death after they refused to leave their homes.[43]

Robert Meininger resisted seeking shelter. Even with the tornado bearing down on him, he chose to stay behind. His family returned to search for him, but it was not until the next day that they found his body buried under his trailer. Rescuers found Ruby Crawford, the Good Samaritan, and her neighbors dead on the opposite side of the park from their homes. No one was sure exactly what happened. The tornado must have caught them out in the open heading for the shelter. A friend found Joe Marks, a loner who lived with his three dogs, dead ten feet from his trailer. Neighbors found two more residents, who tried to escape the storm, dead in a ditch.[44]

Allen Sargent and his family were eating dinner when the tornado approached and he never saw the funnel or heard a siren. Moments later when the tornado was in sight, it was too late. Allen and his wife threw themselves on the floor and ordered their daughters to lie down in the bathtub. When the tornado hit, the trailer disintegrated and Allen blacked out. Elsie and Anton Kemper were watching television when the storm hit. They ran to a storage shed near their trailer. He held tightly to his wife, but the high winds blew her out of his arms.

After the tornado passed, there was complete chaos in the Golden Spur shelter. Residents were still moaning and screaming. As people came out of shelters all across Andover, nothing but dead silence greeted them. They could not believe their eyes. The scene was one of total devastation.

The first thing Tony and Karen McCrary saw was Karen's car upside down in the swimming pool. Fortunately, the McCrary's trailer was one of the few left standing. Allen Sargent's trailer was reduced to a pile of rubble. Allen, who had a spike through his foot, an eighteen-inch gash on his buttocks and was hardly able to walk, still tried to find his family. He found his wife dead in the wreckage of the trailer and his two daughters seriously injured. The force of the wind blew a neighbor so hard against the wall of his trailer that his body left a permanent imprint in the structure.

Up at the Andover strip mall, people began to emerge from shelters. Jim Fairman and son Jimmy found their mother alive in the rubble of the Livingston Restaurant. They worked their way down to the Golden Spur, where they found the bodies of Ronald Kanavy and his son, and the mangled body of their neighbor, Joe Marks. It was quite a shock to Jimmy, a twelve-year-old boy, to find all those bodies.

The storm left one-third of the city's 4,300 residents homeless. The tornado pulled tree trunks from the ground and snapped big trees off at the base like they were toothpicks. Survivors flooded the telephone lines after the storm trying to call loved ones. Medical personnel established a disaster command post across the street at the Countryside Third Addition. A Life Flight helicopter began the task of airlifting the severely injured to hospitals, a painstakingly slow process.[45]

Heavy traffic and emergency vehicles waylaid residents who were not home at the Golden Spur when the tornado hit. One tenant was stopped in traffic for over two hours. Of the 243 mobile homes at the Spur, less than ten were left standing. The next day the residents were stumbling around hugging each other, still stunned with disbelief.[46]

Some Andover residents claimed they did not have adequate warning concerning the storm, and this allegation was probably true. Andover had a siren purchased at a government surplus sale several years before. It never sounded. The siren worked perfect during a test the previous Tuesday, but it malfunctioned that Friday. At some point it could have been struck by lightning and fixed by inexperienced repairmen. Some people thought the flow of emergency radio traffic that night blocked the dispatcher's signal from reaching the siren. Whether this signal or siren would have saved lives or not is debatable. The tornado had been very visiable.[47]

Another controversy arose after city officials allowed workers to use front-end loaders in rescue operations. During the search for victims trapped in the wreckage, heavy equipment destroyed the salvaged property of some homeowners who piled their belongings in the street to be picked up the next day. By the time they were allowed back into the area, the loaders had crushed most of their possessions or hauled them off to the dump.

A footnote: the Golden Spur storm shelter was padlocked at the time of the storm warning, and only three families had the keys. Fortunately, one person with a key was in the park that night to unlock it. If the shelter had remained padlocked, the casualties would have been much higher.[48]

Rescue crews worked until 11:30 p.m. but they had to quit due to another thunderstorm in the area. The next day they still hadn't located all the missing people. One woman, who was allowed back into the trailer park, was sifting through the rubble of her trailer when she lifted a board and found the body of her husband. His arm was lying across his forehead as if shielding his eyes from the sun. She collapsed. Her daughter became hysterical, and workers had to drag her away holding on to her father's cowboy boots.

Tornado approaching El Dorado, April 26, 1991

Cars in the mobile park were smashed and lying on top of crushed trailers. One car was in the swimming pool. A row of trees behind the trailer court became the haven for everything from stuffed bears to housing insulation. Cassette tape, strung through tree limbs like tinsel, glittered in the sun. The storm had scattered tons of litter in a once empty field. Some people stayed the night in makeshift shelters, and some slept in their empty basements or their cars. Merchants tried to clean up and cover the windows of their ruined shops. Utility companies struggled to restore power. Carol Hamill, owner of Carol's Kitchen, moved her operations to the Andover Middle School, where she served hundreds of meals to survivors and workers.

A dark side to the aftermath was the looters. The night after the storm, reports of looters came from all over the area. Sightseers were getting out of their cars, taking certain items, and then driving away. They called it picking up souvenirs, but residents viewed it as looting. Some people even took items off the corpses. Pat Kanavy, who lost her husband and son, claimed that someone took $400 from her husband's pocket and $60 from his billfold. Then there were the weird ones. Around 4:00 a.m. the next day, a strange man walked to the car of one of the residents in the Third Addition. She noted, "Nobody else was around, and I gripped my butcher knife. He knocked on the window and asked if I was OK, and I said, 'Yes, what do you want?' He asked if he could say a prayer for me. I said, 'Well, yes.' He said a prayer out loud and then he left. He just disappeared down the street."

After the tornado passed, rescue operations in Andover were disorganized. Some physicians came to the area to help and reported that everything was chaotic. Dr. Jesus Suerto noted, "Nobody was in charge. We were in the middle of the street. People were bringing bodies on doors or pieces of plywood. Power lines were hanging everywhere. I was afraid I'd be electrocuted… Ambulances couldn't get in because there were huge chunks of concrete in the street. One piece was at least four feet long. Nobody was directing traffic. The police weren't there for a very long time. Nobody assumed command. It was getting dark and starting to rain."

As with many disasters, sightseers often beat the police and emergency crews to the scene, which caused more interference. All hospitals in the area finally implemented their emergency plans and set up temporary morgues. Signs were posted that read "critical," "major," and "minor." In one night five hospitals treated 199 patients.

After leaving the Golden Spur, the tornado moved northeast towards Towanda, paralleling the Kansas Turnpike for miles, forcing cars off the road and drivers into the ditch. Lee Mann and Jack Hughes were heading for Wichita when they saw the tornado coming and pulled their pickup under an overpass. Mann remarked, "It was almost like we were a bull's eye or an 'X' on a map. It was coming straight toward the bridge." Other cars stopped too, and Hughes directed people to take cover under the bridge girders. He watched the storm, which appeared to be moving slowly, and then he joined the others under the girders. Soon the tornado's roar drowned out all the other sounds.

Mann said, "There was a total stillness before it hit. You could still hear the roar, but there was no air movement, there was no wind. There was absolutely nothing just prior to its hitting us." Lightning appeared to be everywhere around them. "I thought this was it," Mann said, "There is no escaping." All types of objects were circulating around the twister. Pink insulation stuck out like bubble gum. When the tornado was over, twenty-five more people climbed out from a culvert down the highway. They all began checking their vehicles. Some had windows and headlights broken and some had contents missing. An 18-wheeler lay on its side.[49]

The storm continued down the turnpike, wrecking cars and destroying homes. This tornado's path was 75 miles long, and it finally lifted in southern Chase County. The tornado was rated an F-4 and averaged one-fourth to one-half mile wide.

In Goddard, the Glenna Fields family looked out their back window around 5:45 p.m. and saw a tornado in their backyard. They barely made it to the basement before the twister removed the roof and the front part of the house. There was no warning. Three other people escaped with their lives when the small tornado hit a custom boat shop, destroying the building.

Another tornado formed in Cowley and Elk Counties, killing two people and demolishing several homes. The storm gained intensity about six miles west of Arkansas City and contained winds over 200 miles an hour. The tornado caught Sam and Helen Tolles by surprise. In their attempt to reach safety, they were hit hard by flying debris. Sam remembered looking straight up into the funnel.[50]

The tornado circled Strother Air Field, tearing up several more homes and destroying Marilyn Decker's mobile home near Winfield. Neighbors found her lifeless body in a nearby field. One family took refuge in a bathtub, and when the tornado tore the roof off, it sucked them into the air and dropped them to the ground, still in the bathtub. The wind rolled the tub twice, throwing them out. They were covered with mud. After the storm passed, the bathtub was nowhere to be found.

In Elk County, a tornado killed a seventy-nine year old great-grandmother, Lucille Jacob. She was doing what she always did each night, crocheting and reading the Bible. The tornado came so fast she didn't stand a chance.[51]

Across the state line in Oklahoma, the storm front produced the largest tornado, a monster F-5. The twister killed Wichita businessman G.D. Davis and his accountant when it tossed their car several hundred yards into a grove of trees.

Late the next morning a funnel moved through Jefferson County, destroying homes in several small towns. This tornado developed just north of the National Weather Service office in Topeka, and it circled the countryside for miles, bouncing back and forth. At Danny Welborns' place near Meriden, the twister destroyed his house. He didn't have time to take cover. After the storm passed, neighbors found Danny sixty feet away thrown against his pickup truck and suffering a broken hip and some cracked vertebrae. On down the road, a weather spotter near Valley Falls reported seeing a tornado on the ground headed for Nortonville, where city officials sounded the sirens and everyone sought shelter.[52]

The weather spotters reported other tornadoes that day in Washington County, passing just west of the town of Washington, near Hanover. At Lanham, a tornado destroyed the office of the Lanham Grain Elevator and smashed several grain bins. In Wabaunsee County near Eskridge, a twister destroyed several cabins at Lake Wabaunsee. After leaving Eskridge, the funnel moved into Shawnee County. Another tornado damaged a section of Rossville and destroyed an old stone church built in 1876 near Maple Hill. Map Available: Appendix 1.

CENTRAL KANSAS, MAY 16, 1991

May 16th was a frightening day for people in Central Kansas. A tornado appeared along the same path that was hit by the devastating Wichita and Andover tornadoes on April 26. One tornado nearly retraced the exact path. Estimated damage was a million dollars after the tornado skipped through the Wichita metropolitan area, demolishing at least twenty homes. Spotters also reported a tornado in Hodgeman County.[53]

MCPHERSON, GALVA, JUNE 15, 1992

A Mitchell County sheriff spotted a tornado, the first of thirteen to hit the county, at 5:22 p.m. four miles west of Tipton. At 6:45 p.m. emergency personnel, police, and the highway patrol knew they were in for a long night. At that time a farmer saw two more tornadoes south of Cawker City and one south of Glen Elder. A storm spotter near Bob Becker's farm could be heard saying, "It's here, it's right in front of us!"[54]

One resident said, "If you drew a 12 mile wide line, from Tipton to Beloit, that would be the area that sustained the most damage. It got a little narrower and a little worse as it got closer to Beloit," where marble-sized hail fell, and the sirens sounded.

In other areas of the county rain, hail, and wind increased. For the next few hours, more tornadoes came and went, and emergency personnel stayed busy keeping up with the tornadoes and checking on the welfare of rural residents.

At 10:12 p.m. tornadic activity hit McPherson County. The storm was moving in a northeasterly direction. It damaged residential property, McPherson College, Kit Manufacturing, and the Mustang Mobile Home Park.

Bryan Hess described it as "a very wide black funnel that looked like it was taking everything in its path; it was that big and wide." Hess was watching the storm from The Cedars Health Care Center. "It was very clear because of the lightning on every side of it. In the middle were blue sparks and yellow sparks," he said. Minutes later he saw the storm northwest of the city. "It looked like it had lightened up in color and then it was more like the rope kind of tornado, a rather big rope, and it was more than one funnel, all rotating together."[55]

At the Mustang Mobile Home Park, Karen and Kevin Pricket left their home to seek shelter, but they returned before the all-clear sounded. They were in their house when Karen looked out and saw the tornado just yards away. They grabbed their daughter and fled, but only got as far as the driveway when their home exploded right before their eyes. Fortunately, they were not injured. Afterwards, they spent the rest of the night wrapped in wet blankets in the street beside the wreckage. For breakfast they lit the barbecue and cooked the only undamaged food they could find – Pop Tarts.

Jim Overstreet was a few blocks from home when he heard the sirens. He made a run for his house, assisted his wife in getting their two children into a shelter, and then went back outside. "I looked out and in the lightning I could see the funnel over at the college. I ran for the shelter, jumped in and slid down across it. I closed the lid and that's when it hit," he said. The Overstreets lost their carport and part of the roof on their mobile home.

Kris Ritchie heard the warning sirens and then contemplated what to do. She didn't have a basement. About that time, her television "went haywire," and she walked over to shut it off.

"Something said 'you better get yourself in the closet,'" she explained. "As I shut the door of the closet, things started flying." After it was all over, the only area left unscathed was the closet in which Kris was hiding.[56]

The tornado moved on toward Galva, where it destroyed some residences. In its fury the storm flipped farm trucks, pushed a semi-trailer 100 feet into a house, and landed a combine upside down atop a tree. Miraculously, no one was hurt. "To have that many houses flattened and not have injuries, it's unbelievable," said a fireman. And as Curtis Walline wryly put it, "I told the kids I'd rather make a trip to the lumber yard than a funeral any day." He lost his mobile home just west of Galva that day.

Pam and Lanny Norstrom headed for a storm shelter when the twister approached. "I could hear the wind was somehow different than anything I'd ever heard before," she said. Then, while hiding below, the family heard glass shattering and wood breaking above them. At first, said Pam, they thought it was hail, but then they realized it was debris. Lanny emerged from the shelter first, and when Pam asked him how bad it was, he said, "You don't want to know." Everything, every building, every vehicle was gone. A half mile east, Cliff Lawless fared a little better. Although the tornado destroyed his mobile home and farm buildings, it missed his farm implements. "Before it hit, it was a dull roar off in the distance," Lawless remembered. "There was 10, 15 minutes of that. Then it started getting closer, it started intensifying. Before I went to the cellar the last time, I was looking at the clouds. There was a hellacious roar, almost a whistle." Lawless said he never really saw a funnel, it looked more like a cloud that came to earth and the air took on "an eerie feeling." He said he could almost smell the storm, "I just picked up a different odor in the air right before it hit." He and his family returned to the shelter. "It wasn't a minute later you could hear tin flying." The next morning their spirit was visible in a proud American flag they mounted atop the trailer's doorway.[57]

Billy Smith lost his entire farm. Describing the storm, he said, "To me, it looked four, five miles wide. It stretched across more than half the horizon, and only in the shadow of lightning, seemed to taper." Across the road from Smith, Friesen rummaged through the rubble that was once his home. He said he was picking out personal belongings and would bulldoze the rest. "By then there was nothing to do but shut off the gas and shut off the water and go drink coffee."

As the storm approached, Dave Clark lit an oil-burning lamp when the power went out. He said he remembered the lamp started to rattle just as he dove for the basement, and he heard a thundering crash when the chimney collapsed on him. Clark freed himself and when he climbed out of the basement, he saw his new 18-wheeler in his living room. He purchased the truck four months before and parked it 150 feet away from the house. He had parked it facing east, but after the storm, it was facing west.[58]

RUSSELL, MAY 7, 1993

A large storm system stretching from Texas to South Dakota passed briefly through Central Kansas near Russell. A tornado touched ground three miles north of Dorrance and went north to Minooka Park at Wilson Lake. When the storm hit the lake area, it demolished Ken's Marine Bathhouse and residence, injuring both Ken Resley and his wife. The wind scattered debris including boat parts, campers, trailers, wheels, fishing rods, and bedding all along the lake road. In Minooka Park one fatality occurred, Helen Bunker drowned. Her son Jimmy Bunker said the tornado struck too fast, without much warning. "Everything is gone," he said, "just that fact—everything, including my motor home, gear, all my stuff."

North of the lake, Ales and Della Herbel lost the roof of their house, and next door the tornado destroyed their daughter Lenice Crawford's home. Mrs. Crawford was away in Lincoln at the time and told a reporter, "We got back late last night after the 'all clear' was given," she said. "We had one bedroom and the bathroom left, so we just stayed the night here. A sheriff's officer kept an eye out from across the road."[59]

About a mile north of Crawford's place at the Randy and Mona Kaufman farm, the tornado blew out all the windows, ripped off the shingles, and leveled a barn. Kaufman and his family eluded the tornado by going to the storm cellar. Randy said, "I saw the tornado come over the hill and I thought for a moment I would just watch for debris from the Crawford and Herbel places, but I changed my mind in a hurry, closed the door and then laid hard against the inside door as the storm passed."

Mona Kaufman said, "We really never heard it, even when all the machines and cars were moved and destroyed." They emerged from the cellar to find their large truck moved 200 yards and their automobile upside down in an embankment 50 yards away. The wind battered Kaufman's new pickup; the entire driver's side was smashed.

Cleanup began the next morning by the US Army Corps of Engineers and volunteers from Russell.[60]

LAWRENCE, JULY 11, 1993

In the midst of torrential rains, severe storms, and floods along the Kansas River, a tornado approached North Lawrence on Saturday morning, July 11, 1993.[61]

On the Roger Pine farm, a tornado twisted and crumpled one of his 45,000 bushel steel storage bins as if it were a soft drink can, and wind-driven hail shredded his corn. Heavy rains flooded portions of the 4,000 acres he farmed in Leavenworth and Douglas counties. One farm was on the flood plain north of the Kansas Turnpike in Lawrence.[62]

In North Lawrence, the tornado tore the roof off the Airport Motel near the airport. The owners of the Bismarck Inn evacuated their hotel because high water was twenty yards from the front door and still rising. At the Jayhawk Motel, travelers on the first floor found their belongings floating around the room.

In a nine-hour period, Lawrence received more than five inches of rain. The city had already received nine inches in the ten days prior to July 11.

KISMET AND MEADE, APRIL 9, 1994

Weird spring weather unfolded throughout Southwest Kansas on April 9, 1993 followed by hail and tornadoes. A twister plowed through Kismet, striking a mobile home park and injuring several people. Less than an hour later, another tornado moved through Meade, damaging houses and barns.

The storm blew away Gene Grano's trailer house, injuring five family members. "We were in Kismet when the weather started getting bad," Gene said. "We drove home and thought we had plenty of time. Just as me and my brother-in-law got to the house, the trailer was lifted into the air. All I remember is dragging my wife out of the car and into a ditch. My brother-in-law got hurt the worst." He suffered severe back injuries after being blown through the front door of the trailer by 150 mile per hour winds.

"The storm picked the trailer house straight up in the air and flipped it three times. Mentally I haven't comprehended this yet. My 4-year old won't leave my side... She was afraid the other night when the wind made the van rock back and forth. She wanted to jump out." Gene said the event was "indescribable" and didn't compare with television footage of a similar incident. "You don't realize the power of those things until you see it live." The storm also moved the car occupied by Grano and his wife. "It scooted the car sideways," he said.

The storm struck the DeKalb farms. "I'm not sure exactly how much damage we suffered," said manager Kelvin Harless. "There were four different farms that were hit. It sucked a lot of tin off the roofs. It rolled or lifted a feed bin, carried it a quarter mile away and stuck it in the side of a building."

DeKalb employees spent the next few days picking up trash, tin, and debris, trying to get things back to normal.[63]

A new method for tracking tornadoes, but is still in the experimental phase, are Seismic detectors, or "Snails." These devices, if spaced correctly, are supposed to send out signals when a tornado has touched down. These detectors are similar in nature to seismographs used to measure earthquakes. A Geophone, buried eight inches deep with spikes pushed into the ground, measures any oncoming tornado that is within a certain distance from the device. Such a method could be effective in recording a tornado on the ground by sending a warning to those cities in its path.

Wichita was one of twenty cities chosen by scientists to test the devices. A network of seismic detectors was installed ten to twenty miles apart in a ring around the city. These detectors would send data back to a central receiving point. Information gathered in Wichita could help determine a common "signature" of a tornado on the ground, which would create a distinct seismic pattern.

In the future, these seismic detectors could provide "ears" to a storm the way Doppler radar provides eyes.[64]

In May of 1996 Warner Brother studios released the movie *"Twister,"* which was based on a tornado outbreak in Oklahoma. While the focus of the movie had nothing to do with Kansas, it popularized tornadoes and aroused the curiosity of the general public. A company near Wichita promised any interested individual, who paid the required fees, a chance to see a real tornado. Some of these tourists, who came from other states and countries, did see a tornado. Most did not. Tornado activity is not that predictable.[65]

Western Kansas tornado near Colby, July 21, 1996

SABETHA, JUNE 13, 1998

A thunderstorm, which started in Wabaunsee County early in the day, quickly progressed through Washington, Republic, Nemaha, and Greenwood Counties. At 9:00 p.m. a tornado touched down three miles west of Reserve in Brown County. An hour later, tornado sirens sounded in Sabetha. The funnel moved down Main Street, damaging eighteen buildings and taking the roof off the three-story city hall, which caused the south wall to collapse. Although the tornado crumbled brick buildings and blew out storefront windows, the American flags and the potted plants in front stayed in place.

Fred and Sherry Frye and son Brandon raced in Fred's pickup truck toward the downtown intersection where he was to pick up his older son. The storm became so severe that both Brandon and Sherry left the truck and took cover inside the city hall just as part of the building "exploded." Fred said he was still in his pickup when the tornado struck him, sliding the truck across the road. "I just grabbed a hold of the wheel and rode it out," he said.

Mack Harvey, who outraced a white wall cloud and drove through falling debris, said the storm would "stick in my mind forever."[66]

WICHITA AND HAYSVILLE, MAY 3, 1999

Many people will remember the video of the destruction left by the Oklahoma City tornadoes of May 3, 1999. In fact, the storms were front-page news. The newspapers barely mentioned the tornadoes that hit the Wichita and Haysville areas. Actually, these storms were severe and deserved more than an off-hand observation. These tornadoes killed six people and injured over a hundred!

During that afternoon a squall line moved from Oklahoma towards Wichita. At 7:44 p.m. a storm spotter reported a tornado twenty-six miles south of Wichita near Mayfield. At 8:15 another spotter saw a tornado on the ground south of Clearwater. Fifteen minutes later they reported severe damage in Haysville. The center of town was a mass of wrecked buildings and downed power lines.

The National Weather Service called the tornado an F4 with wind speeds between 207 and 260 miles per hour. It damaged or destroyed 280 homes and other buildings in Wichita. In Haysville five people lost their lives when the tornado destroyed 150 homes, 27 businesses, four historic buildings, three churches, a library, a nursing home, and the Masonic Lodge.

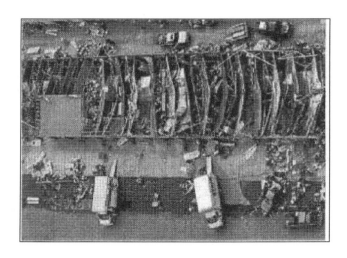

The roof ripped off a Haysville business, May 3, 1999

Eric Peterson looked around a devastated Haysville neighborhood and said in amazement, "I have been in typhoons in the South Pacific, and in hurricanes, but this tops it." Mayor Tim Norton walked through the destroyed historic district. He just received a grant to have cobblestones and old-fashioned lamp posts installed. "You can't recognize there was anything there," he said. "For some of our older residents this will be a real emotional thing."

At the Lakeshore Mobile Homes Resort in South Wichita, the tornado flattened many of the trailers. In the lake floated food and drink coolers, a Tweety Bird doll, a small fishing boat, and parts of broken homes.

In Haysville, the tornado roared as Wayne Maskrid and his wife huddled in their bathtub at the Pacesetter Mobile Home Park. But when the roar stopped, Maskrid went to help. He joined hundreds of others who were searching through the rubble across South Wichita and Haysville minutes after the disaster. They walked up to twisted trailer frames, shouting to anyone who might be inside. They shouted, then paused, hoping to hear a survivor. Then they did hear something, a thump, thump. A man and his pregnant wife lay trapped under debris. Maskrid and five others helped her out of the rubble; she had a few cuts and bruises.

Near a large tree in the park, the rescuers found the body of a bearded man wearing spotless white Nike tennis shoes. He lay on his stomach, his face tilted upward, as if he were propped in front of a television sleeping peacefully. The men called the coroner as soon as possible.

Mari Holton and her daughter Ashlie hid under a desk covered with an overstuffed chair. The next morning they found potatoes soaking in mud puddles on the living room floor, and socks hanging on houseplants like Christmas ornaments. It had been a long night. Still, Ashlie managed to save a few things, including two candles from her high school prom. Etched into the glass of one candle was the phrase: "The Time of My Life." She considered herself lucky; the candle said it all.

To someone who asked Virginia Masters if she was OK, she replied, "As well as you can be when your life is destroyed."

Dale Nelson didn't have time to get to a storm shelter, so he grabbed a sleeping bag and pillows for protection and lay down in the bathtub. He heard a roar. "The whole floor was shaking," Nelson said. "I could feel it push up. A tree went through the living room where I was just at. I just held on and prayed. I'm lucky to be right here."

Sandy Donovan's family stood outside their home and surveyed the damage. "I'm just scared to beat hell, but I'm fine," Donovan exclaimed. The wind blew her husband's truck into a field across the street. Her son Craig heard cries for help and found a car with a man inside who said the tornado blew him 175 feet from the street into the field beside the truck.

Roy and Tammi Ekstrom were in their car. "We couldn't see," said Roy. "Rain and wind were coming so hard. We just hunkered down in the car and held onto each other. It seemed like forever. It was very scary." A utility pole went through the Ekstrom's car, but neither of them was hurt. The next day Larry Behrens spent some time looking for the pieces of his life. From the wreckage he pulled out Barbie dolls and furniture, and stacks of family pictures. Then he yelled out to his wife Terry. "Found my checks, Punkin," he laughed. Larry was wearing shorts and had a nasty cut on his leg. "You should be wearing long britches, Larry," his father-in-law said. But Larry's pants and other clothes were gone. Larry leaned over and picked up the head and shoulders of a statue of Elvis Presley; he tried to put the pieces together, but couldn't. After walking out of the rubble, he looked at the wrecked kitchen. All the new appliances were upside down. Sadly he said, "It was a beautiful home."

A young couple walked west across the tracks, carrying their son. The little boy looked back over this shoulder. "Look what the tornado did," the boy said to anyone who would listen.

"Just look what the tornado did."[67] Map Available: Appendix 1.

PARSONS, APRIL 19, 2000

At 9:00 p.m. on April 19, a tornado moved across Parsons. It was one of four that descended on Southeast Kansas. The weather spotters reported seeing others in Erie, Walnut, and Cherryvale.

In Parsons, the tornado destroyed or damaged dozens of houses and businesses, including the Parsons Police Station and the new Parsons Theater. The storm entered the town from the southwest, and although it did not completely touch the ground, it was low enough to flatten some buildings and tear the roof off others.

Ruins of the Hamilton Chapel, Parsons

It was a shock to see cars tossed into yards, houses, and against buildings and to see large trees flatten homes and other vehicles. The tornado badly damaged some businesses downtown, including Howerter Appliance, the Eagles Club, Time Warner Cable, Parsons Motors, Ace Hardware, Ervin Auto and Marine, and Country Mart. Mayor Tommy McLarty said, "I've had better days, but we're lucky. The warnings were adequate."

Wayne Marlow abandoned his Dad's truck when he saw the tornado and tried to find shelter by squatting next to another car. After a few minutes when the wind quit blowing, he ran to the Country Mart. "I've known fear before, but this is my first experience with terror," Marlow said.

The tornado, from viewing the storm track, did some odd things. It definitely jumped back and forth, damaging at will. These are sometimes the most dangerous of storms because residents are never aware of the location of the tornado at any given time, or whether they are "in the clear." The only situation that is worse is if such a storm occurs after dark.

Just a day or two before the tornado struck Parsons, this picture appeared on the front page of the Parsons Sun, showing the image of an angel. This is the picture that caused the controversy

Downtown the next day, Mike Howerter remarked, "I'm doing real well as long as I'm busy working." The storm flattened the front of his appliance store, but he found a few things worth saving, especially his business records. "We'll reopen when we can find a place. Right now, that's so far ahead of us," Mike said.

Workers at Ace Hardware tried to save the marigolds and begonias buried under bricks and porch swings. "We'll salvage what we can," Roger Sevart said. "Now we're just wiped out."

Dan Gilbreath and wife Kathy both worked at the damaged Country Mart; Kathy was a cashier. "Money's going to be tight," Dan said. He thought it would take about eight weeks for the store to reopen.

Joyce Holmes' home was only half there. Boards propped up the porch where the columns once stood. "It took all but one," Holman said, looking at her porch. "And we found one that was still intact. I stayed here last night because I didn't want to get looted," she stated looking at the damaged second story of the house.

View of significant devastation in Parsons after the tornado

The next afternoon, Violet Radcliff and her daughter Kimberly were working on her brother's wrecked house. "They weren't home when it happened... When they got back, this is what they found." Violet said her son was renting to own the house. "I cried this morning because I know how hard they had worked on it. What's horrible is that he lost his home, his truck and his job all in the same day. He worked at Country Mart," she said.

The twister destroyed Toby's Carnival. Luckily, the crew had taken all the customers off the rides just minutes before the storm struck. "We heard it was up the road. We knew it was coming so we closed all the rides down," Daniel Yarnell said. "We've never encountered anything like this before so we'll tackle it as it comes. It's always hard to take a hit like this. We've gone from one of the nicest carnivals in the Midwest to a pile of junk."

Is it the bright lights of a carnival ride or is it the figure of an angel or Jesus? These are the questions many people asked after seeing a photograph published on the front page of the *Parsons Sun*, just a day or so before a tornado struck the city. In between the red and yellow lights of the "Zipper" ride and the Ferris wheel, there seems to be suspended in the air a ghostly likeness of a figure in a white robe, with white hair and a yellow halo above its head.

It stunned both Sheila Leon and Colleen Eisenbart when they saw the photograph. They thought it was a picture of Jesus or an angel. Yet, some people saw nothing but the lights. Others say the picture was altered, but *Sun* editor Ann Charles said the photo was not altered.

"This is the original picture. I have looked at the negatives and it is the same as the negatives. It is absolutely not a hoax." Ann explained that the picture is of a pendulum-like ride with arms that swing out, and in the sequence of pictures the arms are moving. While she knew the explanation behind the picture, she admitted that she also sees an image. "I feel that God is here with us all the time. I never expected a photographer from the *Sun* to capture Him on film… People often see what they need to see. We're happy if it gives them comfort, but the photograph is still a photograph of a carnival."

Since that day in April of 2000 the city of Parsons has recovered from the effects of the tornado, and the damaged businesses are open once again.[68] Map Available: Appendix 1.

HOISINGTON, APRIL 21, 2001

The tornado at Hoisington left as quickly as it came, for its short path became a scene of controversy for weeks. The controversy—why didn't the National Weather Service warn residents of the impending danger? Again, the citizens viewed this lack of any warning as just another oversight on the part of the National Weather Service. Was this another tornado that wasn't supposed to be there?

The storm originated in Rush County, developing quickly into a severe thunderstorm, but then weakening just as fast. Tornadoes touched down briefly around Rush Center and Timken.

The storm chasers, who were following the storm before it weakened, decided to go to a nearby Great Bend restaurant for something to eat. As the men were beginning their meal, the lights began to flicker. Another super cell thunderstorm developed suddenly, and the storm's intensity surprised the chasers.

Weather spotters and sheriff's dispatchers in Hoisington were so surprised by the storm that they didn't have time to activate the town's warning sirens. Although the tornado struck at 9:15 p.m., the National Weather Service didn't dispatch a tornado warning until 9:22 p.m. However, at 8:00 p.m. a severe thunderstorm warning was issued for the area. When the tornado came roaring through town, it was an F-4 for a brief time.

Hoisington, population 3,000, was left with nearly 900 homeless people. The tornado destroyed or severely damaged the Hoisington High School, the Clara Barton Hospital, and the town's only grocery store. Entire neighborhoods were demolished. The most immediate concern to everyone was the High School prom that was in full swing that night, but the resourceful prom-goers took cover in the basement of the Knights of Columbus building. The only fatality was an elderly man who paused to survey the weather. This brief preoccupation with the oncoming twister cost him his life when his house collapsed around him.

The tornado went from just a thunderstorm to a tornado in a matter of seconds, which is somewhat unusual but not unknown. Less than a mile from where it first touched down, the wind speed in the cell exceeded 200 miles per hour. Power went out immediately, which prompted the police to go to each neighborhood sounding their sirens. Sightseers, downed power lines, and another storm that brought heavy rain and sixty-mile-an-hour winds then hampered rescue efforts. The injured trapped in wrecked houses and the patients from the damaged Clara Barton Hospital needed to be evacuated.

The tornado at Hoisington proved that the most experienced storm spotter and the most sophisticated radar still cannot predict severe weather or tornadoes with 100% accuracy. We have come a long way since the 19th century in the field of meteorology, but we still have a long way to go.[69]

KANSAS CITY, SOUTHERN KANSAS, MAY 4, 2003

One of the most remarkable days in Kansas tornado history was the tornado outbreak of May 4, 2003. This was one of the largest outbreaks to hit this region since the early 1990s. It created multiple tornadoes that stayed on the ground for miles and caused widespread destruction.

The front that caused all the trouble had two major areas of concern: extreme Eastern Kansas and Southeast Kansas. The tornadoes that occurred in extreme Eastern Kansas formed in the worst possible location— just east of suburban Kansas City in Wyandotte County.

Suburban Kansas City had long escaped a direct hit from a tornado despite the growth that occurred from the 1960s forward. On Sunday, May 4, that all changed. A small tornado first touched down just northwest of the Kansas Speedway and moved towards western Kansas City, Kansas. It initially caused minimal damage, but then it rapidly grew in size and strength. Its winds increased to around 200 miles per hour and its size grew to a width of 500 yards as it plowed through town, cutting a wide swath. Cars were flattened, houses unroofed, and people were injured. The tornado may have lifted and dropped several times, as the damage varied. The worst damage may have occurred around 91st & Leavenworth Road, where several homes were flattened to the foundations. An 82 year-old man was killed in his residence. The tornado continued northeast through Wyandotte County, where more severe damage was caused near 79th Street and Cernech. Here four 150-foot metal power poles were flattened to the ground. These poles were designed to withstand 200 mile per hour winds. Either they didn't really withstand the winds, or winds were higher than 200 miles per hour.

The tornado crossed the Missouri River and did considerable damage in Parkville and Riverside, Missouri, and Kansas City North. It continued for several more miles before causing severe damage to college buildings in Liberty, Missouri. Shortly after that, it appears to have lifted. Other severe thunderstorms caused damage and possible tornadoes in Leavenworth and Miami Counties.

Wyandotte County sustained $16 million in damage, including 69 buildings destroyed and 390 damaged. Another four million occurred in Leavenworth County. A forty-six year old woman died from injuries received with this tornado five months later.

This was not the worst that occurred that day. In Montgomery County, another super cell developed and it eventually moved into southwest Crawford County, where it spawned a large and destructive tornado. This tornado laid a path of destruction that was twenty-seven miles long. It killed three people and injured twenty in the eastern part of the county. From here, it moved into Barton County, Missouri, where it continued its deadly path. Here it killed a woman by throwing her from her mobile home while the home disintegrated.

Another super cell moved out of southern Labette County into southwest Cherokee County. Intermittent, brief tornado touchdowns were observed from storm spotters in rural sections of Labette County. The storm eventually produced a long-lived tornado that touched down north of Melrose. It moved through rural areas of central and east central Cherokee County. It killed three people here and injured nineteen. It then moved into Jasper County, Missouri and continued the death and destruction through Southern Missouri.

While this severe storm outbreak was worse in Missouri, it was no picnic in Kansas. The widespread destruction made it one of the worst tornado outbreaks of the decade. It was a wake-up call for Kansas City to realize that they were not exempt from destructive storms. Before the decade was over, the city would be hit again.

RENO COUNTY, JULY 3, 2005

One of the greatest fears in recent decades is if a tornado would ever hit a lake or reservoir during a busy weekend. Thousands of people camping in tents and trailers— it would be a disaster in the making. Such a thing nearly happened on July 3 near Cheney Lake State Park.

A line of severe thunderstorms, which may have produced minimal tornado-force winds, roared across the lake. The marina was badly damaged, as were 125 boats, 35 campers, and several mobile homes. Six people were badly injured and required transport to Wichita hospitals. One fatality occurred— a man was trying out his newly acquired fishing boat, when it capsized and he drowned. His body was not immediately found. Campers that holiday weekend were pretty shook up. The storm developed rapidly and with little warning. Many boaters were caught out in the open at the last minute, not realizing the gravity of the situation.

Governor Kathleen Sebelius declared a state of emergency for Reno County. An estimated 2,500 farm dwellings sustained damage totaling 2.5 million dollars. An estimated 155,000 acres of farmland were a total loss.

GREENSBURG, MAY 4, 2007

There have been a few tornadoes that were so big and destructive that they defy logic. There was the Udall tornado in May 1955 and the Topeka tornado in 1966. The Wichita and Haysville tornadoes in the 1990s also proved to be among the worst that Kansas had to offer.

The worst tornadoes are perhaps those that happen after dark. The main reason is that you can't see them. The Udall tornado occurred after dark, which may have contributed to the high death toll. In similar fashion, the Greensburg tornado occurred just after dark. Despite Barack Obama's claim that "10,000" people died in Greensburg, the death toll was more like 11, thanks to an advanced warning system.

The tornado formed about fourteen miles east of Mullinville around 8:00pm. It stayed on the ground for 26 miles, lifting about an hour later. During that time, it became an F5 tornado and was perhaps 3,000 yards wide at its peak. This would make it one of the widest tornadoes in the history of the state. Unfortunately, the tornado became the most intense right before hitting Greensburg. Over $205 million dollars worth of damage was done in the town, and ninety-five percent of it was leveled. Of the eleven deaths, some were actually in basements. Debris from the tornado slammed into basements, trapping some residents.

The first rescue teams that arrived in Greensburg after the tornado requested three refrigerator trucks, believing that there were hundreds of fatalities. In all, 961 homes and businesses were destroyed, 216 received major damage and 307 received minor damage. It also destroyed a dozen homes and a church south of Greensburg but it did not cause serious injury.

Oddly enough, as the tornado was dissipating, it turned northwest, west, south, and then back east, making a full loop. This was documented on both high resolution Doppler radar and through ground surveys. As the tornado was dissipating, a new circulation occurred northeast of Greensburg. Several oil storage tanks were destroyed, causing an environmental concern. In Greensburg itself, hazardous material was strewn everywhere.

The monumental task of cleaning debris was not completed overnight. Two landfills were filled with debris and this was in spite of the fact that much of the debris was burned. Thousands of dump truck loads were taken out. It was estimated that around 400,000 cubic yards of debris was removed. The major highway through town was closed for a month. Over a hundred and fifty law enforcement officers, some from all over the country, were present. The military was called in to remove debris.

The Greensburg tornado was the first "5" rating on the new enhanced Fujita scale and the first five classification since May 3, 1999, when an F5 tornado ripped through Moore, Oklahoma.

An F3 tornado occurred in Pratt County near Hopewell the same night. It grew to be a mile wide, and it killed one person near Hopewell when a basement wall collapsed on him. Another tornado of similar strength formed near Macksville. It soon became 1,500 yards wide. A law enforcement officer was watching one tornado dissipate and he did not notice that another was rapidly forming. He was unable to get out of harm's way. His car was thrown a quarter mile and was found in an open field. He died several days later with painful injuries received in the crushed vehicle.

Another round of tornadoes occurred the following day across generally the same area. One of these was near Bennington. A woman was killed when her mobile home was destroyed. Nearly 250 pivot irrigation sprinklers were damaged or destroyed during the two-day outbreak. Due to the number of sprinklers involved and the lack of replacements, some farmers would be without service for over a year.

The task of rebuilding Greensburg posed several options. Residents considered rebuilding the town as quickly as possible, but others found this to be an opportunity to rebuild Greensburg as the first all-Kansas "green" community. Since 95% of the town was wiped off the face of the map, the chance to rebuild an environmentally friendly town was the choice of many Greensburg residents. The progress made on this behalf was documented in a TV series on the National Geographic "Green" Channel. Map Available: Appendix 1.

PRATT COUNTY, MAY 23, 2008

A large tornado formed about three miles southeast of Sawyer. Before it was over, the funnel had grown to be 1,500 yards wide. It was not without fatalities. A husband and wife were parked on Highway 54 just east of Cairo. The tornado picked up their car and carried it 1,700 feet into a wheat field. They were not discovered until the following morning at around 9am. The female occupant was ejected and found thirty feet southwest of the wreckage. The male was still strapped in his seat. The car was nearly unrecognizable. A second vehicle was parked twenty yards behind the car. It also went airborne briefly but got lodged on the north side of a ditch. The two male occupants received numerous cuts and bruises but were otherwise unhurt. A home was destroyed about a mile north and the collapsed east wall trapped a male in the bathtub where he had taken cover. Help was needed in lifting the wall off of him but he escaped relatively unhurt.

A strong upper level system was the catalyst to produce what was perhaps the biggest tornado outbreak to ever occur in the Dodge City area. Fifty-five tornadoes were documented during that afternoon and evening. Some of the tornadoes were very large and damaging. The character of the super cell thunderstorms that day had similarities to the storms that produced the Greensburg tornado a year earlier. In fact, there was one tornado that was just as large and perhaps could have been as damaging as it rolled through Kiowa County, but fortunately it turned and dissipated.

EAST CENTRAL KANSAS, JUNE 11, 2008

A series of major storms and tornadoes hit East Central Kansas on June 11, causing widespread damage from Chapman to Manhattan. Three significant tornadoes touched down causing millions of dollars in damage and killing two people.

The first tornado formed a mile southeast of Enterprise. It grew to be 880 yards wide, and it traveled thirteen miles past Chapman in Dickinson County. During that time it grew to an F3 in intensity and it did twenty million in damages. The tornado continued southeast out of Dickinson County and dissipated shortly after entering Geary County.

The primary damage was done at Chapman, where 70 homes were completely destroyed and 215 were badly damaged. When the first news reports came in, the tornado was compared to Greensburg from a year before. Fortunately, it was not quite that bad. In all, three-quarters of the buildings in town sustained damage, including two churches and the town's middle school and high school. About a hundred residents were in the locker rooms of the high school seeking shelter from the storm when the tornado struck. Trees across town were twisted and nearly stripped of leaves and branches. For the most part, the downtown business section received only minor damage.

Debris from the town was littered for several miles. Dozens of individuals sustained minor injuries. Three were critically injured. One death was reported when a tree was blown onto a woman who just put her daughter into a car seat in her vehicle. Over the following weeks, thousands of volunteers took part in the clean-up effort.

The most severe damage occurred in the Miller Ranch neighborhood in Manhattan, where several homes were completely destroyed. Several buildings on the Kansas State University campus were heavily damaged, scaring a number of students who had stayed on campus over the summer months.

Another tornado caused damage and one death near Soldier, Kansas. Here a man was killed in his mobile home when it flipped several times and it was found a few miles from its original location. There was an unoccupied home a few hundred feet from the mobile home. It sustained literally no damage whatsoever. This tornado was considered an F2 and was about 200 yards wide. It started in Pottawatomie County near Havensville, moved to Jackson County and ended up in Nemaha County before it dissipated. For most of its path, it was an F1 at most. Mostly power lines and farm outbuildings sustained damage until it hit Soldier. Map Available: Appendix 1.

Appendix 1: Significant Tornado Paths

General Kansas Map

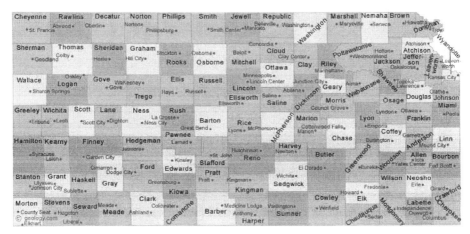

Kansas County Map With County Seats, Courtesy of Geology.com

Cottonwood Falls/ Strong City: 1878

Tornado track, Cottonwood Falls, Strong City tornado, 1878

Irving tornado path: May 1879

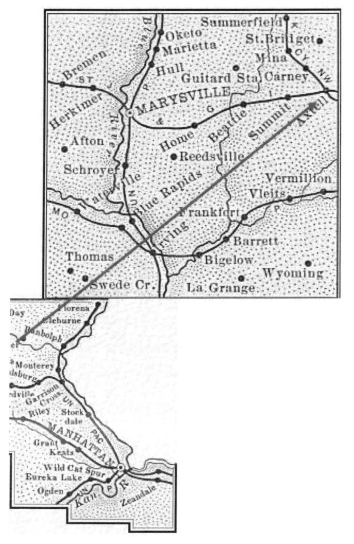

Tornado track of Irving tornado, May 1879.

Tornado Outbreak: June 12, 1881

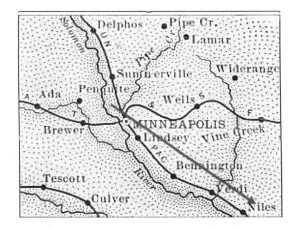

Part of the tornado outbreak of June 12, 1881 in Ottawa County

Phillipsburg Tornado, June 26, 1882

Phillipsburg tornado track, June 26, 1882

Kansas City, Kansas, May 13, 1883

Kansas City, Kansas and Leavenworth tornadoes, May 13, 1883

Tornado Track near Stafford, May 5-7, 1889

Tornado track near Stafford, May 5, 1889

Sumner and Butler Counties, March 31, 1892

Sumner and Butler County Tornado, March 31, 1892

Wellington tornado, May 27, 1892

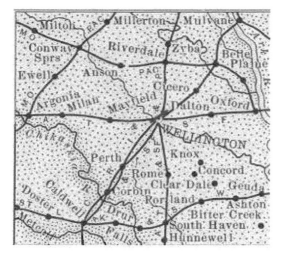

Wellington tornado, May 27, 1892

Perry and Williamstown, June 22, 1893

Perry and Williamstown tornado, June 22, 1893

Cunningham Tornado, May 1898

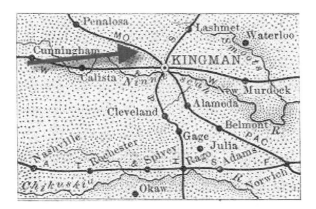

Cunningham tornado, May 1898

Marquette Tornado, May 8, 1905

Marquette tornado, May 8, 1905

Great Bend and Hoisington, May 14, 1909

Great Bend and Hoisington tornado,
May 14, 1909

Emporia and Plymouth, May 1, 1910

Plymouth and Neosho
Rapids tornado, May 1,
1910

Eastern Kansas Tornado, April 12, 1911

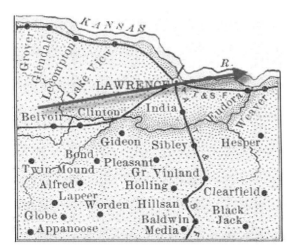

Eastern Kansas tornado outbreak, Douglas County, April 12, 1911

Parker Tornado, June 15, 1912.

Parker tornado, June 15, 1912

November 10, 1915 tornado outbreak: Zyba and Great Bend

November 10, 1915, tornado that hit Great Bend, Barton County

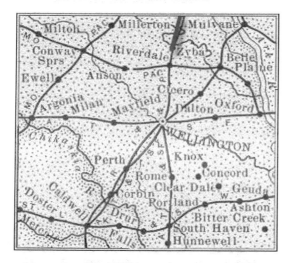

November 10, 1915 tornado outbreak, Zyba

Southern Kansas, May 25, 1917

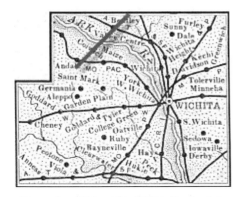

Tornado of May 25, 1917: Sedgwick County track through Andale, Bentley, and others

Registration Day Tornado, June 5, 1917

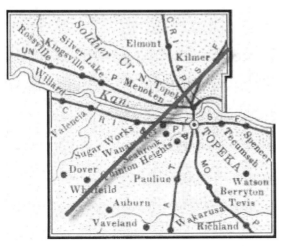

Map of Registration Day Tornado through Shawnee County, June 5, 1917

Registration Day tornado of
June 5, 1917, through
Wabaunsee County

Hays area, May 20, 1918

Tornado of May 20, 1918, through
Trego County

Path of tornado of May 20, 1918, through Rooks County

Augusta, July 13, 1924

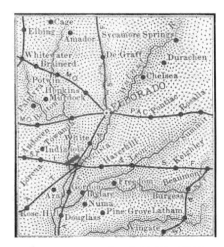

Augusta tornado, July 13, 1924

Pratt, June 25, 1930

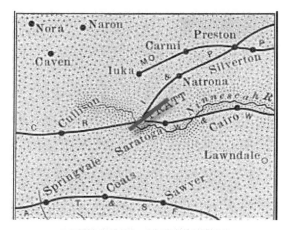

Pratt tornado, June 25, 1930

Washington, July 4, 1932

Washington tornado, July 4, 1932

Independence, February 24, 1935

Independence tornado of Feb. 24, 1935

Oberlin, April 29, 1942

Oberlin tornado, April 29, 1942

WaKeeney, June 27, 1951

WaKeeney tornado, June 27, 1951

Udall, May 25, 1955

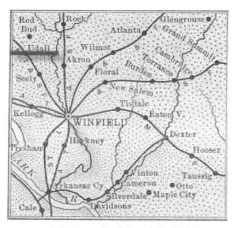

Udall tornado, May 25, 1955

Spring Hill, Ottawa, Ruskin Heights, May 20, 1957

Spring Hill, Ruskin Heights tornado, May 20, 1957

El Dorado, June 10, 1958

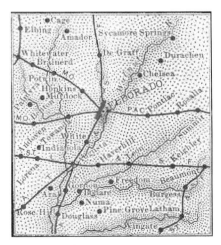

El Dorado tornado, June 10, 1958

Meriden and Elmont, May 19, 1960

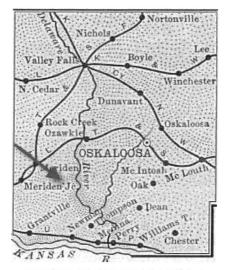

Meriden tornado, May 19, 1960

Holton, August 6, 1962

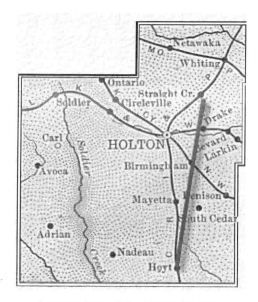

Jackson County tornado, Hoyt to
Birmingham and beyond, August 6,
1962

Topeka, June 8, 1966

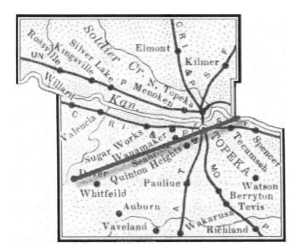

Topeka tornado, June 8, 1966

Emporia, June 8, 1974

Emporia tornado, June 8, 1974

The Whippoorwill, Lake Pomona, June 16, 1978

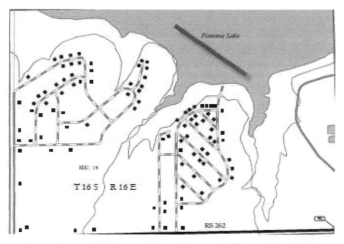

Location of Whippoorwill waterspout, June 16, 1978

Carbondale, October 31, 1984

Tornado, Scranton to Carbondale,
October 31, 1984

Hesston tornado, March 1990

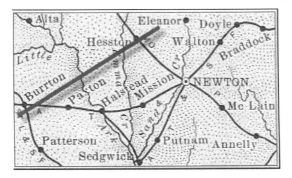

Hesston tornado in Harvey County, March 1990

Wichita and Andover, April 26, 1991

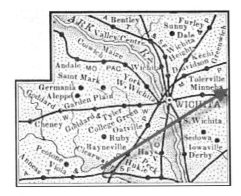

Wichita tornado through Sedgwick County, April 26, 1991

Parsons, April 19, 2000

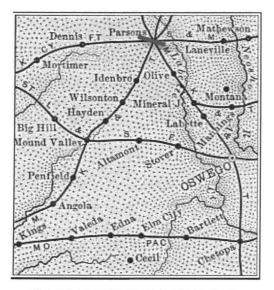

Tornado of April 19, 2000 that struck
Parsons, Labette County

Greensburg, May 4, 2007

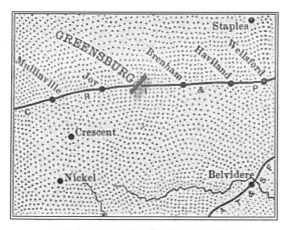

Greensburg tornado, May 4, 2007

East Central Kansas, June 11, 2008

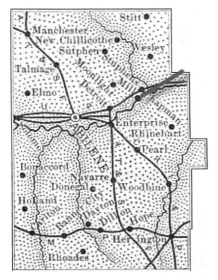

Chapman tornado, June 11, 2008

Manahattan tornado, June 11, 2008

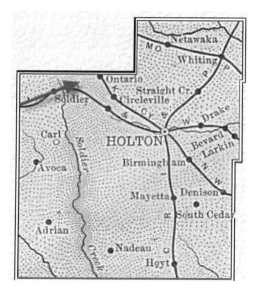

Jackson County, and Soldier, June 11, 2008

Photo Credits

Title Page: Western History Collections, University of Oklahoma Libraries

Pg. 4: Western History Collections, University of Oklahoma Libraries

Pg. 21: National Oceanic & Atmospheric Administration (NOAA) Photo Library, Dept of Commerce

Pg. 22: NOAA Photo Library, Dept of Commerce.

Pg. 58: U.S. Signal Service, Irving Tornado, 1879.

Pg. 77: NOAA Photo Library, Dept of Commerce

Pg. 79: Kansas State Historical Society, Topeka, Kansas.

Pg. 89: Ibid.

Pg. 90: Ibid.

Pg. 101: Ibid.

Pg. 103: NOAA Photo Library, Dept of Commerce

Pg. 106: Gwen Huey, Topeka, Kansas

Pg. 111: NOAA Photo Library, Dept of Commerce

Pg. 114: Kansas State Historical Society, Topeka, Kansas

Pg. 115: Ibid.

Pg. 121: Ibid

Pg. 122: TOP: Kansas State Historical Society, Topeka, Kansas. BOTTOM: NOAA Photo Library, Dept of Commerce.

Pg. 123: Kansas State Historical Society, Topeka, Kansas

Pg. 124: Ibid.

Pg. 125: Ibid.

Pg. 129: Ibid.

Pg. 130: Ibid.

Pg. 134: Ibid.

Pg. 141: NOAA Photo Library, Dept of Commerce

Pg. 143: Kansas State Historical Society, Topeka, Kansas

Pg. 144 and Front Cover: Ibid.

Pg. 146: Kansas State Historical Society, Topeka, Kansas

Pg. 153: Ibid.

Pg. 154: Ibid.

Pg. 155: NOAA Photo Library, Dept of Commerce

Pg. 157: TOP & BOTTOM: NOAA Photo Library, Dept of Commerce

Pg. 159: Kansas State Historical Society, Topeka, Kansas

Pg. 160: Ibid.

Pg. 165: NOAA Photo Library, Dept of Commerce

Pg. 170: Western History Collections, University of Oklahoma Libraries

Pg. 178: Ibid.

Pg. 181: Ibid.

Pg. 186: NOAA Photo Library, Dept of Commerce

Pg. 189: Ibid.

Pg. 190: Ibid.

Pg. 195: Ibid.

Pg. 208: Ibid.

Pg. 215: Western History Collections, University of Oklahoma Libraries

Pg. 217: Kansas State Historical Society, Topeka, Kansas

Pg. 219: Kansas Storm Chasers website

Pg. 221: Kansas State Historical Society, Topeka, Kansas

Pg. 225: NOAA Photo Library, Dept of Commerce

Pg. 226: Kansas State Historical Society, Topeka, Kansas

Pg. 227: Ibid.

Pg. 232: Ibid.

Pg. 241: TOP & BOTTOM: Topeka Capital-Journal.

Pg. 242: Ibid.

Pg. 243: Kansas State Historical Society, Topeka, Kansas

Pg. 244: Topeka Capital-Journal

Pg. 245: Ibid.

Pg. 257: Kansas Storm Chasers website

Pg. 287: Ibid.

Pg. 289: Ibid.

Pg. 290: Tornadoes: Nature's Most Violent Storms (pamphlet), Sept 1992

Pg. 307: Kansas Storm Chasers website

Pg. 308: Ibid.

Pg. 314: Ibid.

Pg. 326: Ibid.

Pg. 328: Ibid.

Pg. 331: Ann Charles, editor, Parsons Sun

Pg. 332: Ibid.

Pg. 333: Ibid.

Selected Bibliography

Barry, Louise. **The Beginning of the West**. Topeka, Kansas: Kansas State Historical Society, 1972. A major resource for significant early tornadoes.

Brewer, Carolyn. **Caught in the Path: The Ruskin Heights Tornado**, May 30, 1957 Kansas City, MO: Leathers Publishing, 1997.

Finlay, Sgt. J.P., "Professional Papers of the U.S. Signal Service, #IV, Tornadoes, May 29 and 30th, 1879, in Kansas, Nebraska, Missouri, and Iowa." Washington D.C.: U.S. Government Printing Office, 1881.

Flora, Snowden D. **Tornadoes of the United States**. Norman, Oklahoma: University of Oklahoma Press, 1954. The main authority for decades on tornadoes. Flora wrote a lesser-known reference book, but just as interesting, called **Hailstorms of the United States**.

Grazulius, T. P., **Significant Tornadoes**. Environmental Films, 1997. A major resource on tornadoes.

Hearth Publ. **Kansas Storms-Destruction, Tragedy and Recovery.** Hillsboro, KS: Hearth Publishing Co., 1991.

Kansas State Historical Society, compilers. **"County Clippings Volumes,"** all counties, all dates. Topeka: Kansas State Historical Society.

Topeka Capital Journal, "The Day the Sky Fell," (Topeka: Stauffer Publications, 1966)

Weems, John Edward. **The Tornado.** Garden City, New York: Doubleday Press, 1977.

Wichita Eagle-Beacon Publishers, **Like the Devil**, Wichita: Wichita Eagle Beacon Publishers, 1991.

Notes

Introduction

i. Weems, John Edward. The Tornado (Garden City: Doubleday Press, 1977) p. 28; Flora Snowden D., Tornadoes of the United States, (Norman, Oklahoma; University of Oklahoma Press, 1954) p. 3. Flora's all-inclusive book on tornadoes was the primary reference source on the subject for over 40 years. In a 1589 edition of a book published by Richard Hakluyt to commemorate and describe notable voyages, one mariner was quoted as saying, "we had terrible thunder and lightning, with exceeding great gusts of raine, called ternados."

ii. Grazulius, T.P. Signficant Tornadoes. Environmental Films, 1997, pp. 3-4.

iii. Ibid., pp. 4-5.

iv. Flora, Tornadoes, p. 54.

v. Ibid., pp,.142-143; Chabaud, Rene, Weather: Drama of the Heavens, pp.29-30.

vi. Flora, Tornadoes, p. 23.

vii. Flora, Tornadoes, pp. 19-22.

viii. Finlay, Sgt. J.P., "Professional Papers of the U.S. signal Service, #IV, Tornadoes, May 29 and 30th, 1879, in Kansas, Nebraska, Missouri, and Iowa." (Washington D.C.: U.S. Government Printing Office, 1881), pp. 52-53.

ix. Flora. <u>Tornadoes</u>, pp. 12-13; Eagleman, Joseph, <u>Thunderstorms, tornadoes, and Building Damage</u>, (Lexington, Mass: Lexington Books, 1975) p. 7.

x. Flora, <u>Tornadoes</u>, pp. 26-27.

xi. Eagleman, <u>Building Damage</u>, p. 8.

xii. Weems, <u>The Tornado</u>, p. 38. You have one chance in 42 in Kansas of being struck by a tornado.

xiii. Flora, <u>Tornadoes</u>, pp. 142-143.

xiv. Ibid., p. 7.

xv. Ibid., pp. 142-143.

xvi. Weems, <u>The Tornado</u>, pp. 25-26.

xvii. Ibid., pp. 25-70; Grazulius, pp. 5-6. Biblical times indicate a tornado about 600 B.C. in Ezekiel 1:4.

xviii. Grazulius, pp. 7-8.

xix. Flora, <u>Tornadoes,</u> p. 142.

xx. Cyclone cellars became popular beginning in the 1870's.

xxi. The southwest corner of the basement proved to be unreliable during the June 8, 1966 Topeka tornado. At the Washburn University auditorium, a crowd inadvertently chose the wrong corner of the basement to seek shelter. The error saved their lives as huge foundation stones collapsed in the actual southwest corner.

xxii. Nearly twice as many women died as men in tornado disasters in the nineteenth century.

xxiii. Engelbert, Phyllis. "Complete Weather Resource," II (New York), 1997, pp. 24-25.

xxiv. "Certain Tornado and Squall Line Features," United Air Lines Meteorology Circular 36.; Flora, <u>Tornadoes</u>, p. 13.

xxv. Flora, <u>Tornadoes</u>, p. 176; Weems, <u>The Tornado</u>, p. 48.
xxvi. Grazulius, p. 17-18; Weems, <u>The Tornado</u>, p. 48.

xxvii. Grazulius, p. 20-21.

xxviii. Animal behavior has often been characterized as erratic before a major storm. Birds and dogs seem particularly prone to strange behavioral twists just prior to severe weather.

xxix. The heat dome is a recent theory as mid-western and southern cities have expanded their boundaries.

xxx. Flora, <u>Tornadoes</u>, pp. 61-62, regarding Codell.

Chapter One

1. Sloane, Eric, <u>Folklore of American Weather</u>, (New York: Duell, Sloan & Pearce, 1963),p. 4.

2. Ludlum, David, <u>The Weather Factor</u>, Boston: Houghton-Mifflin, 1984), p. 10.

3. Ibid., Forrester, Frank, <u>1001 Questions Answered About the Weather</u>, (New York: Dodd-Meade, 1957), p. 341.

4. Forrester, 1001 Questions, p. 341.

5. Chaboud, Rene, Weather, drama of the Heavens, (New York: Times-Mirror Publishers, 1994), p. 129.

6. Chaboud, Weather Drama, p. 30.

7. Hayward, Elizabeth, John McCoy: His Life and Diaries.

8. Barry, Louise, The Beginning of the West, Topeka: Kansas State Historical Society, 1972), p. 489.

9. Ibid.

10. Caldwell, Martha, Annals of Shawnee Methodist Mission (Topeka: Kansas State Historical Society, 1928, reprint 1977) p. 34.

11. Barry, Beginning, p. 636.

12, Parkman, Francis, The Oregon Trail, (New York: Holt, Rinehart & Winston, 1931), pp. 194-196.

13. Kansas City Journal, March 24, 1900.

14. Ludlum, David, Early American Tornadoes, (New York: American Meteorological Society, 1970) pp. 132-133.

15. Ibid.

16. Jefferson County Journal (Adams, New York), May 15, 1895.

17. Ibid.

18. Rich, Everett. Heritage of Kansas, (Lawrence: University Press of Kansas, 1960), p. 118.

19. Ibid.

20. Fitzgerald, Daniel, Ghost Towns of Kansas, A Travelers Guide, (Lawrence: University Press of Kansas, 1988), p. 45.

21. Doran, Thomas F. " Kansas Sixty Years Ago," speech read to Saturday Night Club, Topeka, February 4, 1922.

22. "Reminiscences of Early Settlement of Dragoon Creek, Wabaunsee County," by Stephen Spear, Kansas Historical Collections. Vol. 11 (1910-11), pp. 299-300.

23. "Letters of Peter Bryant, Jackson County Pioneer," edited by Donald Murray and Robert M. Rodney, Kansas Historical Collections, Vol. 15 (1916-17), pp. 439-445.

24. Neosho Valley Register, July 27, 1860.

25. Weems, The Tornado, p. 48.

26. Ibid.

27. Neosho Valley Register, July 27, 1860.

28. Ibid.

29. Ibid.

30. "Ottumwa," in Fitzgerald, Daniel, Ghost Towns of Kansas, Volume Two, (Holton, Kansas: Bell Graphics, 1979), p. 178-179.

31. Leavenworth Daily Commonwealth, October 24, 1860.

32. Malin, James C. "Beginnings of Winter Wheat Production in the Upper Kansas and Lower smoky Hill River Valleys," (Manhattan: Kansas State University, 1941), pp. 12-14.

33. Very little information on early tornadoes is known or available.

34. Newspaper sources remained the main base of information for the earlier Kansas tornadoes.

Chapter Two

1. Chauboud, <u>Weather Drama</u>, p. 137.

2. Forrester, Frank, <u>1001 Questions Answered About the Weather</u>, (New York: Dodd-Meade, 1977), p. 340.

3. Finley, Sgt. J.P. "Professional Papers of the U.S. Signal Service #IV, Tornadoes May 29th & 30th, 1879, in Kansas, Nebraska. Missouri & Iowa," (Washington D.C.: U.S. Government Printing Office, 1881), p. 19.

4. Grazulius, <u>Tornado</u>, p. 4-6; Homan, Dorothy, <u>Lincoln That County in Kansas</u>. (Lincoln: Lincoln County Historical Society)

5. Stratford & Klintworth, <u>The Kingdom of Butler</u>, (El Dorado: Times Publishing Company, 1970), p. 14.

6. Kinner, Emma, "Tornado Tales," Kanhistique Magazine, Vol I, #12, Aril 1976, pp. 1, 3.

7. Kansas State Historical Society Library, comp. "Storm and Cyclone Clippings," Vol. I, (Kansas State Historical Society Library) p. 10.

8. Ibid.

9. Ibid.

10. Travis, Paul D. "Changing Climate in Kansas: A Late Nineteenth Century Myth," Kansas History: A Journal of the Central Plains, Vol. 1, #1, Spring 1978 (Topeka: Kansas State Historical Society) pp. 48-52.

11. Chase County Leader, April 18, 1878.

12. Ibid.

13. Ibid.

14. Ibid.

15. Ibid.

16. Topeka State Journal, July 10, 1878.

17. Finley, "Signal Service," p. 18.

18. If it were not for this report, we would have little to go by regarding this tornado.

19. Finley, "Signal Service," p. 19.

20. Ibid., pp. 20-38, 39.

21. Ibid., pp. 40-42.

22. Ibid., pp. 42-45.

23. Ibid., pp. 46-47, 49.

24. Ibid., pp. 47-48.

25. Ibid., p. 49.

26. Ibid, p. 50; Flora, <u>Tornadoes</u>, pp. 103-105.

27. Finley, "Signal Service," p. 51.

28. Ibid., pp. 51-52.

29. Ibid., pp. 52-53.

30. Ibid., p. 52.

31. Ibid., pp. 52-54.

32. Ibid., pp. 54-55.

33. Ibid., pp. 56-58; Minneapolis Sentinel, June 1, 1879.

34. Finley, "Signal Service," pp. 58, 59, 63-66; Minneapolis Sentinel, June 1, 1879.

35. Finley, "Signal Service," pp. 68-69, 75, 78.

36. Ibid., pp. 73-74.

37. Scientific American Magazine, Vol. XLI, #1, July 5, 1879, p. 1. Today there is a notebook in the town mailbox at the ghost town of Irving where meteorologists from around the world have come to the town and left comments.

Chapter Three

1. Flora, <u>Tornadoes</u>, pp. 65-66; Dary, David, <u>More True Tales of Old Time Kansas</u>, (Lawrence: University Press of Kansas, 1987) p. 177-178.

2. Axtell Standard, May 17, 1934.

3. Kanhistique magazine, Vol. 1, #1, April 1976, p. 3.

4. Ibid.

5. Topeka Capital, April 3, 1880.

6. Topeka, Capital, June 10, 1881.

7. Axtell Standard, May 17, 1934; Topeka Capital, June 11, 1881.

8. Osage City Free Press, June 13, 1881; Finley, Sgt. J.P. "Professional Papers of the U.S. Signal Service, #5, "Tornadoes of June 5 and 18, 1881."

9. Emporia News, Sept. 30, 1881 and October 6, 1881.

10. Stafford Courier, May 5, 1932.

11. Ibid.

12. Ibid.

13. Ibid.

14. Ibid; Kansas State Historical Society, comp., "Storm and Cyclone Clippings", Vol 4. 1932-47, p. 78.

15. KSHS, "Storm and Cyclone," p. 78; Manhattan Mercury, April 14, 1882.

16. Ibid.

17. KSHS, comp., "Storm and Cyclone Clippings," Vol 1, 1880-1910, p. 5.

18. Topeka Daily Capital, June 29, 1882.

19. Medicine Lodge Cresset, April 25, 1883.

20. Ibid.

21. Topeka Daily Capital, may 14, 1883.

22. Holton Recorder, July 17, 1883.

23. Winfield Courier, May 8, 1884.

24. Topeka Daily Capital, April 26, 1887.

25: Ibid.

26. Topeka Daily Capital, May 8, 1889 and May 9, 1889.

27. Wichita Beacon, April 1, 1892.

28. Ibid.

29. Augusta Gazette, April 1, 1938.

30. Augusta Gazette, April 1, 1943.

31. Wichita Beacon, April 1, 1892.

32. Ibid.

33. Ibid.

34. Wichita Eagle, March 31, 1938.

35. Ibid.

36. Wichita Beacon, April 1, 1892.

37. Ibid.

38. Ibid.

39. Wichita Beacon, May 28, 1892.

40. Valley Falls Vindicator, June 22, 1893.

41. Wichita Beacon, May 3, 1895 and May 3, 1918.

42. Topeka State Journal, May 3, 1895.

43. Wichita Beacon, May 3, 1895.

44. Clay Center Dispatch, April 30, 1896.

45. Ibid.

46. Ibid.

47. Ibid.

48. Ibid.

49. Ibid.

50. Ibid.

51. Ibid.

52. Manhattan Mercury, May 18, 1896.

53. Cunningham Clipper, March 20, 1953.

54. Ibid.

55. Clark County Clipper, May 28, 1903.

56. Ibid.

57. Eureka Herald, October 8, 1903.

58. Topeka State Journal, September 2, 1904.

59. Marquette News, May 11, 1905.

60. Ibid.

61. Ibid.

62. Jewell County Republican, May 29, 1908.

63. Ibid.

64. Hoisington Dispatch, May 20, 1909.

65. Ibid.

66. Topeka Capital, April 13, 1911 and April 18, 1911

67, 68, 69– Ibid.

70. Lawrence Journal-World, April 13, 1911 and April 14, 1911.

71. Ibid.

72. Ibid.

73. Ibid.

74. Kansas City Star, April 21, 1912 and Kansas City journal, April 21, 1912.

75. Linn County Republican, June 28, 1912.

76. Ibid.

77. Ibid.

78. Ibid.

79. Flora, Tornadoes, p, 11; Topeka Journal, August 26, 1912.

80. Bader, Robert. Hayseeds, Moralizers and Methodists, (Lawrence: University Press of Kansas, 1988), pp. 24,25; Street Julian, Abroad At Home: American Ramblings, Observatins, and Adventures (New York: Century Company, 1914) p. 35.

81. Wichita Eagle, April 3, 1979.

82. Flora, Tornadoes, p. 98; Kansas City Times, November 11, 1915.

83. Flora, Tornadoes, p. 99; Dary, More True Tales, p. 189.

84. Topeka Daily Capital, April 20, 1916.

85. Ibid.

86. Ibid.

87. Hays Free Press, May 26, 1917.

88. Wichita Beacon, May 26, 1917.

89 thru 93, Ibid.

94. Topeka Daily Capital, June 2, 1917; Coffeyville Daily Journal, June 1, 1917.

95. Coffeyville Daily Journal, June 1, 1917.

96. This tornado has been known as the fastest tornado in history.

97. Flora, Tornadoes, p. 9.

98. Ibid., p. 81. This was the fastest move his employer had ever seen him make!

99. Ibid. p. 83.

100. Topeka Journal, July 31, 1939.

Chapter Four

1. Hays Free Press, May 23, 1918.

2. Porter, marvel. "Three Tornadoes A Year Apart," Kanhistique Magazine, Vol. 2, #3, July 1977, p. 11.

3. Ibid; Flora, Tornadoes, pp. 61-62.

4. Flora, Tornadoes, pp. 61-62; Ellis County News, May 23, 1918.

5. Ellis County News, May 23, 1918.

6. Hays Free Press, May 23, 1918.

7. Hoisington Dispatch, October 9, 1919.

8. Ibid.

9. Ibid.

10. El Dorado Times, July 14, 1924.

11. Ibid; Augusta Daily Gazette, August 15, 1979.

12. Augusta Daily Gazette, August 15, 1979.

13. Hutchinson Herald, May 8, 1927; Topeka Capital, March 2, 1926.

14. Ibid; Topeka Capital, May 9, 1927.

15. Topeka Capital, May 9, 1927; Flora, Tornadoes, pp. 100-101

16. Topeka Daily Capital, July 18, 1927.

17. Ibid.

18. Ibid.

19, Flora, Tornadoes, p. 11; United States Weather Bureau, Monthly Weather Review, May 1930.

20. Flora, Tornadoes, pp. 11-12; USWB, Monthly Weather, May 1930.

21. Weems, The Tornado, p. 50.

22. Topeka State Journal, May 6, 1939.

23. Topeka Capital, June 27, 1930.

24. This was one of the worst dust storms to hit during the 1930's in Kansas.

25. Dary, More True Tales, p. 179-180.

26. Lincoln Sentinel Republican, March 21, 1935.

27. Dary, More True Tales, p. 179-180.

28. Kansas City Weekly Star, July 6, 1932.

29. Ibid.

30. Ibid.

31. Topeka Capital, April 27, 1933.

32. Hearth Publ. *Kansas Storms-Destruction, Tragedy and Recovery*, (Hillsboro, KS: Hearth Publishing Co., 1991), pp. 109-110.

33. Independence Daily Reporter, February 25, 1935.

34. Ibid.

35. Ibid; Coffeyville southern Kansas Tribune, February 27, 1933.

36, 37, 38. Ibid.

39. Atwood Citizen Patriot, July 11, 1935.

40. Bader, *Hayseeds*, p. 75; Dary, *More True Tales*, p. 180.

41. Independence Reporter, March 31, 1938.

42, 43, 44,, 45, 46, 47. Ibid.

48. Wichita Eagle, May 2 and May 3, 1938.

49. Kansas City Times, June 11, 1938.

50. Ibid.

51. Burr Oak Herald, June 15, 1939.

52. Wichita Eagle, June 8, 1941.

53. Ibid.

54. Wichita Eagle, August 26, 1941.

55. Oberlin Herald, April 29, 1942.

56. Ibid; Kansas City Star, April 30, 1942.

57. Iola Register, May 4, 1942.

58. Ibid.

59. Ibid.

60. Topeka Capital, May 11, 1942.

61. Wellington Monitor, June 20, 1942.

62. Ibid; Four days earlier there was a tornado in Finney, Lane and Ness Counties.

63. Wellington Monitor, June 20, 1942; Wichita Eagle, June 22, 1942.

64. Topeka Daily Capital, May 17, 1943.

65. Topeka Daily Capital, June 17, 1945.

66. Topeka Daily Capital, June 27, 1945.

67. Flora, Tornadoes, p. 40.

68. Ibid, p. 41.

Chapter Five

1. Flora, Tornadoes, p. 39.

2. Ibid., pp. 41-42.

3. Ibid., pp. 42-43.

4. Ibid., pp. 44-45; Eagleman, Building Damage, p. 7.

5. Flora, Tornadoes, p. 45.

6. Ibid., p.44.

7. Ibid., pp. 46-48.

8. Ibid., pp. 6, 49.

9. Eagleman, Building Damage, pp. 7-10.

10. Flora, Tornadoes, pp. 52-53.

11. Ibid., p. 53.

12. Ibid., pp. 6-7.

13. Ibid., pp. 7-8.

14. Ibid., p. 81.

15. Topeka Daily Capital, July 18, 1948.

16. Ibid.

17. Topeka Daily Capital, February 13, 1949.

18. Salina Journal, May 20, 1949.

19. Wichita Beacon, May 21, 1949.

20. Ibid.

21. Topeka State Journal, October 19 and 21, 1949.

22. Flora, Tornadoes, p. 99.

23. Topeka State Journal, June 9, 1950.

24. Kansas City Times, May 5, 1951; Topeka State Journal, May 21, 1951.

25. Salina Journal, June 28, 1951.

26. Topeka Daily Capital, June 28, 1951.

27. Topeka Daily Capital, July 3, 1951.

28. Flora, Tornadoes, p. 126.

29. Topeka State Journal, July 3, 1951.

30. Ibid.

31. Lawrence Journal-World, May 23, 1952.

32. Ibid.

33. Salina Journal, August 2, 1952.

34. Anthony Republican, August 6, 1952.

35. Topeka Daily Capital, June 14, 1953.

36. Ibid.

37. Topeka State Journal, July 3, 1953.

38. Ibid.

39. Ibid.

40. Ibid.

41. Flora, Tornadoes, p. 22.

42. Topeka State Journal, March 19, 1954.

43. Topeka State Journal, June 8, 1954.

44. Wichita Beacon, issues of May 26-30, 1955.

45, 46, 47, 48, 49, 50, 51, 52, 53–Ibid.

54. Topeka Daily Capital, May 27, 1955.

55. Topeka Daily Capital, May 26, 1955.

56. Ibid.

57. Garden City Telegraph, June 5, 1955.

58. Independence Reporter, April 3, 1956.

59. Topeka Capital-Journal, April 3, 1956.

60. Ibid.

61. Eagleman, Building Damage, p. 10.

62. Ibid.

63. Ibid.

64. Brewer, Carolyn, Caught in the Path: The Ruskin Heights Tornado, May 30, 1957 (Kansas City, MO: Leathers Publishing, 1997), pp. 1-9.

65. Topeka Daily Capital, May 21, 1957.

66. Lawrence Journal-World, May 21, 1957.

67. Ibid.

68. El Dorado Times, June 11, 1958.

69. Ibid.

70. Ibid.

71. Ibid.

72. Ibid.

73. Topeka Daily Capital, May 25, 1962.

74. Ibid.

75. Ibid.

76. Ibid.

77. Hutchinson News, May 25, 1962.

78. Ibid.

79. Ibid.

80. Ibid.

81. Ibid.

82. Topeka Capital-Journal, May 27, 1962.

83. Holton recorder, August 6, 1962.

84. Topeka Capital-Journal, August 6, 1962.

85. Topeka Daily Capital, July 16, 1977.

86. Kansas City Times, April 13, 1965.

87. Ibid.

88. Kansas City Times, March 18, 1965.

89. Wichita Eagle, May 14, 1965.

90. Ibid.

91. Wichita Beacon, September 4, 1965.

92. Ibid.

93. Ibid.

94. Ibid.

95. Topeka Capital Journal, May 12, 1966.

96. Ibid.

97. Topeka Capital Journal, "Tornado '66" (Topeka: Stauffer Publications, 1966) inside front cover.

98. Topeka Capital Journal, "The Day the Sky Fell," (Topeka: Stauffer Publications, 1966) pp. 2-3, Topeka Capital Journal, "Tornado '66", p. 7.

99. Topeka Capital Journal, "Tornado '66", p. 7.

100. Ibid., p. 8

101. Ibid.

102. Ibid., p. 9.

103. Ibid., inside front cover.

104. Wichita Eagle, March 9, 1974.

105. Ibid.

106. Garden City Telegram, June 24, 1967.

107. Ibid.

108. Salina Journal, June 23, 1969.

109. Ibid.

110. Wichita Eagle, June 20, 1969. On May 27, a waterspout drowned three people near Cheney and on July 9, a tornado hit Eudora in Douglas county.

111. Arkansas City Traveler, March 14, 1973.

112. Clay Center Dispatch, September 26, 1973.

113. Salina Journal, September 26, 1973.

114. Ibid.

115. Clay Center Dispatch, September 26, 1973.

116. Ibid.

117. Ibid.

118. Hanover News, September 26, 1973.

119. Greenleaf Sentinel, September 26, 1973.

120. Ibid.

121. Hutchinson News, May 14, 1974.

122. Topeka Capital Journal, June 9, 1974.

123. Ibid.

124. Emporia Gazette, June 9, 1974.

125. Ibid.

126. Topeka Capital Journal, June 10, 1974.

127. Topeka Capital Journal, June 10, 11 and 12, 1974.

128. Hearth Publishers, *Kansas Storms*, p. 4.

129. Hugoton Hermes, May 26, 1977; Garden City Telegram May 19, 1977; Lawrence Journal-World, May 19, 1977.

130. Holton Recorder, June 5, 1978.

131. Topeka Capital Journal, June 17 and 19, 1978.

132. Clay Center Dispatch, October 19, 1979; Manhattan Mercury, October 19, 1979; Holton Recorder, October 19, 1979.

133. Ibid.

Chapter Six

1. Hearth Publishers, *Kansas Storms*, p. 4.

2. Ibid., p. 5.

3. Ibid.

4. Lawrence Journal World, June 10, 1981

5. Ibid.

6. Topeka Capital Journal, July 19, 1981.

7. Iola Register, March 18, 1982; Yates Center News, March 18, 1982; Eureka Herald, March 18, 1982.

8. Topeka Capital Journal, April 27, 1984.

9. Wichita Eagle-Beacon, April 30, 1984.

10. Topeka Daily Capital, November 1, 1984.

11. Phillips County Review, May 16, 1985; Rooks County Record, May 16, 1985.

12. El Dorado Times, July 5, 1987.

13. Hearth Publishers, Kansas Storms, pp. 9-10, 54-55.

14. Ibid., pp. 9-10.

15. Ibid., p. 11

16. Ibid., p. 15, 19-20.

17. Ibid. p. 23.

18. Ibid., p. 24.

19. Ibid., p. 39.

20. Ibid., pp. 45-48.

21. Ibid. p. 48.

22. Ibid., pp. 50-53.

23. Ibid. pp. 56, 65-66.

24. Hearth Publishers, Kansas Storms, pp. 68-72.

25. Ibid.

26. Emporia Gazette, June 8, 1990.

27. Emporia Gazette, June 8, 1990; Hearth Publishers, <u>Kansas Storms</u>, pp. 73-77.

28. Hearth Publishers, <u>Kansas Storms</u>, pp. 78-79.

29. Wichita Eagle-Beacon Publishers, <u>Like the Devil</u>, (Wichita: Wichita Eagle Beacon Publishers, 1991) p. 71; Hearth Publishers, <u>Kansas Storms</u>, pp. 1-3.

30. Wichita Eagle Beacon, <u>Like The Devil</u>, p. 5.

31. Ibid., pp. 5-6, 14.

32. Ibid., pp. 19-20.

33. Ibid., p. 19.

34. Ibid., pp. 5, 13-14.

35. Ibid., p. 15.

36. Ibid., pp. 15-16.

37. Ibid., pp. 17-19.

38. Ibid., p. 20.

39. Ibid., pp. 21-22.

40. Ibid., pp. 23-25.

41. Ibid., pp. 29-30.

42. Ibid., p. 30.

43. Andover Journal-Advocate, May 2, 1991; Wichita Eagle Beacon, Like The Devil, pp. 31-32.

44. Wichita Eagle Beacon, Like The Devil, pp. 32-33.

45. Ibid., pp. 35-36.

46. Ibid., pp. 39-40.

47. Ibid., p. 40.

48. Ibid., p. 42.

49. Ibid., pp. 46-47.

50. Ibid., pp. 31-32.

51. Wichita Eagle beacon, April 27, 1991.

52. Topeka Capital Journal, April 27, 1991.

53. Wichita Eagle Beacon, Like The Devil, pp. 74-75.

54. McPherson Sentinel, June 16, 1992; Topeka Capital Journal, June 17, 1992. These were 16 tornadoes tracked outside of McPherson that day. An inland hurricane in Jewell county did extensive damage.

55. McPherson Sentinel, June 16, 1992; Topeka Capital Journal, June 17, 1992.

56. Ibid.

57. Ibid.

58. Ibid; Beloit Daily Call, June 16, 1992; tornadoes also hit Glen Elder and Beloit that night.

59. Russell Daily News, May 8, 1995.

60. Ibid.

61. Lawrence Journal World, July 12, 1993.

62. Ibid.

63. Southwest Daily Times, Liberal, April 11, 1994.

64. Wichita Eagle, April 6, 1998.

65. Ibid.

66. Topeka Capital Journal, June 14, 1998.

67. Wichita Eagle, May 3, 1999.

68. Parsons Sun, April 19 and April 20, 2000

69. Wichita eagle, April 22, 23, 25, 26, 2001; Great Bend Tribune, April 22, 2001.

Index to Kansas Tornado Locations

Abbyville, 228

Abilene, 47, 197, 204

Aetna, 147

Agra, 283

Alameda, 182

Albert, 81, 85, 196, 204

Aliceville, 104

Allen County, 175, 276

Alma, 180

Altamont, 207

Altoona, 192

Andale, 128, 129, 182, 300

Anderson County, 214, 234, 276

Andover, 27, 263, 272, 301, 302, 307, 308, 309, 311, 312, 314, 315, 318, 401

Anthony, 182, 202, 214, 303, 393

Argonia, 182

Arkansas City, 215, 252, 316, 397

Ashville, 66

Atchison, 38, 39, 76, 279

Atlanta, 252

Attica, 182

Atwood, 165, 390

Auburn, 242

Augusta, 81, 84, 145, 146, 384, 388

Aurora, 200

Axtell, 59, 63, 382, 383

Baileyville, 98

Barber County, 147, 148

Barton County, 73, 295

Barton Courts, 196

Baxter Springs, 204, 215

Beattie, 59

Belle Plaine, 89, 203, 236

Beloit, 195, 218, 319, 402

Belvue, 180

Bennington, 66, 254, 341

Bentley, 128, 300

Bird City, 218

Birmingham, 232

Bismarck Grove, 116

Bison, 117, 118

Blodget, Lorin, 30

Bluff City, 182

Bogue, 51, 253

Bonner Springs, 200, 201

Bourbon County, 207

Brookville, 203, 251

Brown County, 98, 199

Brown, O.C., 36

Bryant, Peter, 39

Bucklin, 199

Burden, 252

Burdick, 203

Burlingame, 149

Burlington, 39, 40, 41, 160, 166

Burnett, Chief Abram, 241, 242

Burnett's Mound, Topeka, 12, 28, 104, 217, 241, 242, 243, 244

Burr Oak, 172, 218, 390

Burrton, 228, 288, 293, 294

Bushton, 296, 297

Butler County, 81, 203, 300

Cairo, 341

Caldwell, 182, 203, 378

Canton, 71, 93

Carbondale, 281, 282

Cawker City, 318

Cedar Point, 195

Chanute, 132, 205

Chapman, 47, 69, 342

Chase, 47, 193, 195, 381

Chase County, 48, 316

Cheney, 182, 397

Cheney Lake State Park, 338

Cheney Reservoir, 300

Cherokee County, 64, 338

Cherryvale, 86, 87, 330

Chetopa, 65, 168

Cheyenne County, 203

Cimarron, 199

Claflin, 143, 216, 296

Clark County, 102

Clay Center, 71, 93, 94, 95, 97, 147, 255, 256, 268, 385, 397, 398

Clay County, 94, 97, 98, 102, 255, 268

Clearwater, 182, 303, 327

Clifton, 98

Clinton, 135

Cloud County, 93, 94, 97, 200, 204

Coburn, Foster, 120

Codell, 27, 139, 140, 377

Coffey County, 78

Coffeyville, 119, 132, 133, 204, 275, 387, 390

Coldwater, 194

Colony, 176, 192

Columbus, 65, 167, 168, 169, 192

Colwich, 182

Concordia, 110, 218

Conway Springs, 182, 204

Cook Field, 280

Coolidge, 203

Corbin, 182

Corwin, 182

Cottonwood Falls, 48, 49, 203

Cottonwood Station, 48, 49, 50

Council Grove, 204

Cow Creek, 73

Cowley County, 66, 235, 316

Crawford County, 64, 199, 337

Cunningham, 99, 169, 385

Danville, 182

David, John, 47

Dearing, 119

Decatur County, 199, 203, 207

Delphos, 59

Derby, 85, 124

Derringer, J.J., 95

DeSoto, 200, 201

Dexter, 205

Dickinson County, 69, 71, 102, 250, 342

Dodge City, 177, 190, 205, 214, 295, 342

Doran, Thomas F., 38

Dorrance, 322

Doubrava, Anna and Frank, 46

Douglas County, 33, 134, 135, 234, 323

Douglass, 74, 81, 243, 285

Dover, 242

Downs, 218

Dust Devils, 25

Eagleman, Joe, 247

Effingham, 279

El Dorado, 44, 45, 47, 220, 221, 222, 314, 380, 388, 395, 399

El Dorado Lake, 285

Elk City, 119

Elk County, 316, 317

Elkhart, 197

Ellinwood, 125, 153, 154

Ellis, 108, 122, 124, 141, 193, 283, 388

Ellis County, 141, 295

Ellsworth, 250

Ellsworth County, 295

Elmont, 134, 135, 136, 137, 224, 225, 226, 240

Emmett, 164, 265

Emporia, 28, 51, 68, 111, 112, 149, 187, 192, 199, 203, 215, 242, 259, 261, 262, 263, 267, 297, 299, 383, 398, 400

Englewood, 102

Enterprise, 47, 69, 257, 342

Erie, 191, 330

Eskridge, 112, 134, 318

Espy, James, 43

Eureka, 103, 104, 385, 399

Evans, Col Elwood, 131

Fairmont Park, 110

Fall River Reservoir, 276

Fancy Creek, 52

Farm Ridge, 119

Fawbush, Lt Col E.J., 188

Finley, J.P., 18, 27, 52, 53, 56, 58

Finley, James, 27, 43, 44, 52, 60, 380, 381, 382, 383

Flora, Snowden, 13

Florence, 195

Ford County, 102

Fort Leavenworth, 30, 32

Fort Riley, 47, 71, 180

Fort Row, Missouri, 30

Fort Scott, 125, 214

Fort Snelling, Minnesota, 30

Frankfort, 98

Franklin County, 218

Fujita, Dr. Theodore, 25

Fujita, T. Theodore, 263

Gale, Dorothy, 54

Game Fork Creek, 53

Garden City, 197, 205, 248, 249, 264, 373, 375, 394, 397, 398

Garden Plain, 182

Garfield, 214

Garnett, 78, 169, 234

Geary County, 342

Germantown, 112

Geuda Springs, 235

Girard, 64

Glasco, 66, 125

Glen Elder, 318, 402

Goddard, 182, 251, 316

Goessel, 292

Golden Spur Mobile Home Park, 309, 310

Goodland, 190, 205, 206, 253

Gorham, 193

Gothenburg, 154, 155

Gove County, 198

grasshopper invasion, 45, 46

Gray County, 249

Great Bend, 109, 110, 123, 124, 125, 196, 204, 215, 285, 335, 402

Greenleaf, 72, 257, 258, 397

Greensburg, 11, 13, 144, 152, 339, 340, 341, 342, 343

Greenwood County, 103, 276, 326

Grenola, 132, 215

Gretna, 283

Gypsum, 251

Hallowell, 275

Halstead, 92, 228, 236

Hamilton County, 203

Hanover, 256, 318, 397

Harper, 182

Harper County, 203, 204

Harvey County, 290, 292, 300

Haven, 20, 81, 235, 256, 287

Havensville, 343

Hays, 127, 139, 253, 387, 388

Haysville, 280, 303, 327, 328, 339

Hayward, Elizabeth, 32

Hazleton, 182

Heat Dome, 27

Heizer, 110

Herington, 206, 293

Herington Reservoir, 293

Hesston, 229, 263, 271, 286, 287, 289, 290, 291, 292, 293, 294, 297

Hiawatha, 112, 113, 199

Hill City, 204

Hodgeman County, 102, 318

Hoisington, 109, 125, 142, 143, 204, 295, 334, 335, 336, 386, 388

Holcomb, 197

Hollis, 110

Holton, 39, 77, 112, 231, 232, 233, 265, 269, 379, 384, 395, 398

Holyrood, 296

Hopewell, 340

Horton, 154, 192, 206

Hoyt, 126, 127, 195, 232, 278

Hugoton, 203, 398

Hutchinson, 91, 131, 147, 148, 206, 207, 214, 228, 229, 230, 258, 301, 388, 395, 397

Idana, 268

Independence, 32, 39, 119, 163, 165, 192, 207, 390, 394

Independence, Missouri, 32

Inman, Henry, 63

Iola, 176, 234, 276, 391, 399

Irving, 17, 27, 43, 51, 53, 54, 57, 58, 59, 60, 62, 63, 66, 71, 72, 382

Jackson County, 39, 195, 224, 231, 265, 269, 343, 379

Jacobs Creek, 50

Jefferson County, 36, 69, 134, 224, 227, 317, 378

Jennings, 199

Jewell County, 108, 386

Johnson County, 207, 214

Jones, H.L., 20, 189

Junction City, 71, 285

Kanopolis Reservoir, 250

Kanorado, 218

Kansas City, 11, 26, 32, 75, 77, 110, 120, 149, 190, 199, 204, 212, 218, 220, 240, 265, 303, 336, 337, 338, 373, 378, 386, 387, 389, 390, 393, 394, 395, 396

Kansas Cyclone, 22

Kansas State Historical Society, 13, 369, 370, 371, 373, 378, 380, 381, 383

Kearny County, 249

Keller, Will, 151

Kensington, 204

Kimeo, 72

Kincaid, 91, 176

Kingman, 147, 182, 202, 205, 300

Kingman County, 147, 199, 205

Kinner, Emma, 46, 64

Kiowa, 182, 203

Kismet, 324

Kurtis, Bill, 244

Labette County, 207, 338

LaCrosse, 201

LaHarpe, 175, 177

Lake Kahola, 203, 215

LakePomona, 267

Lakin, 197, 249

Lamont, 199

Lanham, 318

Larkinburg, 127

Lawrence, 11, 34, 36, 69, 91, 113, 114, 115, 116, 199, 200, 234, 264, 272, 274, 302, 323, 378, 379, 382, 386, 387, 393, 394, 398, 402

Layman, C.E., 135

Leanna, 175

Leavenworth, 76, 190, 224, 227, 234, 337, 379

Leavenworth County, 224, 234, 323, 337

Lebo, 149, 171

Leedey, Oklahoma, 186

Lehigh, 147

Leona, 192

Leoti, 197, 249

Leroy, 39, 41

Leverrier, Urbain, 31

Lewis, 215

Liberal, 162, 163, 181, 203, 402

Liberal Army Air Field, 181

Liberty, Missouri, 76

Lincoln, 119, 156, 203, 322, 380, 389

Lincoln County, 199

Lincolnville, 173

Lindsborg, 203, 251, 297

Linn, 239, 256

Linn County, 79, 118, 386

Logan, 162

Louisville, 265, 268

Lucas, 202, 288

Ludlum, David, 36, 39

Madison, 218

Maize, 182

Malin, James C, 42

Manhattan, 36, 47, 69, 195, 199, 202, 214, 268, 293, 342, 343, 380, 383, 385, 398

Mankato, 215

Maple City, 216

Marienthal, 197

Marion County, 195

Marquette, 105, 297, 386

Marshall County, 39, 53, 98, 102, 205

Martin City, Missouri, 218

Marysville, 39, 40, 71, 205, 265

Mayday, 72

Mayfield, 182, 327

McConnell Air Force Base, 27, 237, 302, 303, 306, 307

McCoy, John, 32, 378

McLouth, 286

McMillan, Al, 69

McNulty, Rich, 274

McPherson, 147, 192, 195, 204, 250, 294, 295, 401

McPherson County, 147, 195, 196, 319

Meade, 324

Meeker, Jotham, 32

Melrose, 338

Melvern, 67, 68

Mennonite Disaster Service, 291

Menoken, 135

Meriden, 135, 224, 225, 226, 227, 240, 317

Miami County, 34, 118, 224, 337

Micro Bursts, 25

Milan, 182

Miller, Maj R.C., 188

Miltonvale, 97, 204

Minneapolis, 38, 67, 382

Minooka Park, 322

Missouri City, 76

Mitchell County, 198, 203, 318

Monett, 119

Monotony, 120

Moore, Ely, 34

Moran, 175, 176

Morganville, 94, 95, 98

Morris County, 250

Morse, 43, 132, 133

Morse, Samuel F.B., 43

Morton County, 102, 263

Mound Valley, 133

Moundridge, 92, 93, 259

Mount Hope, 199

Mount Washington, 110

Mt. Hope, 92

Mt. Hope, 300

Mulberry, 275, 277

Mullinville, 122, 339

Mulvane, 178, 180

Murdock, 182

Mustang Mobile Home Park, 319

Nashville, 169, 182

National Severe Storms Forecast Center, 303

National Severe Storms Forecasting Center, 188

National Weather Service, 16, 86, 185, 188, 274, 281, 303, 335

Nelson, William Rockhill, 120

Nemaha County, 98, 199, 326, 343

Neodesha, 119

Neosho County, 191, 207

Neosho Rapids, 111

Ness City, 253

New Albany, 132

New Cambria, 254

New Salem, 205

Newton, 128, 229

Nickerson, 228

Niles, 254

North Lawrence, 200

North Topeka, 200

Norton, 110, 111, 204, 328

Norton County, 102, 110, 198, 199

Nortonville, 318

Norwich, 182

O'Herin, 133

Oak Hill, 255

Oakland, 246

Oakley, 215

Oatville, 128, 182

Oberlin, 174, 175, 390

Oil Hill, 220

Olathe, 132, 133, 203

Olivet, 67

Omaha, Nebraska, 119

Oneida, 98

Oronoga, 76

Osage City, 90, 213

Osage County, 66, 67, 90, 282, 383

Osawatomie, 36, 214

Osborne, 215

Osborne County, 198

Oskaloosa, 224, 227

Ottawa, 65, 66, 67, 192, 203, 218, 219, 254, 285

Ottawa County, 66

Otto, 172, 216

Ottumwa, 39, 41, 379

Overland Park, 205

Oxford, 212

Ozawkie, 224, 240

Palco, 199

Parallel, 72

Park City, 301

Parker, 98, 118

Parkman, Francis, 33

Parkville, Missouri, 337

Parsons, 192, 330, 331, 333, 334, 372, 402

Parter, Marvel, 140

Partridge, 259

Pawnee County, 195, 199, 214

Pawnee Rock, 202

Peabody, 147

Peck, 182

Penalosa, 182

Perry, 47, 91, 203

Perth, 182

Phenis Creek, 51

Phillips County, 198, 283, 295

Phillipsburg, 72, 73, 204, 218

Pilsen, 293, 297

Pittsburg, 192, 240

Plainville, 200, 205, 252

Plymouth, 112

Pomona, 133, 257

Pomona Reservoir, 266

Pottawatomie County, 102, 224, 343

Pratt, 71, 80, 154, 300

Pratt County, 71, 80, 301, 340

Prescott, 79, 80

Pretty Prairie, 182, 287

Quenemo, 68

Ramona, 204

Randolph, 52, 53, 66

Rantoul, 220

Rawlins County, 165, 203

Reading, 69

Registration Day tornado, 24

Reno County, 147, 286, 287, 300, 301, 339

Republic County, 326

Reserve, 326

Rice County, 73, 80, 193, 196, 198, 295

Riley County, 98, 102

Riverdale, 182

Riverside, Missouri, 337

Rock Creek, 127

Roeland Park, 149, 150

Rooks County, 139, 198, 200, 283, 399

Rose Hill, 280, 285

Rossville, 224, 226, 318

Rozel, 193, 195

Rush Center, 195, 335

Rush City, 192

Rush County, 195

Ruskin Heights, 27, 185, 218, 219, 220, 373, 394

Russell, 193, 195, 322, 323, 402

Sabetha, 98, 199, 326

Safford, 51

Salina, 65, 166, 193, 205, 207, 249, 250, 251, 253, 392, 393, 397

Saline County, 102, 250

Satanta, 203

Sawyer, 341

Schilling Air Force Base, 250

Scott City, 197

Scottsbluff, Nebraska, 25

Scranton, 281

Sedan, 119

Sedgwick, 121, 128, 131, 280, 300, 301

Sedgwick County, 121, 128, 280, 300

Seismic detectors, 325

Seneca, 98

Sharon, 182

Sharon Springs, 215

Shawnee County, 133, 134, 135, 224, 240, 286, 318

Shawnee Heights, 286

Shawnee Methodist Mission, 32, 378

Sherman County, 199, 203

Sherman Field, 190

Silver Lake, 224, 277, 278, 279, 280

Silverdale, 252

Smith Center, 295

Soldier, 77, 343

Solomon City, 65, 66

Sorter, William, 84

Spear, Stephen, 39

Spivey, 182

Spring Creek Valley, 40

Spring Hill, 218

St. Bridget, 59

St. Leo, 191

Stafford, 47, 69, 70, 80, 383

Stafford County, 195

Stark, 214

Stevens County, 199, 203, 263

Stites, Ada, 63

Stockdale, 59

Stockton, 283

Street, Julian, 120

Strong City, 48, 49

Strother Air Field, 317

Sublette, 199, 207

Sumner, 38, 81, 121, 199

Sumner County, 204, 209, 235

Sun City, 74

Sylvan Grove, 202

Syracuse, 203, 207

Tampa, 293

Thayer, 191, 214

The Cyclone State, *43*

Tipton, 318, 319

Topeka, 11, 12, 22, 23, 27, 28, 38, 65, 72, 77, 79, 87, 91, 104, 110, 119, 133, 135, 136, 147, 185, 187, 190, 192, 199, 202, 205, 206, 213, 214, 216, 217, 224, 227, 230, 231, 240, 241, 242, 243, 245, 246, 247, 248, 264, 274, 282, 286, 317, 339, 369, 370, 371, 372, 373, 376, 378, 379, 381, 383, 384, 385, 386, 387, 388, 389, 391, 392, 393, 394, 395, 396, 397, 398, 399, 401, 402

tornado

definition of, 11, 12, 13, 15, 16, 17,

descriptions of, 18, 19, 20, 21, 22, 24, 25, 26, 27, 28, 29, 32, 34, 35, 36, 38, 39, 40, 41, 42, 43, 44, 46, 47, 48, 49, 50, 51, 52, 53, 54, 55, 56, 57, 58, 59, 60, 61, 62, 63, 64, 65, 66, 67, 68, 69, 71, 72, 73, 74, 75, 76, 77, 78, 79, 80, 81, 83, 84, 85, 86, 87, 88, 89, 90, 91, 92, 93, 94, 95, 96, 97, 98, 99, 100, 101, 102, 103, 104, 105, 106, 107, 108, 109, 110, 111, 112, 113, 115, 116, 117, 118, 119, 120, 121, 122, 124, 125, 126, 127, 128, 129, 130, 131, 132, 133, 134, 135, 136, 139, 140, 141, 142, 143, 144, 145, 146, 147, 148, 149, 150, 151, 152, 153, 154, 155, 159, 160, 161, 162, 163, 164, 165, 166, 167, 168, 169, 171, 172, 173, 174, 175, 176, 177, 178, 179, 180, 181, 182, 183, 185, 186, 187, 190, 191, 192, 193, 194, 195, 196, 197, 198, 199, 200, 201, 202, 203, 204, 205, 206, 207, 208, 209, 210, 212, 213, 214, 215, 216, 217, 218, 219, 220, 221, 222, 224, 225, 226, 227, 228, 229, 230, 231, 232, 233, 234, 235, 236, 237, 239, 240, 241, 242, 243, 244, 245, 246, 247, 248, 249, 250, 251, 252, 253, 254, 255, 256, 257, 258, 259, 260, 261, 262, 263, 264, 265, 266, 268, 271, 272, 273, 274, 275, 276, 277, 278, 279, 280, 281, 282, 283, 284, 285, 286, 287, 288, 289, 290, 291, 292, 293, 294, 295, 296, 297, 298, 299, 300, 301, 302, 303, 304, 305, 306, 307, 308, 309, 310, 311, 312, 313, 315, 316, 317, 318, 319, 320, 321, 322, 323,

324, 325, 326, 327, 328, 329, 330, 331, 333, 334, 335, 336, 337, 338, 339, 340, 341, 342, 343, 376, 377, 381, 387, 391, 397

tornado, 15

Toronto, 215

Towanda, 81, 83, 84, 86, 220, 223, 315

Trego County, 198

Tribune, 197

Tri-State Tornadoes, 20

Turkey Creek, 75

Tuttle Creek Reservoir, 62

Twister, 18, 325

U.S. Signal Service, 18, 27, 30, 52, 66, 86, 369, 373, 380, 383

U.S. Weather Bureau, 15, 204, 233

Udall, 11, 185, 203, 207, 208, 209, 211, 212, 214, 221, 240, 308, 339

Ulysses, 199, 264

Uniontown, 132

Valley Center, 300

Valley Falls, 69, 317, 385

Vaughn's Acres, 276

Vesper, 202

Villas, 192

Viola, 182

Wabaunsee County, 134, 224, 318, 326

Wakarusa, 206

WaKeeney, 139, 198

Wakefield, 59, 60

Waldron, 182

Wallace County, 102, 203

Walnut, 330

Wamego, 81, 85, 86, 181, 224, 293

Washington, 30, 72, 88, 98, 159, 162, 187, 373, 375, 380

Washington County, 239, 256, 318, 326

Waterville, 59, 72

Wauneta, 119

Weather Channel, 15

Weather Data, Inc, 294, 303

Webster Lake, 283

Weller, Norman, 217

Wellington, 81, 89, 90, 182, 203, 391

Page 416

Westport Field, 192

Westport, Missouri, 32

Whippoorwill, 265, 267

White City, 205, 293

White Deer, Texas, 191

Whitewater, 172

Whiting, 113

Wichita, 27, 74, 81, 83, 85, 121, 123, 131, 144, 146, 182, 190, 192, 203, 205, 208, 212, 214, 235, 236, 240, 252, 271, 280, 300, 301, 302, 303, 304, 305, 315, 317, 318, 325, 327, 328, 338, 339, 374, 384, 385, 387, 390, 391, 392, 394, 396, 397, 399, 400, 401, 402

Williamstown, 91

Willowbrook, 301

Wilmore, 193

Wilson County, 125

Wilson Lake, 322

Winfield, 204, 235, 285, 317, 384

Wizard of Oz, *54*, *166*

Woodbine, 47, 69

Woodson County, 125, 276

Woodward, Ok, 191

Wyandotte County, 337

Yates Center, 125, 276, 399

Yoder, 287, 288

Zenda, 182

Zuni Indians, 29

Zurich, 200

Zyba, 121, 124

Made in the USA